CAVES OF
THE PEAK DISTRICT

Compiled by
David W. Gill & John S. Beck
on behalf of the Derbyshire Caving Association

Dalesman Books

1991

The Dalesman Publishing Company Ltd.,
Clapham (via Lancaster), LA2 8EB

First published 1964
(as "Caves of Derbyshire")
Fifth edition 1984
This edition 1991
© David W. Gill & John S. Beck
ISBN 1 85568 034 3

Typeset by Lands Services, East Molesey, Surrey
Printed by Peter Fretwell & Sons Ltd, Goulbourne St., Keighley, West Yorkshire

CONTENTS

Cover photograph: The pitch from Millers Chamber, Eldon Hole.
Photograph by Paul Deakin.

Cave Surveys appear on the following pages:

ACKNOWLEDGEMENTS

The authors would like to acknowledge the assistance of the following for help with the revisions for this edition:

D. Arueschoug, I. Barker, K. Bentham, F. Brown, P. Chandler, J. Cordingley, N. Dibben, K. Drakeley, T.D. Ford, J. Gunn, M. Loftus, P.T. Mellors, M. Milner, D. Nixon, G.W. Peppit, J.E. Potts, D. Warriner, J. Wilmot.

Grateful thanks are due to the many cave surveyors who have allowed their work to be used in the production of the plans herein, and to many other cavers who have helped by supplying information.

INTRODUCTION

This edition is largely based on previous editions compiled by T.D.Ford, D.Allsop, R.Travis, D.W.Gill, and numerous other cavers.

It was decided that it would be more helpful to list the caves in alphabetical order within the various areas, and the area boundaries were drawn by defining the catchment areas of major resurgences or rivers. In some cases, such as the central River Wye, several small areas have been grouped together as there are few caves. The small number of caves found in the Churnet catchment have been included in the Hamps/Manifold chapter, as have the small areas of karst that protrude into the Dove catchment.

Cited references are by no means exhaustive (for instance there are hundreds of references to Peak Cavern alone), but the major works are included. It is essential that future discoveries are recorded so that the information is accessible, for instance in the Derbyshire Caving Association Newsletter, or in the journals of the larger clubs.

Access details can be found at the beginning of the various descriptions where known, and should be strictly adhered to. Failure to do this may result in access being denied to all cavers. Where no access information is given, it does not mean that there is a right of way. Permission should be sought from the owners or tenants of the land.

Single Rope Techniques (SRT) are now used exclusively in a few of Derbyshire's more vertical systems. In most cases only basic information is given as rope lengths vary considerably depending on the number of re-belays used etc. Bolt belays deteriorate with age, and should be treated with great caution. Only those cavers proficient in the use of SRT should attempt such descents. The authors consider that such cavers will have the knowledge and expertise to use their own initiative in deciding on rigging techniques, the amount of tackle required, and the safety and position of the belays used in order to carry out a safe descent.

The authors, the Derbyshire Caving Association, or the publishers cannot accept any responsibility for errors or inaccuracies in this guide, although every effort has been made to make the guide as accurate as possible. It would help if omissions or inaccuracies could be notified to D.W.Gill, 54 Lower Lane, Chinley, via Stockport, Derbyshire, or to J.S.Beck, Glebe Cottage, Eyam, via Sheffield, Derbyshire.

The British Cave
Research Association

BCRA is the official scientific body for British caving. Membership is open to any individual or club with an interest in speleology. It publishes a quarterly magazine, "Caves and Caving", with up to date news on caving at home and abroad. Its scientific publication, "Cave Science", is published on a regular basis and offers articles on the science of speleology and detailed expedition reports from all over the world.

"Current Titles in Speleology" is published yearly, and contains bibliographies on almost everything written on the subject of caves throughout the world.

Anyone with a serious interest in caves is advised to consider joining. The contact address is BCM–BCRA. London WC1N 3XX.

The Derbyshire Caving Association

The Association was formed in 1960, and membership is open to any caving club or individual interested in caves and caving in the Southern Pennines and adjoining areas.

Its main function is to maintain access to the caves and mines, promote conservation, and provide a united negotiating body to deal with the ever increasing pressure on our caves. It is directly responsible on behalf of the national body for caving (at present the National Caving Association) for all access and conservation matters on a regional basis. The D.C.A. also disseminates information to its members by means of a regular newsletter and through its meetings.

Enquiries should be addressed to the Secretary, The Derbyshire Caving Association, c/o The Sports Council, 26 Musters Road, West Bridgeford, Nottingham.

Current addresses for all Derbyshire caving clubs can be obtained from the above address.

The Derbyshire Cave Registry

The Cave Registry was set up in order to collect all available data on Derbyshire caves. It is constantly updated, and provides a source of up to date information for both sporting cavers and researchers.

The Registry is, of course, only kept up to date by cavers reporting their discoveries. The current Cave Registry Secretary is John Beck, Glebe Cottage, Eyam, via Sheffield. S30 1RB, who will be pleased to receive any amendments or additions.

The Cave Diving Group

The exploration of flooded passages should only be attempted by qualified cave divers. It is essential that anyone remotely interested in this aspect of cave exploration should join the C.D.G., the official British body for cave divers. They run extensive training courses and publish a regular newsletter on recent discoveries.

The contact address for the Cave Diving Group is: Hon. Chairman, Mike Jeanmaire, Elm Cottage, Peak Forest, Derbyshire.

Cave Conservation in Derbyshire

Caves form a unique and vulnerable part of our natural heritage. It takes tens of thousands of years for cave passages to form, along with beautiful and delicate calcite formations and sediments, and to allow their cave life to colonise and develop. It takes only a moment for all this to be destroyed or damaged. Their conservation is important on three main grounds:

Caves are a nationally rare and integral part of our natural heritage and are worthy of conservation in their own right.

We have a duty to conserve caves for the benefit and enjoyment of future generations.

Caves provide a valuable scientific resource.

Caves are at risk from two directions – those activities occurring outside the cave, eg. quarrying, landfill, and some land management practices, and from internal activites resulting from the use of caves.

Internal pressures

From the moment caves are discovered, deterioration of the cave begins. Some damage will inevitably occur as a result of exploration and the passage of cavers. Conservation is about limiting or avoiding this damage. If cavers follow a number of simple guidelines, as an integral part of normal caving, then much of this damage can be minimised.
* Observe taped routes.
* Treat calcite formations with greater care – avoid breakage.
* Do not leave litter.
* Do not dump carbide.
* Take care not to disturb cave life, especially bats.
* Sediments are vulnerable. Do not trample needlessly on undisturbed deposits.
* Archaeological and palaeontological features should be left undisturbed.
* Take an active interest in cave conservation.
* Digging should take place in a responsible manner.
* Artificial aids should be kept to a minimum.

External Threats

Quarrying represents one of the most serious threats to caves, as it can completely remove the passages. Landfill can also lead to the loss of access to caves, and can result in the pollution of the system. Some land management practices such as moor gripping can have an impact on caves, resulting in increased flood risk and increased deposition of silt from the sediment laden waters. Land reclamation and tipping can lead to the blocking of cave entrances. The tipping and discharge of farm effluent can result in the pollution of the cave system.

Statutory Protection – Nature Conservancy Council and SSSIs

The Nature Conservancy Council is the government's statutory advisory body on nature conservation. Under the Wildlife and Countryside Act (1981) it has a duty to notify any land which, in its opinion, is of special interest by reason of its fauna, flora, geological or physiographical features, ie. a Site of Special Scientific Interest.

This allows NCC to be consulted over any planning application on an SSSI or any application which may affect an SSSI. NCC therefore has a statutory input to such activities as quarrying.

NCC also has a duty to notify the owner/occupier of an SSSI of any activity which may affect the interest of the site – Potentially Damaging Operations (PDOs). This provides a mechanism for consultation over various activities within an SSSI not covered by planning laws. This allows some activities such as tipping and pollution to be controlled.

SSSIs in the Peak District

Castleton, Stoney Middleton Dale, Bagshawe Cavern, Lathkill Dale, Pooles Cavern, Masson Hill.

Further information from DCA Conservation Officer or NCC, Earth Science Division, Northminster House, Peterborough PE1 1UA.

If caves are going to be conserved for the future, cave conservation must take a far higher priority than at present. The practical conservation of our underground heritage is primarily the responsibility of the caver – this duty must be taken seriously.

J.R.Wright,
Earth Science Division,
Chief Scientist Directorate,
Nature Conservancy Council.

RADON DAUGHTER CONCENTRATIONS
IN DERBYSHIRE CAVES

Radon is a naturaly occurring, colourless and odourless radioactive gas, the most significant isotope of which is radon-222, a decay product of uranium. When radon in turn decays, it forms very small particles of other radioactive substances which are collectively known as radon daughters. The particles may be inhaled and deposited in the lungs, where they emit radiation.

Exposure to high concentrations of radon daughters has been shown to increase the risk of lung cancer and possibly also other cancers such as acute myeloid leukaemia. The "normal" radiation dose in the UK is about 2.5 mSv (millisiieverts) although some people receive much higher doses as a result of living in areas where houses have a high radon concentration. Workers are allowed to receive up to 15 mSv per year, and classified radiation workers up to 50 mSv per year. These figures are likely to be revised downwards in the near future as a result of recent research which has shown the risk of cancer as a result of exposure to radiation to be greater than previously thought.

Rightly, there are no regulations governing exposure to radon as part of recreational pursuit, and it is highly unlikely that any will be introduced. The writer believes that radon should be accepted as one of the risks of caving, but it is a risk which must be spelled out and assessed just as one would assess the risk of rock fall or flooding.

As yet only a small number of caves have been tested, but initial measurements have shown that radon daughter concentrations vary spatially (from cave to cave and from site to site within a cave) and temporally (seasonally, daily, and diurnally). The highest concentrations occur in summer in caves in the Castleton area, Giant's Hole having the highest concentrations in Britain and possibly in the world. Much more work is needed, but at least some of the caves in other parts of the Peak District also have high concentrations in summer. When concentrations are at their highest a few hours caving would be sufficient to accumulate the "normal" annual radon dose of 2.5 mSv, and regular summer cavers may well receive a radiation dose in excess of that received by classified radiation workers.

During the winter months, when cold low radon air is blowing into the caves, the concentrations are generally much lower and initial measurements suggest that regular winter cavers are unlikely to receive a high radiation dose. A programme of measurement is currently (May 1990) under way, and the results will be published in the main caving journals. In the meantime anyone concerned about the radon risk may contact either the writer at the address below, or Dave Edwards (Chairman of the NCA Cave Radon Working Party) at the Whitehall Centre, Buxton.

Finally, it should be noted that the radon daughter concentrations in tourist caves and mines are regularly monitored, and the radiation dose received by a member of the public on a guided tour would be negligible.

John Gunn,
Limestone Research Group,
Manchester Polytechnic.

The Grading System

These grades should be applied by fit and properly equipped cavers, and can only be regarded as an approximate indication of severity. Novices should bear these facts in mind when undertaking a caving trip. What is to them a Grade 5 will only be a Grade 3 to an expert.

Grade I:	Easy caves. No pitches or other difficulties.
Grade II:	Moderate caves and small potholes.
Grade III:	Caves and potholes without any hazardous, difficult, or dangerous sections.
Grade IV:	Caves and potholes which present some hazard or difficulty such as a long underground pitch or a long wet crawl.
Grade V:	Caves and potholes which include very strenuous sections, wet underground pitches, or tight and long wet crawls.
Arch:	Caves that have been or could be archaeologically excavated.
Dig:	Any site of speleological interest which has been or could be dug.
Dive:	Accessible only to fully equipped divers.
Lost:	Site destroyed or entrance buried.
Mine:	Mines or caves that have been modified by mining.
Show:	Show caves open to the public.
Spring:	A rising with no associated cave passage.

Safety

A PLAN TO BE SAFE

All parties should be properly organised, equipped, and supervised by a responsible and experienced leader.

Pick a cave or mine well known to the leader and within everyone's capabilities.

Let others know where you are going.

Ask for permission to enter sites on private land, and securely replace gates, grills, and shaft cappings.

No less than 3 in the party, and no more than 3 novices for each experienced leader makes sense.

Take notice of the weather forecast before going down caves where water flows.

One helmet and reliable cap lamp for each person.

Beware of disturbing stacked rock, loose boulders or props, especially in mines.

Ensure that ladders, belays, ropes are rigged properly before hanging your life on them.

Someone should carry emergency lights, food and first aid.

Act sensibly – do not drop stones down mine shafts or cave pitches.

Falls, loose boulders, flood water, exhaustion and being cold and wet cause most accidents – take care.

Exit takes more effort than entry, especially on long trips – plan with the return in mind.

In the event of an accident underground

1 Decide whether outside help is needed or not.

2 To summon help, send competent persons to the surface with reliable information for passing to the authorities (see paragraph 5 below).

3 Administer First Aid. Bearing in mind the inevitable delay before rescuers arrive, encourage injured persons who are still mobile to start moving towards the surface. At all events, reassure and keep injured persons warm.

4 To call out the D.C.R.O. telephone 999 and ask for Cave Rescue.

5 Useful initial information for passing to the Police:-

    i.   Identity of person telephoning and where calling from.

    ii. Name of cave or mine and its location.

    iii. Wheareabouts in the cave or mine the accident occurred.

    iv. Time and nature of accident and injuries sustained.

    v. Number of persons still underground at the scene.

6 The caller should be prepared to stay within reach of a phone to give any further information required.

Weather Information

Some of the Peak District caves are susceptible to flooding during adverse weather conditions, and can flood rapidly to the roof or become impassable.

Mountaincall Peak District give three to five day weather forecasts with daily updated messages on weather and ground conditions in the Peak District National Park. Weather information is supplied by the Met. Office, and ground conditions by the National Park Wardens.

Cavers descending flood-prone caves can phone this service on 0898 500 433.

Abbreviations

BCRA	British Cave Research Association
BSA	British Speleological Association
CDG	Cave Diving Group
CRG	Cave Research Group
DCC	Derbyshire Caving Club
DCA	Derbyshire Caving Association
DSG	Derbyshire Speleological Group
DUG	Disley Underground Group
EEG	Eyam Exploration Group
EPC	Eldon Pothole Club
MSG	Moldywarps Speleological Group
OCC	Orpheus Caving Club
OMMRE	Operation Mole Mines Research and Exploration
PAS	Peakland Archaeological Society
PDMHS	Peak District Mines Historical Society
STPC	Stoke on Trent Pothole Club
SUSS	Sheffield University Speleological Society
TSG	Technical Speleological Group
TVCG	Trent Valley Cave Exploration Group

Further Reading

A considerable amount of more extended information on the caves listed will be found in:

"Limestones and Caves of the Peak District" by T.D.Ford and others, published by Geo Books, c/o Geo-Abstracts Ltd., University of East Anglia, Norwich. 1977.

Details of sumps will be found in the Cave Diving Group's "Derbyshire Sump Index".

Details of the archaeological background will be found in "The Archaeology of the Peak", by Don Bramwell, published by Moorland, Ashbourne, Derbyshire, 1977.

A survey by R.Jenkinson of all the archaeological caves of the Creswell area on the Derbyshire Nottinghamshire border has been published for the Creswell Crags Visitor Centre by Notts. County Council Leisure Department, and detailed surveys of the Creswell Caves are in "The Upper Palaeolithic of Britain" by J.Campbell, Oxford University Press, 2 vols. 1978.

A short history and itineraries of the lead mining areas are available in "Lead Mining in the Peaks" by T.D.Ford and J.H.Rieuwerts, published by the Peak Park Board, Bakewell. Further details of the Matlock area are in "Caverns and Mines of Matlock Bath, 1", by R.Flindall and A.Hayes, published by Moorland, Ashbourne, Derbyshire 1976.

In addition to these general works, there are numerous articles in caving club journals and newsletters, and several organisations have compiled libraries of these. In particular the libraries of the former British Speleological Association (Derbyshire material only), the Peak District Mines Historical Society, and the Derbyshire Caving Association are deposited in the Derbyshire County Reference Library at Matlock, where they are available during normal working hours. In addition, collections largely of mining documents are to be found in the Derbyshire County Records Office, Matlock.

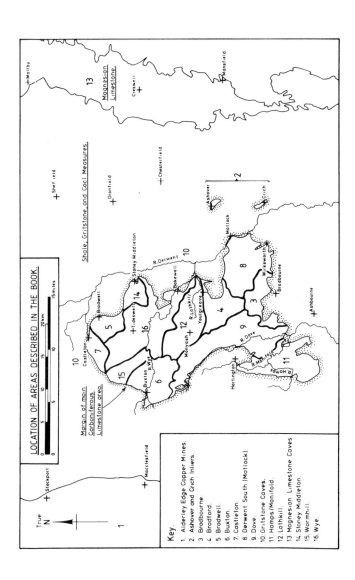

LOCATION OF AREAS DESCRIBED IN THE BOOK.

Key.
1. Alderley Edge Copper Mines.
2. Ashover and Crich Inliers.
3. Bradbourne.
4. Bradford.
5. Bradwell.
6. Buxton.
7. Castleton.
8. Derwent South (Matlock).
9. Dove.
10. Gritstone Caves.
11. Hamps/Manifold.
12. Lathkill.
13. Magnesian Limestone Caves
14. Stoney Middleton.
15. Warmhill.
16. Wye.

Shale, Gritstone and Coal Measures.

Magnesian Limestone

Margin of main Carboniferous Limestone area.

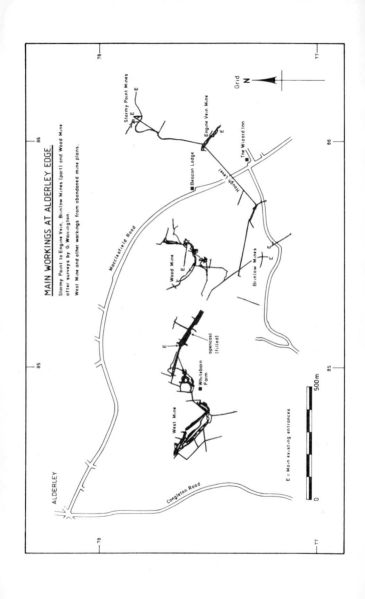

MAIN WORKINGS AT ALDERLEY EDGE

Stormy Point to Engine Vein, Brinlow Mines (part) and Wood Mine after surveys by G. Warrington.

West Mine and other workings from abandoned mine plans.

Stormy Point Mines
Engine Vein Mine
Beacon Lodge
The Wizard Inn
Hough Level
Wood Mine
Brinlow Mines
Macclesfield Road
ALDERLEY
opencast (filled)
Whiteban Farm
West Mine
Congleton Road

Grid N

E = Main existing entrances

500 m

ALDERLEY EDGE COPPER MINES

The mines at Alderley Edge are not unique, as there are several similar sites around the Cheshire/Shropshire basin. Nevertheless, Alderley has long proved of interest because of the extent of the mines and the variety of minerals found there. Geologically, Alderley Edge is a horst of Triassic sandstone, capped with the base of the harder Helsby (Keuper) Sandstone series, but formed mainly of softer Wilmslow (Bunter) Sandstone. The minerals are mainly carbonates of copper and lead, although a considerable amount of galena is also present. Cobalt was mined at times. The history of mining is unknown before 1700, although there is evidence of probable Bronze Age origins. After 1700, the mines were worked sporadically until 1919 with the most productive period being between 1857 and 1877. The mines were blocked off in the 1960's, and have been reopened from 1970 onwards by the Derbyshire Caving Club.

Access. Except for West Mine, all the mines are on National Trust property and have been reopened by the D.C.C. According to the terms of the lease of the mines to D.C.C., all entrances are securely locked. Please contact D.C.C. to arrange access.

References: Paxton, S.R.A. 1951. B.S.A. Cave Science Vol.3. No.4. pp.71 – 82. Survey.
Warrington, G. 1965. Mercian Geologist Vol.1. No.2. pp.111 – 129.
Warrington, G. 1980. Amateur Geologist Vol.3. No.2.
Warrington, G. 1981. Jour. Chester Archaeological Soc. Vol.64.

BRINLOW MINE   NGR SJ 8555 7723   Grade II (Mine)
Alt. 510ft (155m)   **Length: 980ft (300m)**   **Depth: 80ft (25m)**

A hand picked level leading from Brinlow Dell.

Entrance level leads to a small old mine cut through at depth by the Hough Level. After 330ft (100m) take the right branch (straight on is dead end) to ledge over 35ft (10m) drop. Fixed ladders lead up to three levels above and shaft entrance (covered). Fixed ladder leads down 35ft (10m) to blockage on Hough Level (qv). Passage is accessible in both directions.

ENGINE VEIN   NGR SJ 8605 7747   Grade II (Mine)
Alt. 640ft (195m)   **Length: 2500ft (750m) approx.**   **Depth: 200ft (60m)**

Exposed workings in woods near the Edge. Entrance is hinged door on side passage to S side.

Walking passage leads onto main passage after 165ft (50m). Climb down of 10ft (3m). Turn right (east) to short drop into chamber that was once in open air, now covered with concrete slab. Vein can be seen in roof at end and in following chamber. Steep descent leads to ore chute (now blocked) that connects to Hough Level. Return past climb for steep slope down to drop (8m fixed ladder) to floor of main chamber. Old timbering in roof before drop. At bottom follow curve of main chamber round past hole in roof and down slope to end of mine at this level. Just before the end, a low passage on the right leads to Blue Shaft. Quick way to Blue Shaft is to turn opposite way at bottom of ladder and follow a stooping passage down a slope.

Bear Pit (165ft/50m) is seen on left, leading from surface to the bottom of the mine where access can be gained to Brinlow Mine. Just beyond is the top of the inclined Blue Shaft, which also leads to Hough Level at bottom of mine. There is a climbing route that avoids the top section of Blue Shaft. Returning to the main chamber, there is an easy climb up to a continuation with further access to Bear Pit. At the end are some small coffin levels and a run-in from surface. Most of Engine Vein is either excavated on the fault (17th/18th C) or to the S of the fault (19th C).

HOUGH LEVEL   NGR SJ 8622 7781   Grade III (Mine)
Alt. 440ft (134m).   Length: 5000ft (1500m) approx.

In the 19th century all the mines were connected at depth by the Hough Level. The blocked entrance was near West Mine. It can be entered from Wood Mine, Stump Shaft, Brinlow, Engine Vein, Square Shaft, or below Stormy Point.

The section in Wood Mine is a branch tunnel meeting the main Hough Level near its W limit. Heading SE, waist deep water is met which ends at a blockage from above. This can be passed to another section of deep water, which becomes shallower until Brinlow is reached. There, the water becomes deeper again and shortly after the passage turns NE and heads straight towards Engine Vein for 1300ft (400m). Under Engine Vein a short branch leads to a well preserved ore chute. After the bottom of Bear Pit, Blue Shaft is passed. Another 820ft (250m) on is Square Shaft, and 18th century shaft to surface (165ft/50m). The passage then takes a number of turns before emerging on the surface below Stormy Point.

WEST MINE   NGR SJ 8519 7760   Grade III (Mine)
Alt. 480ft (146m)   Length: 6.25 miles (10000m) approx.   Depth: 165ft (50m)

Access is by arrangement with the owner of the entrance, Mr P.V.R. Sorensen, and can also be arranged through the D.C.C.

West Mine consists of a series of large tunnels on three levels following the dip down towards the WSW and then turning NW on the strike towards the end of the mine. The description is of the main route only.

Entrance is a hinged steel cover. Fixed ladders lead to the Main Chamber. This can be followed to an end after 460ft (140m). The main branch (The Canyon) leads off on the south side after about 300ft (90m). Above and to the north are a series of older, smaller passages known as the Roman Galleries. These can be reached from the N side by a climb after 330ft (100m) or by a climb on the opposite side and cross-over passage. Following on down the Canyon leads past a junction (E side) at 165ft (50m) where the Railway Tunnel enters. This is a short cut back to the entrance. At this junction a passage leads S into Twisted Pillar Cavern, while the main passage continues SW to Sphinx Chamber. The Sphinx was a prominent rock that was vandalised in the 1950's. Above this route is another large stope reached from the Cavern of the Twisted Pillar and ending in a covered shaft to surface above Sphinx Chamber.

The mine is cut in two after Sphinx Chamber by a major N-S fault. At Sphinx Chamber a short climb (fixed chain) leads to a steep incline up to the bridge across the infamous Plank Shaft. From here two routes can be followed that converge on the Great Arroyo, the first large stope after Plank Shaft. At the end of the Great Arroyo, which runs NE-SW, a second fault is met, and the mine turns NW again. At this point is Chain Shaft, an inclined shaft on a fault, connecting all levels.

When the mine was working, a railway level led from the Sphinx Chamber, through the bottom of Plank Shaft and Chain Shaft to the end of the mine. This level is partly flooded, and accessible from Chain Shaft and the Bottom Level (see below).

A bypass to Chain Shaft leads round the W side of it. Chain Shaft can be free climbed upwards with the use of a fixed chain, and downwards with a 10m ladder to descend to the railway level. At the top of Chain Shaft, the Top Level can be followed to the NW limit of the mine. Below this and connected to the Top Level at Chain Shaft and 650ft (200m) further along is the Middle Level route to the end of the mine. The next level runs straight across Chain Shaft, and joins the old railway level after a gentle slope down. Just after joining the railway level is a prominent rock known as The Dog or The Lion. From here, access is possible by some easy climbs and devious routes to the Middle and Top Levels. The Bottom Level can also be followed to the stopes at the NW end of the mine. 330 ft (100m) before the end, a branch leads W. below Doctor's Shaft to a steep incline up to the Top Level.

There are a number of branch tunnels on the NE side of the three main levels in the further part of the mine.

WOOD MINE

WOOD MINE	**NGR SJ 8544 7760**	**Grade III (Mine)**
Alt. 525ft (160m)	Length: 1.5 miles (2400m)	Depth: 100ft (30m)

Entrance is a steel manhole in Windmill Wood.

Entrance drops into the roof of the original entrance adit that leads E. to a T-junction. N. (left) leads 360ft (110m) to the N. Boundary fault and North End Chambers. S (right) leads across a bridge to Sand Cavern. From here three routes lead off. To the SW is a passage heading to Rabbit Caverns, and then turning W to meet the lower hauling level. This level leaves the mine in a S direction to join the Hough Level (qv). W and down dip from the junction with the hauling level leads to a flooded stope, the Blue Lake. N from this junction leads to the deepest point in the mine, where trial passages and workings head off on two levels to the NW. Turning E, the Railway Level can be followed through Key Chamber and the Stream Passage for about 650 ft (200m) to re-emerge in North End Chambers. Leaving Sand Cavern on the S side leads to Junction Shaft (fixed 8m ladder) which drops into a complex of passages under Sand Cavern. These can be followed SW to join the Railway Level at Key Chamber, or NE via the Green Waterfalls to rejoin the main top level on the way to North End Chambers. A third route from Sand Cavern (13ft/4m fixed ladder) leads to the Green Waterfalls by a shorter route.

COBALT MINE
NGR SJ 8594 7727 & 8594 7733   Grade II (Mine)
Alt. 625ft (190m)   **Length: 3300ft (1000m)**   **Depth: 52ft (16m)**

There are three entrances, one an old well directly behind the Wizard Restaurant. All three are connected underground by a compact mine formed on a N-S fault at several shallow levels. There are signs of there having been several shaft entrances at 10-20m intervals. Excavation to extend the mine continues as there are surface traces for another 1/2 mile (800m) to the south.

OTHER MINES   NGR SJ 85 77

Apart from the mines described above, there are two in Brinlow Dell, one behind the Wizard Inn, and three at Stormy Point.

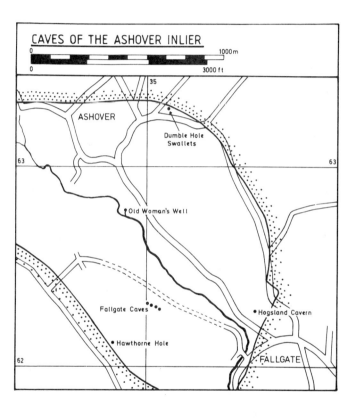

CAVES OF THE ASHOVER INLIER

ASHOVER

Dumble Hole
Swallets

Old Woman's Well

Fallgate Caves

Hogsland Cavern

Hawthorne Hole

FALLGATE

THE ASHOVER AND CRICH INLIERS

These small isolated limestone outcrops lie to the east of the main White Peak area. They are completely surrounded by the later Namurian rocks. There are a number of old mines, but accessible caves are few.

Near Crich, Wakebridge Cavern was documented in lead mining records, and was re-entered recently by cavers. This is the only listed cave in the Crich Inlier.

The Ashover Inlier, a little further to the north, boasts a group of small swallets, which feed water to a rising 150ft (46m) lower. None of these has been penetrated for any distance, but there is the possibility of a system of limited size here. The Fallgate Caves, in the cliff on the east side of the River Amber, are of no great extent, but here again digging may be repaid.

DUMBLE HOLE SWALLETS   NGR 352 632   Digs
Alt. 650ft (198m)

No access restriction. Owner is Mr C. Chapple, Grange Farm, Ashover.

In a tree-lined depression near the Black Swan Inn.

Three small swallets taking a small amount of water, known as Spout Swallow Hole, Bull Hole, and Tunnel Hole. The water was dye tested in 1968 to Old Woman's Well, Demonsdale, Ashover, approximately half a mile (0.8km) away and 150ft (46m) lower.

FALLGATE CAVES   NGR 350 623   Grade I
Alt. 600ft (180m)

Land owner is Mr Wilmot, Hilltop Farm, Hilltop Road, Ashover. Prior permission not needed.

Four entrances in the cliff face across the river from Fall Hill. Caves are numbered from left to right facing the cliff.

CAVE NO. 1   NGR 3507 6228   Grade I
Length: 60ft (18.2m).

Large entrance leads directly into a chamber with one crawl leading off 5ft (1.5m) off the ground. Crawl leads to small chamber and exit between boulders close to entrance No.2.

CAVE NO. 2   NGR 3505 6229   Grade I
Length: 57ft (17.3m)

Large entrance leads into walking sized passage which turns sharply right. Passage soon lowers to crawl over earth fill. Can be seen to continue, but requires removal of earth fill to proceed.

CAVE NO. 3   NGR 3504 6230   **Grade II**
Length: 100ft (30m)

Climb 12ft (3.6m) up cliff face leads to a tight meandering rift cave with formations. It ends in a small decorated chamber near the surface, which was being dug by persons unknown in 1988.

CAVE NO. 4   NGR 3503 6230   **Grade I**
Length: 36ft+ (11m+)

Low crawl under fractured rock (care needed) leads directly into small chamber with two ways off. Small passage straight ahead soon ends, and contains an animal sett. Other passage is small and narrow but can be seen to enlarge slightly. Not explored.

HAWTHORNE HOLE   NGR 3484 6211   Grade I
Alt. 650ft (195m)   **Length: 51ft (15.5m)**

Land owner is Biwater Pipes and Castings (ex Clay Cross Company), Clay Cross.

Difficult to find. Behind a bush in a field south east of Overton Hall. Short level nearby with fence round entrance.

A single chamber with a crawl leading off. The nearby mine level is best avoided as it is rather unstable.

HOGSLAND CAVERN & MINE   NGR 3558 6227   Lost

No access. Owner lives at "Spath Fluor" house, Milltown. Shaft capped with concrete.

A cavern struck in the workings down the Hogsland lead mine shaft and now under water. Exact position not known but believed to lie in a series of pipe-vein workings some 200ft (61m) below the surface under the east side of Fall Hill. The grid reference given is for Hogsland Mine Shaft.

OLD WOMAN'S WELL   NGR 3488 6278   Spring
Alt. 510ft (155m)

A rising on the north east bank of the River Amber. The resurgence of water which sinks at the Dumble Hole Swallets.

WAKEBRIDGE CAVERN   NGR 339 558   Grade II (Mine)
(Bacchus Pipe)

No access at present.

In the workings of Wakebridge Mine. A large cavern struck in the workings of the Wakebridge Mine, and once drained by a sough. Rediscovered by Wirksworth Mines Research Group.

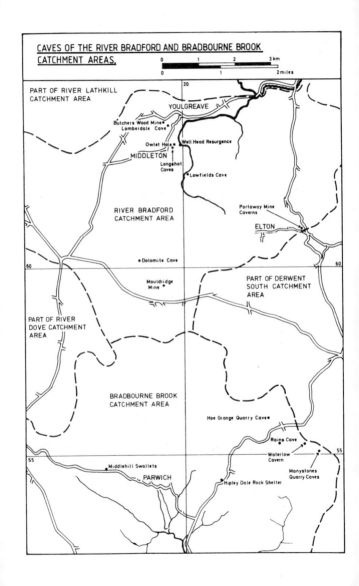

CAVES OF THE RIVER BRADFORD AND BRADBOURNE BROOK
CATCHMENT AREAS.

THE BRADBOURNE BROOK
CATCHMENT AREA

At the southern extremity of the White Peak lies the seldom visited area which, topographically, drains to the Bradbourne Brook. It is dominated by reef limestones, with distinctive dolomites to the west which can be seen as the periglacial weathered tors of Rainster and Harborough Rocks. To the south lies the small isolated Kniveton – Bradbourne limestone inlier.

Of geological interest is the Tertiary Brassington Formation, preserved as silica sand pockets up to 43m thick in large solution collapse hollows scattered over a 4km wide area from Parsley Hay to Brassington.

Along the limestone margin small sinks lie to the west of Parwich, but their risings are unknown. Small springs feed the Bletch and Havenhill Dale Brooks, as at Parwich, Ballidon and Brassington, but some drainage from the area may go westwards to rise in the Dove.

Also of interest are the dry valleys and gorges at Hipley Dale and Ballidon.

It seems unlikely that large penetrable caves exist, but digging at the sinks, coupled with a dye testing programme, may yield interesting results.

HIPLEY DALE ROCK SHELTER NGR 210 543 Grade I
Alt. 650ft (195m)   **Length: 15ft (5m)**

Close to the Bakewell-Ashbourne road on the south side.

Two obvious shelters, broken into by quarrying. One has good bedding anastomosis.

HOE GRANGE QUARRY CAVE
NGR 223 560   Grade I (Arch)
Alt. 1100ft (335m)   **Length: 20ft (6m)**

Entrance 25ft (8m) up in lower quarry face.

Yielded Pleistocene mammal remains, now almost all quarried away. Only a 20ft (6m) crawl remains. Quarry exhibits a variety of solution features along joints and bedding.

Reference: Bemrose, H.A. and Newton, E. 1905. Quart. Jour. Geol. Soc. Vol.61. pp.43-62. Survey.

MANYSTONES QUARRY CAVES   NGR 237 551   Lost
Alt. 1050ft (320m)

Small solution caves in a large disused limestone quarry. All now buried under industrial waste.

One small blind solution tube and small tubes high up.

MIDDLEHILL SWALLETS   NGR 178 546   Digs
(Parwich Sink)
Alt. 660ft.(201m)

Two active sinks in hollows beside the Parwich-Alsop road.

The more northerly sink was forced in 1971 to a small muddy chamber, but the entrance has since collapsed and dumped farm rubbish obscures much of the site. The swallet nearest the road is choked with masonry from collapsed former barn (shown on earlier maps as "Tithe Barn"). Resurgences not known.

References: Mellors, P.T. 1971. D.C.A. N/L No.11. pp.3-4, Potts, J. 1976. D.C.A. N/L No.27. p.6.

RAINS CAVE   NGR 226 553   Grade I (Arch)
(Longcliffe Fissure)
Alt. 1100ft(330m)   Length: 30ft (9m)

Behind large boulders at the east end of Longcliffe Crags, about 100 yards (91m) west of Observer Corps Box.

A sloping chamber with crawls off. Incompletely excavated. Numerous animal remains and some prehistoric pottery found.

References: Ward, J. 1889. Derbys. Arch. Jour. No.11. pp.31-45. Plan. Ward, J. 1892. Derbys. Arch. Jour. No.14. pp.228-250. Section. Ward, J. 1893. Derbys. Arch. Jour. No.15. pp.161-176.

WATER LOW CAVERN   NGR 233 553 approx.   Lost

The hill between Manystones Quarry and Longcliffe is unnamed on the 6 inch map, but was once known as Waterlow. It is presumd to be the site of the cavern explored by the Derbyshire Pennine Club in May 1907.

A 6ft (1.8m) by 4ft (1.2m) mineshaft 30ft (9m) deep led to a natural chamber 10ft (3m) wide, 30ft (9m) high and 30ft (9m) long. A further climb down of 16ft (5m) led to a small continuation to the south east which became too tight.

At the north end, a climb up led into a passage 18ft (5.5m) high by 3ft (1m) wide. A climb down a narrow slot for 10ft (3m) entered a passage which ended at a small chamber. The continuation from here was dug, but soon choked.

Would be an interesting dig if the site could be located.

Reference: Smithard, W. 1st June 1907. Nottinghamshire Guardian.

THE RIVER BRADFORD CATCHMENT AREA

The main catchment for the River Bradford is the shale and sandstone upland to the east, but a small proportion of its flow emerges from active risings in its south and west banks. No known swallets feed these risings: the nearest swallets are the small ones at Duckett Wall and Astonhill, in the Derwent South Catchment. These could be associated with the Bradford risings, but no dye tests have been carried out to confirm this.

Gratton Dale has a small wet-weather rising, but for the most part the dale has no surface flow.

There has been some suggestion that the flow of the River Bradford has declined since the driving of the Hillcar Sough.

Speleologically, very little is known, and there is a very large blank area on the map containing no known caves. However a dip slope of limestone rises gently westwards from the river, and it is possible that an integrated underground drainage system lurks beneath it awaiting the lucky explorer. Determined digging in the vicinity of the risings, or at the Longshot Caves, may well bring some worthwhile discoveries.

ALPORT QUARRY FISSURE   Lost

A fissure which yielded red deer remains according to Bemrose.

References: Bemrose, H.H.Arnold. Victoria County History of Derbyshire. p.36.

BUTCHER'S WOOD MINE
NGR 195 639   **Grade II (Mine)**
Alt. 825ft (251m)   **Length: 70ft (21m)**   **Depth: 40ft (12m) approx.**

On hillside opposite Needleseye Corner on the B5056 road.

Stooping adit entrance. Walking for 30ft (9m) to lip of first pitch in natural pot. 20ft (6m) sloping descent to sloping boulder floor of small chamber which forms the northern end of an enlarged rift running at right angles to the entrance passage. 2nd Pitch of 12ft (3.2m) is off perched boulders in the rift which then drops steeply to terminal silt choke in floor. Good active formations in the lower section of the mine.

Tackle – 1st Pitch, 20ft (6m) ladder; 30ft (9m) lifeline. 2nd Pitch, 12ft (4m) ladder; 20ft (6m) lifeline.

DOLOMITE CAVE   NGR 188 602   Grade I
Alt. 900ft (270m)   Length: 15ft (5m)

In branch of Long Dale near the dolomite/limestone junction.

A small cave exposed by collapse, with an outer and an inner chamber connected by a squeeze.

LOMBERDALE CAVE   NGR 196 638   Grade I
Alt. 770ft (235m)   Length: 15ft (5m)

Entrance in south side of dale, 100 yards (91m) or so west of Youlgreave road.

A scramble down into a wide low bedding plane with roof pendants and a channel in the floor. Becomes too tight for progress without excavating the floor.

LONGSHOT CAVES   NGR 198 633   Grade II
(Rusden Caves)
Alt. 580ft (176m)   Length: 200ft (61m) total

Two slot entrances one above the other at the foot of the cliff, behind excavated material visible from the footpath in Middleton Dale.

Low bedding crawls ending in chokes. The upper passage trends south, becoming too tight after 70ft (21m) in gour pools and flowstone. This passage is thought to be an old outlet for water rising at Well Head nearby in the main valley. The lower passage lies parallel to the dale side. Right hand branch ends at blocked hole in the floor close to the cliff face. The left branch develops into a vadose modified tube soon becoming too tight in partial fill of mud and rock. A strong draught at times.

References: Christopher, N.S.J. & Mellors, P.T. 1977. Bull. B.C.R.A. No.17. pp.16-19. Mellors, P.T. 1972. D.C.A. N/L No.13. pp.2-3.

LOWFIELDS CAVE   NGR 201 625   Grade I
(Badger Hole)
Alt. 600ft (180m)   Length: 30ft (9m)

On the east bank of Rowlow Brook, well hidden.

A low bedding cave. May be a former outlet for sinks higher up the scarp. It soon becomes too tight.

MOULDRIDGE MINE   NGR 1943 5952   Grade 2 (Mine)
Alt. 900ft (274m)   Length: 500ft (152m)

The adit entrance is fitted with a grill, and spanner for shaft entrance obtainable from Mr Walker, Keeper's Cottage, Astonhill. Other shafts close by have been sealed.

Obvious adit entrance by tips in the south branch of upper Gratton Dale.

A complex maze of worked out pipe veins and scrins, with links to surface via a number of partially blocked shafts. The site was last worked for ore in the 1950's. The shaft entrance is blocked at 90ft (27m) but has workings opening off it at 30ft (9m) and 50ft (15m).

Reference: Pearce, A. et al, 1984. Bull. P.D.M.H.S. Vol.9. No.2. pp.108-122.

OWLET HOLE   NGR 198 633   Grade I (Arch)
(Owlet Hole Cave)
Alt. 600ft (183m)   Length: 10ft (3m)

High in the cliff face seen from the footpath down Middleton Dale.

A prominent entrance. The roomy threshold closes down to a vadose slot too tight for entry. Archaeologically excavated. Animal remains found.

Reference: Bramwell, D. & Wood, C. 1947. Northwestern Naturalist Vol.22. pp.235-239.

PORTAWAY MINE CAVERNS
NGR 232 610 to 234 607   Mines
Alt. c.800ft (244m)   Depth: over 300ft (91m)

Permission rarely given.

Between Winster and Elton. Access via deep shafts.

A very extensive series of pipe vein caverns and workings, last worked in the 1950's.

WELL HEAD RESURGENCE   NGR 1995 6325   Spring
Alt. 550ft (168m)

The largest of a series of risings on the west bank of Rowlow Brook between Smerrill Grange and Youlgreave. The outlet is a wide low impenetrable bedding plane beside the footpath through the dale. Flow is held back by a small concrete dam which diverts some of the water along an iron pipe to a ruined pumping station at the foot of Middleton Dale. The spring dries up in mid to late summer, and Rowlow Brook has been seen to sink into its bed close by.

Reference: Christopher, N.S.J. & Mellors, P.T. 1977. B.C.R.A. Bull. No.17.pp.16-20.

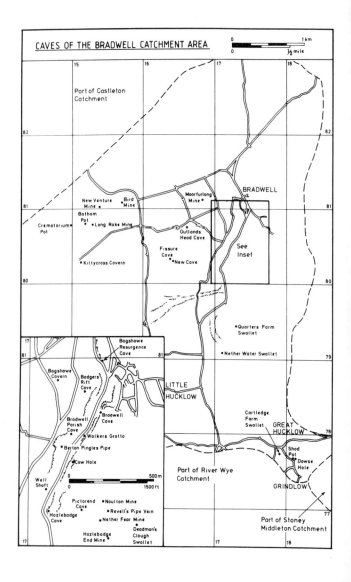

CAVES OF THE BRADWELL CATCHMENT AREA

Part of Castleton Catchment

BRADWELL

New Venture Mine
Bird Mine
Moorfurlong Mine
Bothom Pot
Crematorium Pot
Long Rake Mine
Outlands Head Cave
See Inset
Fissure Cave
New Cave
Kittycross Cavern

Quarters Farm Swallet

Nether Water Swallet

LITTLE HUCKLOW

Cartledge Farm Swallet

GREAT HUCKLOW

Bagshawe Resurgence Cave
Bagshawe Cavern
Badgers Rift Cave
Bradwell Parish Cave
Bradwell Cave
Walkers Grotto
Berton Pingles Pipe
Cow Hole
Well Shaft

Shod Pot
Dowse Hole

GRINDLOW

Part of River Wye Catchment

Pictorend Cave
Noulton Mine
Revell's Pipe Vein
Hazlebadge Cave
Nether Fear Mine
Hazlebadge End Mine
Deadman's Clough Swallet

Part of Stoney Middleton Catchment

0   1 km
0   ½ mile

0   500m
0   1500 ft

THE BRADWELL
CATCHMENT AREA

Bradwell Dale contains many small caves, but none is of any great extent. Running subparallel to the dale on the west side, however, is Bagshawe Cavern, a system of mature passages consisting mainly of a flood overflow route. The large stream is only briefly seen in a short stretch of streamway at the southern end of the system, close to the level of the resurgence cave in Bradwell village. The cave ends at deep sumps, and there are very few good digging prospects.

A look at the map soon reveals that there is a very large cave system waiting to be found upstream of Bagshawe Cavern. The size of the stream itself suggests an extensive system, and the geography of the catchment area confirms it. In a similar manner to the Stoney Middleton and Castleton areas, there is a line of sinks along the shale margin from which water must follow the strike of the beds to the resurgence.

The farthest swallet is Dowse (or "Duce") Hole at Grindlow, 400ft (122m) above the rising, and over 2 miles (3.5km) distant. There is a very large unexplored area in between. In addition to the route from swallet to resurgence, there must be a number of large tributaries from the west, where the limestone rises gently onto the summit of Bradwell Moor. Digs in smaller swallets at Grindlow and Hucklow have so far proved inconclusive, but Dowse Hole is being actively dug (1991).

The Bradwell area is thus one of the best areas of future potential, probably second only to the Wormhill area. It may take years to find it, but the cave is there waiting.

BADGER'S RIFT   GR 173 808   Grade I
Alt. 630ft (192m)   **Length: 60ft (18m)**

In field above Bagshaw Resurgence Cave.

Partly excavated fissure passage descends to a choke. The entrance may be covered with rocks, which should be replaced.

Reference: Orpheus Caving Club Hut Log. 1978.

BAGSHAWE CAVERN
NGR 1714 8088   Grade III (Part Show)
Alt. 770ft (235m)   **Length: 1.9 miles (3km) approx**

Show Cave. Adventure trips etc. Details from the proprietor, Mr. P. Revell, 12 Bradwell Head Road, Bradwell.

On southern outskirts of Bradwell village.

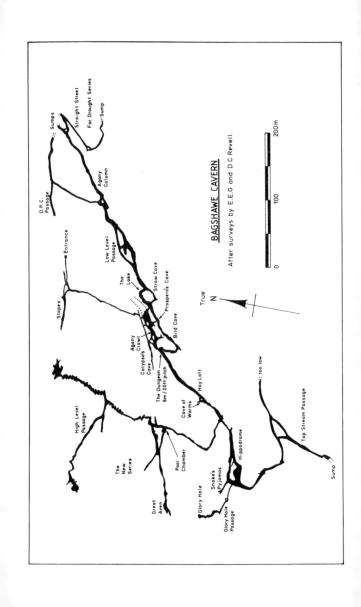

BAGSHAWE CAVERN

After surveys by E.E.G and D.C.Revell.

Upper Levels

Old workings at and below entrance formerly known as Mulespinner Mine. Entrance covered by a small stone building. Descend steps in vein, then turn left along obvious passage following tourist path for 540ft (165m) to the junction with Calypso's Cave, 180ft (55m) long to a choke. Tourist path turns left, passing the wide low Agony Crawl on the left. Just beyond, steps lead down to the top of the Dungeon, an 18ft (5.5m) pitch. The main passage continues beyond the Dungeon for 295ft (90m), and lowers to a crawl. To the right is the Cave of Worms, where a climb down boulders rejoins the main route, which continues as a large passage for 460ft (140m) to the Hippodrome, a wide boulder-strewn chamber.

Turning left at the Hippodrome, a sloping muddy passage leads to the streamway. Left downstream has been dived in a tight bouldery sump for 60ft (18m) containing one air bell. Right (upstream) can be followed with minimal air space for 220ft (67m) to Sump 1, 30ft (9m) long, followed by a 70ft (21m) crawl leading to a 15ft (4.5m) duck. 40ft (12m) of larger passage follows to Sump 2, 25ft (8m) long. 50ft (15m) of canal passage leads to Sump 3 which has been dived to a gravel choke 500ft (150m) from base at a depth of 100ft (30m).

An oxbow on the west side of the Hippodrome leads to a short climb down into Glory Hole Passage, a phreatic joint-controlled inlet which descends to a duck, then rises again to the head of an impressive pothole, 45ft (14m) deep to water, the Glory Hole. The water level in the Glory Hole falls considerably in dry weather. It has been inconclusively dived. Just to the right of Glory Hole Passage is a crawl, which gradually lowers until it is too tight.

Lower Series

From the bottom of The Dungeon 330ft (100m) of crawling and walking leads to a chamber where the Agony Crawl enters at roof level. Shortly beyond is The Lake, a waist deep pool. A further 1000ft (305m) of varied passage leads to a sump, which becomes a duck in dry weather. 300ft (91m) of passage follows, mostly crawling, to a permanent sump. Just before the sump, a passage on the right is the entrance to the Far Drought Series, first entered in 1989, consisting of 395ft (120m) of stooping and crawling to a sump. Shortly before the duck, a left hand branch can be followed for 500ft (152m) to another sump. The sumps lie close to the level of the nearby resurgence at the head of the Bradwell Brook.

The New Series

On the right of the Upper Series between the Cave of Worms and the Hippodrome, a gate leads to an ascending hands and knees crawl. After a tight squeeze the passage enlarges, in places to walking size, and leads to a junction. To the left a crawl (flooded in winter) leads to a series of passages with high avens, while to the right the route soon lowers to an unpleasant restricted muddy duck. Beyond the duck the passage soon becomes larger, and further branches lead up-dip to the left. The main route continues until it lowers and ends at clay chokes close to the entrance vein.

Tackle:	Ladder	Belay	Lifeline
Dungeon	18ft (5.5m)	Spreader	30ft (9m)
Glory Hole	50ft (15m)	20ft (6m)	70ft (21m)

References: Baker, E.A. c.1910. Moors, Crags and Caves of the High Peak. Chapter XXV. Survey. Farr, M. 1977. CDG N/L No.45. pp.18-19. Ford, T.D., Burek, C., and Beck, J.S. 1975. Trans B.C.R.A. Vol.2. No.3. pp.133-140. Survey.

BAGSHAWE RESURGENCE CAVE
NGR 174 811   Grade 1 & Dive
(The Yeld, The Lumb).
Alt. 600ft (183m)   Length: 100ft (30m)

Entrance is in masonry once supporting a water wheel for the lead smelter, at the head of Bradwell Brook.

The resurgence of the Bagshaw Cavern stream. More water resurges here per annum than the combined flow of Peak Cavern and Russett Well.

Main entrance is normally a 23ft (7m) sump above the waterfall, reduced to a duck in dry weather, but free diving inadvisable. An alternative entrance is a dry culvert crawl 3ft (1m) to the right. Both routes join at a partly natural chamber, followed by a short passage to Sump 2 (Boulder Sump). This flooded pot has been excavated by C.D.G. for 16ft (5m). Rubble removed from here has filled the blind ending 25ft (8m) long level beyond.

In the chamber near the entrance is a very low bedding on stream left leading after 30ft (9m) to Sump 3, which is too low.

References: Cordingley, J.N. 1987. D.C.A. N/L. No.64. p.12. Survey. Murland, J.D. 1978. CDG N/L Nos 46,47 & 48 & D.C.A. N/L No.37.

BATHAM POT   NGR 152 808
(Pigeon Hole, Moss Pot)
Alt. 1250ft (375m)

100ft (30m) west of Long Rake Mine on Bradwell Moor.

A large open pot 100ft (30m) long and 50ft (15m) deep, now largely filled in. Easy scramble down the east end. Old mine workings to the west and abortive dig in floor. Probably communicated with natural caverns in Long Rake Mine (q.v.).

700ft (210m) to the north east a mine shaft 30ft (9m) deep led to a large natural cavern 60ft (18m) high and 40ft (12m) wide. (NGR 153 808). It has now been obliterated by fluorspar working.

100ft (30m) further east-north-east is a group of shafts and natural pots some 30ft (9m) deep (NGR 154 810).

Reference: Tottle, P. 1957. The Lyre Vol.1. No.2. pp.38-41. Survey.

BERTONS PINGLES PIPE   NGR 1719 8053   Grade II
(Shawley Cave)
Alt. 700ft (213m)   Length: 525ft (160m)

On the west side of Bradwell Dale, a short distance up the dale from Bradwell Parish Cave. A narrow entrance at the base of the cliff in the quarry floor.

The narrow entrance gives access to 250ft (76m) of dry passage. A 30ft (9m) shaft descends to lower flooded workings. The shaft drops straight into the sump pool with two ways on. C.D.G.divers have explored 140ft (42m) of sump to three run-in chambers where the air is suspected to be bad. At right angles to this sump another sumped passage continues to a junction. Left has been dived for approx 120ft (36m) with no end in sight, right terminates in boulders after 15ft (4.5m).

References: Buckley, A.L. 1974. DCA N/L No.21. Drakeley, K. 1978. DCA N/L No.37.

BIRD MINE   NGR 157 811   Grade III
Alt. 1130ft (339m)   **Depth: 328ft (100m)**

A mine shaft some 200ft (60m) west of the top Castleton-Tideswell road south west of Earle's Quarry.

The shaft is 328ft (100m) deep with levels off at 110, 193, and 263ft (33, 58 and 79m). The first level extends into a rift now blocked. The second extends into a short series of flat workings and a natural rift chamber 70ft (21m) high. The third level is short and goes into workings only, whilst at the bottom there is only a short trial level.

The shaft can be descended directly, or the levels can be entered and interconnecting winzes can be descended to the bottom.

Tackle:

Direct descent	330ft (100m) ladder	350ft (107m) lifeline
SRT	350ft rope	

Reference: Lord, P.J. & Thompson, S.J. 1969. Jour. S.U.S.S. Vol.1. No.4. pp.166-169. Survey.

BRADWELL CAVE   NGR 174 807   Grade I
Alt. 663ft (200m)   **Length: 106ft (32m)**

On east side of Bradwell Dale, 130ft (40m) north of the lay-by north of Walker's Grotto. Scramble up a series of ledges to an obscure cave entrance in the cliff some 50ft (15m) above the road.

A low crawl descends down dip, becoming larger before ending at a mud choke. A few small side passages all quickly become too low. There is another small cave entrance high in the buttress on the east side of the dale near the village tip immediately south of Bradwell. This is said to extend for 30ft (9m) although access is not allowed.

BRADWELL PARISH CAVE   NGR 172 805   Grade I
(Old Brook Cave)
Alt. 640ft (195m)   **Length: 130ft (40m)**

Large truncated phreatic tube in the abandoned quarry to the west of the track up from the road opposite layby near Bradwell Cave.

Obvious entrance continues as an easy passage up dip to a low section over calcited rocks and gravel. Beyond the squeeze the cave ends at a complete choke.

References: Crabtree, P.W. 1964. Cave Science Vol.5. No.36. Survey.
Turner, D. 1950. British Caver Vol.21. p.22.

CARTLEDGE FARM SWALLET NGR 1791 7774 Grade I
Alt. 1010ft (308m)   Length: 55ft (17m)   Depth: 45ft (14m)

Access not normally granted.
  In garden of Cartledge Farmhouse, in the centre of the lawn.
  A collapse close to the house took a considerable stream from an ancient
land drain. Excavated for 25ft (8m) to bedrock by Eyam Exploration Group
in 1988. Paving slab covers short drop into concrete culvert, leading to 23ft
(7m) concrete shaft. Short descending passage with shale roof leads to 15ft
(5m) climb down narrow rift to a very tight continuation.

COW HOLE   NGR 1725 8044   Grade I
Alt. 780ft (238m)   Length: 130ft (40m)

Large entrance overlooking Bradwell Dale from the east.
  A large mined out chamber, partly natural, leads to a short passage.
  Reference: Crabtree, P.W. 1964. B.S.A. Cave Science Vol.5. No.36.
pp.188 & 190. Survey.

CREMATORIUM POT   NGR 150 808   Dig
Alt. 1250ft (380m)   Depth: 40ft (12m)

In field north west of Batham Pot (Pigeon Hole).
  A natural pothole which has been dug for 40ft (12m) to a descending mud-
filled passage. A resistivity survey suggested the presence of a large chamber
50ft (15m) below the surface.
  References: Anon. 1979. Jour. S.U.S.S. Vol.3. No.1. p.59. Lord, P.J.
1970. Jour. S.U.S.S. Vol.1. No.6. p.229.

DEADMAN'S CLOUGH SWALLET   NGR 176 801   Dig
Alt. c.800ft (244m)

About 1/4 mile (400m) east of Hazlebadge Hall, near Old Pig Tor End Lead
Mine.
  A choked swallet which takes little water now owing to reservoirs higher
up.

DOWSE HOLE   NGR 1812 7767   Grade III
(Duce Hole)
Alt. 1000ft (305m)   Length: 370ft (113m)   Depth: 40ft (12m)

Permission from Mr. Ollerenshaw at the farm. Please park in a manner that
does not obstruct roads or entrances.
  Immediately north of Grindlow, near Great Hucklow. Two streams sink.
Shod Pot is a 20ft timbered shaft in the field nearest to the road, taking a
stream.
  A sizeable stream which includes farm sewage flows down over boulders
into a chamber, and on down a short stretch of roomy stream passage. The
original entrance lies above the stream sink, and led through very tight

squeezes to drop into the roof of the streamway. Stream drops down impenetrable hole in second chamber, littered with three generations of old digging gear.

Passage lowers to a crawl, and becomes narrow beyond a short incline. Enlarged joint passage continues to end of railway approx 230ft (70m) from entrance. Sharp right hand bend is followed by muddy squeeze and crawl through boulders. Tight sump can be bypassed by climbing above pool into chamber with tight passage running back towards entrance. Way on from chamber is very awkward and loose squeeze into flat out crawl in stream, which flows into low bedding. Climb above into final rift where stream flows into a tight sump. Currently (1990) being dug by Eyam Exploration Group.

There is some confusion over the name. Farey (1811, p.295) noted Dowse Hole, Grindlow, near Eyam, a deep open hole. He also refers (p.293) to "Duss Pit, in Eyam". Duss Pit is likely to be Hungerhill Swallet, near Dustypit Mine. There is evidence to suggest that the hole known as "Duce" or "Dowse" was blown in early this century, and local people refer to it as "The Dowse". It is called "Dowse Hole" on the earliest Ordnance Maps, but the name seems to have changed to "Duce Hole" on maps of the late 1800's.

References: Batey, A. & Lord, P.J. 1970. Jour. S.U.S.S. Vol.1. No.6. p.246-247. Survey. British Speleological Association Records. 1959-1960. Farey, J. 1811. A general view of the Agriculture and Minerals of Derbyshire. p.293 & 295.

HARTLE DALE CAVES
(Gelly Dale Caves)

Permission from Hartlemoor Farm.

NEW CAVE   NGR 1644 8031   Grade I (Arch)
(Upper Hartle Dale Cave, Upper Gelly Dale Cave)
Alt 980ft (299m)   Length: 50ft (15m)

On the south side of the valley on a bench a short distance above the valley floor.

Entrance 6ft (1.8m) high and 6ft (1.8m) wide, diminishing to a crawl for about 50ft. There is little doubt that this is the "New Cave" referred to by Pennington in 1877.

FISSURE CAVE   NGR 1642 8033   Grade I (Arch)
(Lower Hartle Dale Cave, Lower Gelly Dale Cave)
Alt 975ft (297m)   Length: 10ft (3m)

30 yards (27m) north west of New Cave.

An obvious fissure with a tiny bedding plane passage directly above. The fissure is about 13ft (4m) high, dwindling from several feet wide at the top to a few inches at the bottom. There is no doubt that this is the "Fissure Cave" referred to by Pill (1963) and Turk (1966).

TOP CAVE   **Lost**

Top Cave could well be New Cave, and it is possible that two lots of archaeological material in the last century came from the one place, with additional material being excavated in the 1960's from Fissure Cave. Despite extensive search in 1979 "Top Cave" was not found.

References: Pennington, R. 1877. Quart. Jour. Geol Soc. pp.240-241. Pill, A.L. 1963. B.S.A. Cave Science Vol.V. No.33. pp.25-35. Turk, S.M. 1966. B.S.A. Cave Science Vol.V. No.40. pp.426-439.

HAZLEBADGE CAVE   NGR 1711 8019   Grade II
Alt. 700ft (213m)   **Length: 391ft (119m)**   **Depth: 54ft (16m)**

Gated. Limited access. Contact D.C.A. for up to date information.

Situated on hill spur 600ft (182m) north of Hazlebadge Hall and 180ft (55m) east of the road.

A short mine level ends at the base of a run in shaft which lies beneath a blocked depression on the surface. Near the end of the level is a shaft 24ft (7m) deep. 12ft (4m) down this shaft a short level can be entered which gives access to the top of the main chamber. From the bottom of the shaft an upward level ends after 20ft (6m) while down the slope a series of short climbs (rope useful for novices), gives access to the main chamber which is natural. The passage to the left ends after 10ft (3m) while a low muddy tube on the right can be followed southward for 50ft (15m) into a high tight rift passage terminating in a small chamber. From a ledge above the chamber a small tube becomes too tight, and a bedding plane to the west can be followed for a short distance.

The way on from the main chamber is straight ahead through a muddy crawl, or climb above which drops to the same point. A couple of sporting climbs follow (rope useful). The cave terminates at the top of a steeply ascending rift in a chamber with a flowstone cascade. A short distance before this a climb in the roof gives access to a narrowing decorated crawl.

Tackle:

Entrance Pitch	25ft (8m) ladder	30ft (9m) lifeline
Climbs:	20ft (6m) handline useful.	

References: Crabtree, P.W. 1964. B.S.A. Cave Science Vol.5. No.36. pp.180,183, & 185. Survey. Farey, 1811. A general view of the agriculture and minerals of Derbyshire. p.296.

HAZLEBADGE END MINE
NGR 1745 8015   **Grade I (Mine)**
Alt. 780ft (238m)   **Length: 100ft (30m)**

Permission from Hazlebadge Hall. Unlikely.

At extreme south end of limestone hill behind Hazlebadge Hall, a few yards north east of Pictor End Mine.

Entrance from mined trench, by sliding down among boulders. Single natural but mined out chamber, with a crawl through boulders at the end.

Reference: Crabtree, P.W. 1964. B.S.A. Cave Science Vol.5. No.36. pp.183,184, & 186. Survey.

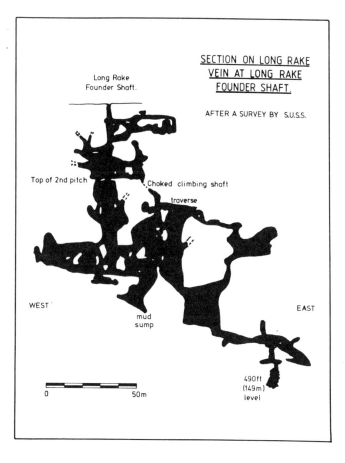

Long Rake
Founder Shaft.

SECTION ON LONG RAKE
VEIN AT LONG RAKE
FOUNDER SHAFT.

AFTER A SURVEY BY S.U.S.S.

Top of 2nd pitch

Choked climbing shaft

traverse

WEST

EAST

mud
sump

0   50m

490ft
(149m)
level

KITTYCROSS CAVERN   NGR 151 803   Grade III (Mine)
Alt. 1275ft (388m)   **Depth: 450ft (137m)**

Mine shaft east of Moss Rake spar-washing plant.

At bottom of main shaft a short passage leads into narrow natural fissure with a 10ft (3m) drop into a single chamber in the top of a decomposed lava.

Tackle – 450ft (137m) ladder; 480ft (146m) lifeline.
SRT: 480ft (146m) rope.

Reference: Ford, T.D. 1951. British Caver. Vol.22. pp.45-48. Survey.

LONG RAKE MINE   NGR 153 808   Grade V (Mine)
(Long Rake Founder Shaft)
Alt. 1235ft (310m)   **Depth: 500ft (150m)**

Warning: Mine contains many unstable stacked deads. Treat with extreme caution.

An obvious mine shaft about 100ft (30m) east of Batham Pot.

First pitch of 130ft (40m), partly a ginged mine shaft, partly a worked out vein. Levels off at 30, 69, and 92ft (9, 21, and 28m) into natural cavities and stopes. Second pitch follows soon, 170ft (50m), in a vein cavity with a ledge and short level at 120ft (37m) down. Main level runs east-west at 300ft (92m) depth, with short pitches downwards. Climbing at the western end leads into a large stope with a steeply sloping floor to the head of the third pitch, 48ft (15m) into a large oval chamber with stemples opposite. A short climb down below these leads into another large cavern 50 x 90ft (15 x 27m) with short stalactites. A stream can be heard and digging has reached a short pitch to a chamber with a washed out lava bed and no way on. The stopes can be climbed for 120ft (37m) to a level which enters another chamber 40ft (12m) long and 130ft (40m) deep. A ledge round this leads to another chamber and a series of climbs down to lower levels.

Tackle:	Ladder	Lifeline
First Pitch	130ft (40m)	150ft (46m)
Second Pitch	170ft (52m)	190ft (58m)
Third Pitch:	50ft (15m)	70ft (21m)

Ropes and climbing gear useful in stopes.

References: Lord, P.J. & Thompson, S.J. 1968. Jour. S.U.S.S. Vol.1. No.3. pp.104-111. Lord, P.J. & Worthington, S.R.H. 1969. Jour. S.U.S.S. Vol.1. No.5. pp.181-185. Survey.

MILL DAM CAVERN   Lost

In the vicinity of Great Hucklow, on the Hucklow Edge Vein.

A large cavern found during mining operations said to be "as big as Tideswell Church".

Reference: Kirkham, N. 1963. Bull. P.D.M.H.S. Vol.2. No.1. p.32.

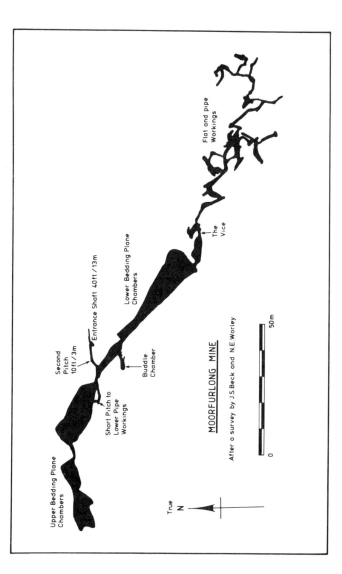

Upper Bedding Plane Chambers

Short Pitch to Lower Pipe Workings

Second Pitch 10ft/3m

Entrance Shaft 40ft/13m

Buddle Chamber

Lower Bedding Plane Chambers

The Vice

Flat and pipe Workings

True N

MOORFURLONG MINE

After a survey by J.S.Beck and N.E.Worley

0   50m

MOORFURLONG MINE & CAVERNS
NGR 1683 8120   Grade II (Mine)
Alt. 943ft (287m)   **Length: 700ft (210m)**   **Depth: 70ft (21m)**

Permission from Within Farm, above the road.

In corner of field almost opposite the entrance to Within Farm.

Entrance shaft 44ft (13m) with ancient metal ladder. A short passage leads to the second pitch of 12ft (4m). At the bottom a series of pipe workings and natural caverns extends to the south east and north west. The longer series is to the south east, running for some 600ft (180m) and bending round to the east, via old buddle pools and "The Vice" crawl. Passages beyond The Vice consist of a network of crawls. To the north west of the entrance is about 100ft (30m) of large bedding cave.

Tackle:

Entrance pitch	45ft (14m) ladder	55ft (17m) lifeline
SRT	55ft (17m) rope	
Second Pitch	12ft (4m) ladder	20ft (6m) lifeline

References: Marsh, A.L. 1953. The Speleologist. Vol.1. pp.3-8. Survey. Beck, J.S. & Worley, N.E. 1976. Trans. B.C.R.A. Vol.3. No.1. pp.49-53. Survey.

NETHER FEAR MINE   NGR 1740 8015   Grade II (Mine)
Alt. 800ft (240m)   **Length: 120ft (36m)**   **Depth: 110ft (34m)**

280 yards (256m) north east of Hazlebadge Hall.

A 100 ft (30m) shaft leads to a ledge with a scramble down to worked out pipe vein with some natural chambers leading eastwards to a muddy crawl into rifts. Probably no longer accessible.

Tackle – 100ft (30m) ladder. 110ft (34m) lifeline.

Reference: Crabtree, P.W. 1964. B.S.A. Cave Science Vol.5. No.36. pp.184 & 186. Survey.

NETHERWATER SWALLET   NGR 171 791   Dig
Alt. 790ft (237m)

100 yards (91m) below Netherwater Farm, immediately below the fluorspar mine.

A choked swallet. Has been used in attempts to dispose of water pumped from the mine, though it is also thought that it leads flood water into the mine. Water probably reappears at Bagshaw Cavern.

NEW VENTURE MINE AND CAVERN
NGR 1540 8104   Grade IV (Mine)
Alt. 1250ft (381m)   **Depth: 220ft (67m)**

Shaft No.6. on New Venture Vein, 100 yards (91m) north of and parallel to Long Rake.

First pitch, a ginged shaft, is 80ft (24m) deep to a level, which leads east to link with a single cavern reached from the adjacent Shaft No.5. A shaft in the floor leads to further pitches to the lower workings. The second pitch is almost under the first, and at a depth of 50ft (15m) it reaches a four way junction. Here miners levels run east and west, and a natural cave trends from north to south. To the north a single chamber is nearly full of miners' debris, but to the south a well decorated fissure can be climbed for 80ft (24m). Whole system rather unstable.

Tackle:	Ladder	Lifeline
First Pitch:	80ft (24m)	100ft (30m)
Second Pitch:	50ft (15m)	70ft (21m)
Lower Stopes:	100ft (30m)	120ft (37m)

Reference: Wright, A. and Worthington, S. 1971. S.U.S.S. Jour. Vol.2. No.1. pp.21-23. Survey.

NOULTON MINE   NGR 1742 8025   Grade II (Mine)
Alt. 790ft (241m)   Length: 207ft (63m)   Depth: 41ft (12m)

Approximately 400 yards (366m) north east of Hazlebadge Hall.
   A 41ft (12m) shaft leads to worked out pipe vein caverns, leading north north west. Partly removed by opencast mining.

Tackle – 40ft (12m) ladder. 50ft (15m) lifeline.

   Reference: Crabtree, P.W. 1964. B.S.A. Cave Science Vol.5. No.36. p.187. Survey.

OUTLANDS HEAD CAVE   NGR 166 808   Grade II
Alt. 1150ft (350m)   Length: 1215ft (370m)   Depth: 86ft (26m)

No access at present. Contact D.C.A. for further details.
   In floor of Outlands Head Quarry.
   Explored and surveyed by E.P.C. 1973. Two entrances in quarry floor, each needing 20ft (6m) handline. Original entrance drops into small unstable chamber, leading to stooping sized phreatic passage. Eventually passage breaks into large high cross rift with passage continuing on the far side to end at a clay blockage after about 400ft (122m). Climb up left wall of cross rift leads to large passage which after a short distance becomes a hands and knees crawl, eventually becoming too low.
   There are seven other small caves in the quarry, one of which, the Frantastic Way, has a strong draught. These will probably be lost to land-filling.
   References: Bentham, K. 1989. Descent No.91. p.14.
Gill, D.W. 1973. D.C.A. N/L No.17. p.2.
Gill, D.W. 1976. E.P.C. Jour. Vol.9. No.1. pp.13-14. Survey.
Gill, D.W. 1989. Descent No.88. p.16. Survey.
S.U.S.S. N/L No.21. May 1973.

PICTOREND CAVE   NGR 173 802   Grade II (Mine)
Alt. 800ft (244m)   Length: 200ft (61m)   Depth: 45ft (14m)

Entrance in old surface lead workings 70ft (21m) south of walled Pictorend Mine Shaft (200ft/61m deep).
   15ft (4.5m) climb leads into a large chamber 30 x 60ft (9 x 18m) with crawls beyond. Right leads into partly collapsed old workings. Left to window into mine shaft 40ft (12m) below surface. Partly removed by opencast mining.
   Reference: Ryder, P.F. 1973. S.U.S.S. Jour. Vol.2. No.2. pp.25-27. Survey.

PIPPIN HOLE

The Pippin at Hazlebadge is referred to only in passing by Farey. It is likely to have been Quarters Farm Swallet. He certainly wasn't referring to Little Waterfall Swallet, or an obliterated hole behind Glebe Mine, Eyam. Other "Pippin" holes, swallets etc are mentioned, (eg. by William Wood, in his "History of Eyam"), which cover such possibilities at Eyam.

References: Farey, J. 1811. A general view of the agriculture and minerals of Derbyshire Vol.1. p.296.

QUARTERS FARM SWALLET   NGR 1730 7945   Dig
(Hazlebadge Swallow)
Alt. 750ft (229m)

In trees some 200 yards (183m) north of Quarters Farm.

A sink in a tree-lined shakehole. Was dug in 1937, and again in 1949 by Eccles Grotto Group (Turner, 1950). Only narrow fissures were found, but the dig was only opened to a depth of 15ft before being abandoned. A slight draught was reported. May have been Farey's "Pippins Hole" or "Hazlebadge".

References: Farey, J. 1815. View of the Agriculture and Minerals of Derbyshire Vol.1. p.290 & 296. Turner, D. 1950. B.S.A. Cave Science No.14. p.250.

REVELL'S PIPE VEIN   NGR 1745 8020   Grade I (Mine)
Alt. 780ft (238m)   **Length: 386ft (118m)**

Permission rarely granted.

A few yards north of Hazlebadge End Mine.

Two low entrances at the base of a small scar. The more southerly may have been a trial, but the other entrance leads into the pipe, trending south east. Several crawls lead to mined out caverns with a short climbing shaft to lower levels and another to the surface.

Reference: Crabtree, P.W. 1964. B.S.A. Cave Science Vol.5. No.36. pp.184,187, & 189.

SHOD POT   NGR 1809 7767   Dig
Alt. 1000ft (305m)

Permission from adjacent farm.

In a prominent hollow close to Dowse Hole.

A small swallet excavated by Stockport Caving Group. A timbered shaft was sunk through what appears to be road widening debris. It must therefore have been a large open hole and may have been part of the original "Dowse Hole" referred to by Farey.

References: Beck, J.S. 1978. Bull. P.D.M.H.S. Vol.7. No. 2. pp.106-115. Farey, J. 1811. A general view of the agriculture and minerals of Derbyshire. p.293.

WALKER'S GROTTO   NGR 173 806   Grade I
(Bradwell Dale Cave. Nickerlow Cave)
Alt. 630ft (189m)   Length: 130ft (40m)

Obvious entrance at foot of cliff, across the valley from Bradwell Parish Cave, and south of the first lay-by coming from Bradwell village.

Immediately inside, a tight crawl to the right is blocked after 16ft (5m). The main passage follows a calcite vein to a large and muddy chamber with flowstone deposits, now sadly vandalised. A hole in the floor of the chamber is choked, as is the continuation of the chamber in the roof at the end. In wet conditions a temporary lake forms at the base of the chamber.

50ft (15m) to the south of Walker's Grotto is a low tube choked with mud after 14ft (4m)

References: Crabtree, P.W. 1964. B.S.A. Cave Science Vol.5. No.36. Survey. Turner, D. 1950. British Caver Vol.21.p.22.

WELL SHAFT   NGR 1710 8032   Grade II (Mine)
Alt. 650ft (198m)   Length: 200ft (61m) approx.   Depth: 50ft (15m)

Concrete capped shaft a few yards west of the road in Bradwell Dale.

Crawl under the south side of the lid into the shaft. Shaft is 50ft (15m) deep, usually to water. Natural passage off at 30ft (9m) to the west, ending at a gravel and rock choke, dug unsuccessfully. Opposite this is a passage leading under the road to a further run-in. Workings at the bottom of the shaft, when accessible, are very unstable.

Reference: Whitehouse, R.H. 1966. E.P.C. Jour. Vol.7. No.1. pp.23-24.

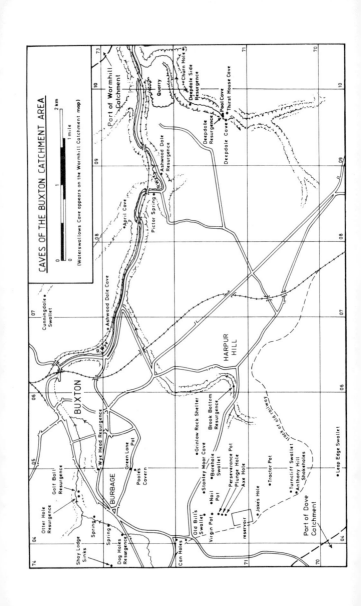

CAVES OF THE BUXTON CATCHMENT AREA

0   1 mile

0   1   2 km

(Waterswallows Cave appears on the Wormhill Catchment map)

Part of Wormhill Catchment

Churn Hole
Quarry
Deepdale Side Resurgence
Deepdale Resurgence
Pool Cave
Thirst House Cave
Deepdale Cave

Ashwood Dale Resurgence
April Cove
Pictor Spring
Ashwood Dale Cove
Cunningdale Swallet

BUXTON
BURBAGE
Wye Head Resurgence
Otter Hole Resurgence
Golf Ball Resurgence
Spring
Shay Lodge Sinks
Dog Holes Resurgence
Can Holes
Old Bill's Swallet
Virgin Pot
Nail Pot
Stanley Moor Cave
Grinlow Rock Shelter
Borehole Swallet
Perseverance Pot
Plunge Hole
Axe Hole
Brook Bottom Resurgence
Green Lane
Pooles Cavern
Jokes Hole
Tractor Pot
Turncliff Swallet
Anthony Hill Shakeholes
reservoir
track of old railway
HARPUR HILL
Part of Dove Catchment
Leap Edge Swallet

Spring

THE BUXTON
CATCHMENT AREA

The River Wye rises on the shales and sandstones of Axe Edge Moor, and first encounters the limestone just west of Buxton. It does not sink, but flows on the surface through the town. It is augmented by numerous springs before continuing eastwards down Ashwood Dale. Further springs swell the river here. Some appear to be in the river bed itself, and may be fed from the Water Swallows area to the north. Digging here only revealed a narrow fissure, and it seems unlikely that a penetrable cave system exists to the north of the river although little serious work has been done.

The majority of the risings in the Buxton area lie on the south bank, and are fed from the swallets of Stanley Moor. The hydrology is complex, but most of the drainage goes to Wye Head Resurgence via Poole's Cavern. Dye tests have also revealed connections to Brook Bottom and Otter Hole Resurgences.

Prior to deepening of the Wye Valley, Poole's Cavern may have been the main outlet, but today the water rises at Wye Head, 46m lower. The drainage route between the two is immature, and it is doubtful if it would be penetrable.

The swallets have been dug over the years, but a large vadose system has not been entered. This may be due to the existence of the north-south Grin Low Anticline, leading to adverse dips in the Stanley Moor Region. The swallets lie to the south west of the anticline, and the upstream end of Poole's Cavern is only 20m below the lowest points reached in the swallets. The chances of entering an extensive vadose system do not seem hopeful, but there is scope for further work.

The other drainage system of interest is the Shay Lodge–Dog Holes Resurgence system, which seems to run down dip, and may well repay further work.

The large Ashwood Dale Resurgence appears to be fed by percolation water from a large area of limestone to the south, as are smaller risings issuing from the valley floor in Deep Dale. Little work has been attempted in Deep Dale, and a protracted dig at Thirst House Cave, above the risings, may bring results.

ANTHONY HILL SHAKEHOLES   NGR 047 703   Dig
Alt. 1250ft (375m)

Two small wet weather swallets close together south of Stanley Moor Reservoir, a few yards east of the railway line and near Turncliffe Swallet.
Possible dig?

APRIL CAVE   NGR 082 727   Grade I
Alt. 980ft (299m)   Length: 36ft (11m)

A short distance up Cunning Dale from the River Wye in disused quarry.

Discovered by EPC in 1969. Enlarged entrance to 10ft (3m) high passage with large mud bank up to roof. At roof level two passages diverge. Right hand passage closes down after 7ft (2.1m) and left hand passage curves round to where daylight can be seen, too tight to exit.

References: Bridger, R. 1976. D.C.A. N/L No.30.

ASHWOOD DALE CAVE   NGR 069 730   Grade I
Alt. 1000ft (300m)

On north side of dale, immediately east of sewage works. Go up path under bridge and cave is high up on right.

15ft (4.5m) passage, squeeze past boulder into small chamber. Might repay archaeological digging as it is probably the cave which yielded a few Romano-British remains to Salt in 1895.

References: Turner, W. 1899. Ancient Remains Near Buxton. p.75.
Haverfield, F. in Victoria County History of Derbyshire. p.238.
Eldon Pothole Club Newsletter Vol.4. No.1.
Eldon Pothole Club Newsletter Vol.5. No.10. S.

ASHWOOD DALE RESURGENCE
NGR 0895 7222   **Dig**
Alt. 820ft (246m)

A large volume of water rises immediately south of the A6 from a cave entrance and lower fissures. It was used for a water supply. The source is unknown.

In dry weather can be forced in a very tight passage for approx twenty feet to where it becomes too tight. It emits a very strong draught when dry.

References: Needham, J. 1966. Eldon Pothole Club Journal Vol.7. No.1. pp.9-12

AXE HOLE   NGR 044 713   Grade II
Alt. 1250ft (375m)   Length: 200ft (60m)

In first shakehole north of Stanley Moor Reservoir. Squeeze down for 12ft (4m), then tight rift 8ft (2m). Further sideways squeeze for 10ft (3m). Left turn into walking passage for 20ft (6m), terminating in muddy sump. Crawl beyond in muddy 3ft (1m) high passage round several bends and undulating to final chamber. Climbing into roof leads to small chambers with straw stalactites. Turning right at entrance rift it is possible to squeeze into sandy crawl for 60ft (18m). Tight connection with Plunge Hole. Rope is useful at the entrance and down the rift, 50ft (15m).

Dye tested to Brook Bottom, Otter Hole, Wye Head via Pooles Cavern.

BOREHOLE SWALLET   NGR 049 715   Dig
Alt. 1160ft (384m)

50 yards upstream from the Borehole pump house.

Stream sinks under a wall. Dug out (assisted by collapse) to 15ft (5m) to uncover a tight passage blocked after a few feet. Now filled in.

Dye tested to Wye Head via Pooles Cavern.

Reference: Eldon Pothole Club N/L Vol.5. No.7.

BROOK BOTTOM RESURGENCE 1, 2, & 3
NGR 056 710, 0575 7115, 057 713   **Digs**
Alt. 1025ft (312m)

Three risings to the west of the road. The two southerly ones have been dye tested from the Stanley Moor Swallets. The third is probably local drainage above a lava bed.

CAN HOLES   NGR 041 721 & 040 718   **Digs**
Alt. 1200ft (366m)

Small sink near the Macclesfield-Buxton and Leek-Buxton road junction, and another at 040 718 which takes more water in wet weather.

At the first swallet water can be seen falling through boulders for 5ft (1.5m).

References: Gilman, J. 1985. Karst Hydrology of the Buxton area, Derbys. Unpublished BSc. Thesis. Manchester Polytechnic.

Gunn, J. & Edmans, A. 1989. The Wye Head systems – some hydrological observations. Caves & Caving No.45. p.35.

CHURN HOLES   NGR 1054 7186   **Grade I**
Alt. 880ft (264m)   Length: 200ft (60m)

At head of Marl Dale, the southern branch of Deepdale near Topley Pike.

Two pothole entrances drop into a chamber, with 200ft (60m) of partly excavated low passage, passing a number of cross joints.

References: Drakeley, K. 1981. Churn Holes. The Lyre No.5. pp.23-26.

Turner, W. 1899. Ancient Remains near Buxton. p.78.

CUNNINGDALE SWALLET   NGR 073 738   **Dig**
Alt. 1000ft (305m)

At head of Cunningdale, just past allotments in middle of waste ground.

The sink takes a small stream largely composed of sewage from a pig farm.

DEEPDALE CAVE   NGR 0962 7129   **Grade I**
(Nettle Cave)
Alt. 975ft (292m)   Length: 70ft (21m)

The name strictly applies to a cave opposite and higher than Thirst House Cave (q.v) but the name has often been applied to the latter.

A bedding plane crawl, extensively dug by Orpheus Caving Club in the 1950's.

Above Deepdale Cave is a rift in the wood once dug.

Reference: Smith, P. 1956. Lyre No.1. pp 13-14.

DEEPDALE RESURGENCE   NGR 097 713   Dig
Alt. 875ft (267m)

In the floor of Deepdale, a short distance downstream of Thirst House Cave.

A large volume of water rises from an indeterminate source among the boulders in the valley floor.

DEEPDALE SIDE RESURGENCE   NGR 098 718   Dig
Alt. 860ft (262m)

Resurgence in the floor of Deepdale.

DOG HOLES RESURGENCE   NGR 041 727   Dig
Alt. 1000ft (300m)

Behind two small cottages at Dog Holes.

A large resurgence, which has been dye tested from Shay Lodge Sinks.

Reference: Gunn, J. & Edmans, A. 1989. BCRA Caves & Caving No.45 p.35.

GOLF BALL RESURGENCE   NGR 047 733   Dig
Alt. 1000ft (305m)

A small rising at river level which sometimes acts as a sink. The source is unknown.

GREEN LANE POT   NGR 050 726   Grade II
Alt. 1000ft (305m)   **Length: 80ft (24m)**   **Depth: 70ft (21m)**

Permission required from Borough Surveyor.

Entrance through manhole in road a few yards uphill from Poole's Cavern.

An unsafe wooden ladder leads to a platform 30ft (9m) down. (Use a 70ft (21m) ladder belayed to car or lamp post). The bottom of the pot is usually flooded to a depth a several feet. In drought a tube can be entered, 30inches (0.8m) high and two thirds full of liquid mud. Apparently part of the Poole's Cavern to Wye Head system.

Tackle – 70ft (21m) ladder; 80ft (24m) lifeline.

References: Eldon Pothole Club Newsletter Vol.5. No.10. Survey.

GRINLOW ROCK SHELTER   NGR 052 717   Grade I
Alt. 1150ft (345m)   **Length: 10ft (3m)**

In crags halfway between Solomon's Temple and the road, to the south west of the Temple. A tight passage for 10ft (3m) between boulders, then too narrow.

JAKES HOLE   NGR 0445 7080   Grade III
Alt. 1250ft (380m)   **Length: 80ft (24m)**   **Depth: 35ft (11m)**

In deep shakehole near the south wall of Stanley Moor Reservoir. Shakehole has large limestone slab at one side.

Tight 6ft (2m) crawl down slope. Squeeze over boulder to top of 25ft (8m) pitch. Very tight. Belay to iron bar in floor. 10ft (3m) square chamber at the bottom is very muddy. Tight squeeze into 20ft (6m) silted passage on left. Cave is difficult to get out of. Only for thin agile cavers!

Tackle – 25ft (8m) ladder; 30ft (9m) lifeline.

JAKES HOLE (Lower)　　　　NGR 0445 7080　　　　Dig
Alt. 1250ft (380m)

In same shakehole as Jakes Hole.

A small stream sinks among boulders. This has been dug and penetrated for 20ft (6m) but was considered to be impossible for further work.

Dye tested to Otter Hole, & Wye Head via Pooles Cavern.

References: Eldon Pothole Club N/L Vol.5. No.10.

LEAP EDGE SWALLET　　　　NGR 0490 6975　　　　Dig
(Dale Head Swallet)
Alt. 1275ft (389m)

South of Stanley Moor. Active swallet taking a fair sized stream down an impenetrable hole. Dye tested to Brook Bottom.

NAIL POT　　　　NGR 045 715　　　　Lost
Alt. 1250ft (375m)　　　Length: 50ft (15m) approx.　　　Depth: 50ft (15m)

50 yards (46m) south of Stanley Moor Cave.

Contained about 50ft of passage. Partly collapsed in 1962, and now filled in for safety.

Reference: Anon. 1963. The Caves of Stanley Moor. E.P.C. N/L. Vol.5. No.10/11 p.63. Survey.

OLD BILL'S SWALLET　　　NGR 044 716　　　Grade I Dig
Alt. 1300ft (390m)　　　Length: 10ft (3m)

At base of rock outcrop on Stanley Moor.

A small cave 10ft (3m) long. A small stream sinks among boulders in wet weather. An impenetrable crack to the right.

OTTER HOLE RESURGENCE　　NGR 046 733　　Grade II
Alt. 1025ft (312m)　　　Length: 120ft (37m)

In field by Otter Hole Farm.

A powerful resurgence. Dug by Eldon Pothole Club 1962/3. Crawl in the stream for 35ft (11m) to a flake dividing the passage. Pass on left, then squeeze lying on side in water. Follow stream crawling to duck which can be passed, and 5ft (1.5m) on is crawl into chamber with tin bath jammed in hole in roof! Stream flows out of silted up bedding plane and is known to come from Resurgence Swallet 120ft (37m) away. Dye tests were positive from the Stanley Moor Swallets.

Reference: Eldon P.C. N/L Vol.5. No.2. & Vol.5. No.10. Survey.

PERSEVERANCE POT   NGR 044 714   Grade III
Alt. 1250ft (381m)   **Length: 120ft (37m)**   **Depth: 90ft (27m)**

In third shakehole north of Stanley Moor Reservoir.

Dug by Eldon Pothole Club in 1962. 6ft (1.8m) drop between boulders to 20ft (6m) slope, then further 6ft (1.8m) drop into passage at right angles. Turn left and cross two holes in the floor (care – 40ft/12m deep). Continue to hole on left which is 25ft (8m) pitch. Pitch tight and ends on muddy slope of 15ft (4.5m). Then short iron ladder to short muddy passage and three muddy chambers. Has been dug in vain.

Tackle – 25ft (8m) ladder; 40ft (12m) lifeline.

References: Downhill, C. 1964. Eldon P.C. N/L Vol.5. No.10/11. p.64. Survey. Dunn, J.A. & Hockenhull, C. 1963. Eldon P.C. N/L Vol.5 No.4. pp.11-12.

PIGTOR SPRING   NGR 0867 7230   Dig
(Pictor Spring, Cowdale Spring)
Alt. 840ft (256m)

On the south west side of the A6 just north of the Cowdale turning.

A small pumphouse lies on the spring, which is used as a domestic water supply. The flow does not vary greatly in floods, and rarely (if ever) dries up.

Reference: Beck, J.S. 1980. Speleogenesis in the Carboniferous Limestone of North Derbyshire. Unpublished PhD Thesis. Univ. Leicester. p.243.

PLUNGE HOLE   NGR 044 713   Grade II
(Ladmanlow Cavern?)
Alt. 1220ft (372m)   **Length: 30ft (9m)**   **Depth: 50ft (15m)**

Second shakehole from the north wall of the Stanley Moor Reservoir, where the stream runs into boulders.

Crawl under large boulder into a small chamber with a large boulder apparently blocking the way on. Route is under this (care) into 40ft (12m) deep rift (rope or ladder useful) which it is possible to climb down. Stream at bottom. Downstream after 20ft (6m) is too narrow. Upstream for 10ft (3m) to boulders through which the stream enters. Low crawl leads to small chamber, then tight squeeze into 5ft (1.5m) deep hole with choked bedding plane. Tight connection made with Axe Hole. Dye tested to Brook Bottom, Otter Hole, and Wye Head via Pooles Cavern.

Reference: Anon. 1950. British Caver No.20. p.83. Reprinted Manchester Evening News 17-1-50.

POOL CAVE   NGR 0968 7133   Grade I
Alt. 850ft (259m)   **Length: 30ft (12m)**

Mine level below Thirst House Cave which was pumped dry and found to be blind.

POOLE'S CAVERN   NGR 050 725   **Show**
Alt. 1100ft (335m)   Length: 800ft (244m)

Show Cave. Most of cave seen on normal tourist trip.

In Green Lane, Buxton.

An archaeological show cave. Romano-British animals and artefacts on show in museum attached. Roman Chamber a short distance from the entrance. Stream is seen sinking in large passage with fine stalactites and stalagmites. One of the chambers is 100ft (30m) high. Once lit by gas, now electric. After leaving the public section it is possible to crawl upstream into a boulder choke. Above the choke are two further chambers, roots from surface being seen in upper one. Stream originates from the Stanley Moor Swallets, and sinks in the cave to reappear at Wye Head. Stalagmites three inches long grew on the victorian gas pipes.

References: Adam, W. 1838. Gem of the Peak. pp.307-309 in 1973 reprint by Moorland Publishing, Hartington. Dawkins, W.B. 1874. Cave Hunting. pp.126-127. MacMillan, London. Ford, T.D. & Allsop, D. 1975. Pooles Cavern Guide Book. Survey. Glennie, E.A. 1953. C.R.G. N/L No.48. pp.12-13. Glennie, E.A. 1953. C.R.G. N/L No.45. pp.5-10. McIntosh, J. 1972. E.P.C. Jour. Vol.8. No.1. p.13. Survey. Pitty, A. 1969. Proc. B.S.A. No.7. pp.7-15.

RESURGENCE SWALLET   **Grade II**
Alt. 1200ft (366m)   Length: 120ft (37m)

In centre of fairway on Cavendish Golf Course.

Dug by Eldon Pothole Club in 1963. Stream runs across floor of shakehole. Possible to squeeze into bedding in sink in passage 2.5ft (76cms) high. Possible to crawl and swim for 120ft (37m) when water is low. Has been dived but became too low. Water reappears at Otter Hole.

Reference: Anon. 1963. E.P.C. N/L Vol.5. No.2. pp.23-24. & No.10, p.48. Survey.

SHAY LODGE SINKS   NGR 035 729   **Grade III.**
Alt. 1300ft (396m)   Length: 150ft (46m)   Depth: 90ft (27m)

The area around Shay Lodge Farm above Burbage, Buxton has 3 sinks.

One cave can be entered by a series of squeezes to a free-climbable pitch of 33ft (10m). A crawl follows after a further awkward squeeze which has been dug, but is still blocked by boulders. Dye testing has shown that the water rises at Dog Holes.

Reference: Needham, J. 1963. E.P.C. N/L Vol.5. No.4. pp.9-10. Dickinson, S. 1983. E.P.C. Jour. Vol.9. No.3. p.11.

STANLEY MOOR CAVE   NGR 047 716   Grade I
Alt. 1220ft (372m)   Length: 70ft (21m)

In large shakehole on Stanley Moor.

Discovered by Eldon Pothole Club in 1958. Slope of 10ft (3m) into entrance chamber. Tight passage on left slopes down into two small chambers with boulder chokes. 6ft (2m) hole on right of entrance chamber leads into fine grotto with curtains and straw stalactites. Further sloping passage for 20ft (6m) to choke.

Reference: Anon. E.P.C. N/L No.10. p.67. Survey.

SWALLOW HOLES   Lost

An unknown cave near Buxton referred to by Cox, 1878.

Reference: Cox, J.C. 1878. The Tourist Guide to Derbyshire. p.43.

THIRST HOUSE CAVE   NGR 0970 7124   Grade I (Arch)
Alt. 890ft (271m)   Length: 190ft (58m)

An obvious entrance on the east side of Deepdale well above the dry bed. Opposite is Deepdale Cave, and Thirst House has often been incorrectly called Deepdale Cave.

A large entrance 15ft (4.5m) high and 20ft (6m) wide. Height soon drops to 6ft (2m) and after 72ft (22m) the floor descends to a second chamber. Hole in floor amongst boulders descends to a short crawl and a rift with a pool below. Both chambers have been archaeologically excavated.

References: Cox, Rev. J.C. 1890. Arch. Jour. Vol.12. pp.228-230. Cox, Rev. J.C. 1891. Arch. Jour. Vol.13. pp.194-199. Turner, W. 1899. Ancient Remains near Buxton. pp.7-71. Survey. (Largely reprinted from Derbys. Arch. Jour.). Ward. J. 1894. Arch. Jour. Vol.16. pp.185-189. Ward. J. 1895. Arch. Jour. Vol.17. pp.60-81. Survey.

THREE J'S CAVE   NGR 109 717   Grade I.
Alt. 920ft (280m)   Length: 160ft (49m)

A mine level high on the east side of Deep Dale, on a steeply hading vein. Little evidence of natural solution.

Reference: Gunn, J. 1985. D.C.A. N/L No.57. pp.3-4. Survey.

TRACTOR POT   NGR 048 707   Lost
Alt. 1300ft (396m).

A hole which appeared under a tractor. Now refilled for safety.

TURNCLIFF SWALLET   NGR 0472 7034   Dig
Alt. 1200ft (366m)   Length: 10ft (3m)

Stream comes from under embankment and sinks. Not to be confused with large pool fed from a leat just off the limestone at 0460 7005.

A 6ft drop between boulders into a bedding cave blocked by a boulder. Could be a productive dig. Dye tested to Brook Bottom, Otter Hole, and Wye head via Pooles' Cavern.

VIRGIN POT   NGR 044 715   Dig
Alt. 1250ft (381m)   **Depth: 45ft (14m)**

In fourth shakehole north of Stanley Moor Reservoir.

Dug in 1962 by Eldon Pothole Club. A short drop between boulders to a tight oval hole in the floor for 25ft (8m), followed by a 20ft (6m) drop. Then too narrow. Entrance now blocked with large boulders.

Tackle – 25ft (8m) ladder; 50ft (15m) lifeline.

Reference: Anon. Undated. Eldon P.C. N/L Vol.5. No.10/11. Survey.

WATERSWALLOWS CAVE   NGR 079 749   Grade I.
Alt. 1100ft (335m)   **Length: 25ft (8m)**

In middle of field south of the Buxton – Wormhill Road.

A stream sink, now capped and culverted. The stream flows into a tight bedding plane, opened by blasting for 25ft (8m) into a narrow rift which closes up. The stream was dye tested, and reappeared in the bed of the River Wye (exact location unknown).

References: Woodall, B. 1972. E.P.C. Jour. Vol.8. No.1. pp.42-43.

WYE HEAD RESURGENCE   NGR 0499 7304   Digs
Alt. 1000ft (305m).

On the north side of Macclesfield Road, Buxton.

The River Wye appears from several places among rocks. Eldon Pothole Club penetrated 15ft by clearing boulders but were stopped by unstable roof under the road. Now blocked again.

Water sinks at Stanley Moor Swallets and flows via Pooles Cavern.

Reference: E.P.C. N/L. Vol.5. No.10.

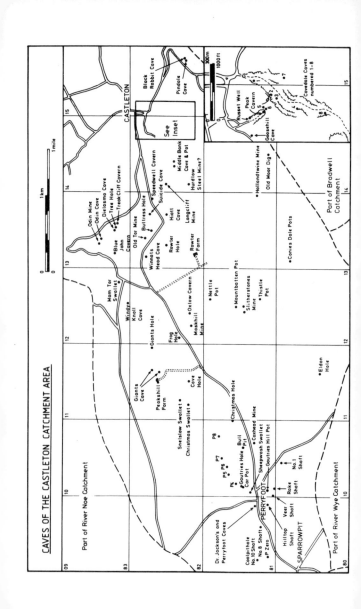

CAVES OF THE CASTLETON CATCHMENT AREA

CAVES OF THE CASTLETON CATCHMENT AREA

The Castleton area is the best known caving area in Derbyshire. It was first noted by Charles Leigh in 1700 that the water from the Rushup Edge Swallets was that which emerged in the Peak Cavern gorge, and Lloyd and King's survey of Eldon Hole in 1772 was one of the first detailed cave surveys to be published.

Many streams enter swallet caves on the shale/limestone junction to the west of Castleton, and all this water drains to the Peakshole Water by way of either Peak or Speedwell Cavern. Topographically, the Rushup Vale should drain down Perry Dale, Dam Dale, Monks Dale etc. to the River Wye, but the underground drainage is diverted eastwards by the underlying structure to cross the surface watershed.

Water flows eastwards, its path determined by the large east-west mineral veins, which happen to line up quite nicely with the maximum hydraulic gradient. It surfaces at the low point on the shale margin at Castleton where the reef belt is thin, and where a series of joints have provided an easy passage.

The Peak–Speedwell Cave System consists of two major stream passages, with a complex network of tributaries and high level fossil passages. Most of the swallet water flows via the Speedwell Streamway, while the Peak Streamway carries percolation water from the limestone area to the south.

Exploration of the main Speedwell route ends upstream at a very deep and spectacular sump, Main Rising. This lies at roughly the same elevation as the East Canal in Giants Hole, and there may be a very large flooded area in between. However, many of the swallet caves are still unexplored because the swallets themselves are choked with debris from the gritstone escarpment to the north, so that there may be many inlets to explore on the way.

The best prospects for extensions lie in some very remote digs at the western limits of the Peak–Speedwell system, in excavation of some of the unexplored swallets, and possibly in digging some of the smaller dry caves and dolines which abound in the area. Exploration of the Castleton area is far from finished, and although many of the most promising sites are only available to experienced divers, the inquisitive explorer may still stumble upon interesting leads to follow.

BLACK RABBIT CAVE   GR 157 823   Grade III
Alt. 800ft (244m)   **Length: 500ft (152m)**

Warning: The lower chokes are VERY UNSTABLE and it is inadvisable to enter them.

Opposite Pindale Cave at the north west end of the quarry.

Trends south east. SYCC dig through entrance boulder choke leads after 60ft (18m) to a tight squeeze. Wide low bedding cave beyond leads after 20ft (6m) to a further tight squeeze into a further low area with the main passage to the left and a choked passage to the right. Main passage is a wide crawl over boulders to a junction where the passage enlarges to walking size, but soon ends in a huge boulder choke. Right hand passage about 60ft (18m) long.

A way down through the choke was found in 1985. A small stream and a short and very unstable extension were found.

References: Noble, M. 1983. T.S.G. N/L No.10. p.10. Survey. Cordingley, J.N. 1985. T.S.G. Members newsletter p.2.

BLUE JOHN CAVERNS NGR 1319 8320 Grade II (Show)
Alt. 1250ft (375m)   **Length: 4180ft (1274m)**   **Depth: 296ft (90m)**

Generally no access beyond the show cave. Most of the cave is seen on a tourist trip.

A mile west of Castleton on the Mam Tor Road.

Artificial entrance for 18ft (5m) then descent of steps to Ladies Walk, sloping passage to 90ft (27m) high Crystallised Cavern. Second stairway leads to Stalactite Cavern and Lord Mulgrave's Dining Room, 140ft (43m) high and 30ft (9m) wide, where water is met in a fissure. These caverns make a very large and impressive vadose canyon. Several passages lead off, one to Fairy Grotto and Stemple Cavern, also reached from Stalactite Cavern. Show route ends in Variegated Cavern, over 100ft (30m) high and 30ft (9m) wide, seen from ledge 20ft (6m) up. Large passage continues beyond with rock barrier passable by muddy Rabbit Burrow into final chamber. Descent to final sump requires a 30ft (9m) ladder. Climbs of 48ft (15m) and 26ft (8m) reach to Superior Gallery. Branch passage leads up to choke where one can communicate with Fairy Grotto.

References: Barnes & Holroyd, 1896. Trans. Manch. Geol. Soc. Vol.XXIV. Ford, T.D. 1955. Proc. Yorks. Geol. Soc. Vol.30. Survey. Martel, E.A. (transl. Winder, F.) The Caverns of Castleton. Survey. Royse, J. 1943. Ancient Castleton Caves. Survey. Westlake, C.D. 1979. Eldon P.C. Jour. Vol.9. No.2. pp.3-6. Survey. Whitehouse, R.H. 1970. Eldon P.C. Jour. Vol.7. No.3. pp.33-42. Survey. Winder, F. 1938. An Unconventional Guide to the Caverns of Castleton. Survey.

BULL PIT   NGR 1064 8143   Grade I
Alt. 1185ft (335m)   **Depth: 80ft (24m)**

600 yards (546m) east of Perryfoot, north of the road.

A deep open pothole choked at the bottom with large boulders. Easy scramble down south east side. Various digs in the bottom. Shaft No.1. is 20ft (6m) deep, then 30ft (9m) crawl in side passage to chamber. Downward passage and 20ft (6m) pitch leads to second chamber. Passage over leads to T-junction and left is over jagged rocks to a third chamber containing a stream. Other passage leads back to entrance pitch through natural and mined passages. Digging now abandoned and shaft hidden.

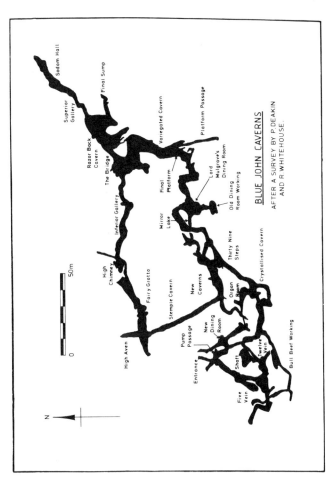

BLUE JOHN CAVERNS

AFTER A SURVEY BY P. DEAKIN
AND R. WHITEHOUSE.

Sodom Hall

Final Sump

Superior Gallery

Razor Back Cavern

Variegated Cavern

The Bridge

Final Platform

Platform Passage

Inferior Gallery

Mirror Lake

Lord Mulgrave's Dining Room

High Chimney

Old Dining Room Working

Fairy Grotto

Thirty Nine Steps

High Aven

Stemple Cavern

New Caverns

Organ Room

Crystallised Cavern

Pump Passage

New Dining Room

Twelve Vein

Entrance

Shaft

Bull Beef Working

Five Vein

N

50m

0

BUTTRESS HOLE NGR 135 827 Grade I
Alt. 1072ft (326m) Length: 30ft (9m)

High on prominent buttress on north side of Winnats Pass.
Obvious round hole leads to single chamber with muddy crawl to the left.

CAR POT NGR 101 814 Grade I
Alt. 1040ft (317m) Length: 50ft (15m)

Permission from Perryfoot Farm.
In the Gautries Hole shakehole, just west of Gautries entrance.
A hands and knees crawl to the east, choked with silt. A short crawl on the left ends close to Gautries Hole.
Reference: Salmon, L.B. and Boldock, G. 1948. B.S.A. Cave Science Vol.1. No.6.

CAVE DALE CAVE No 1 NGR 1502 8264 Grade I
Alt. 730ft (219m) Length: 20ft (6m)

Immediately on the right on entering the dale, under an overhanging rock.
A short mine level with evidence of solutional activity.

CAVE DALE CAVE No 2 NGR 1495 8254 Grade I (Arch)
Alt. 875ft (262m) Length: 15ft (4.5m)

At top of slope under south side of Castle Keep.
A bedding cave 8ft (2.5m) wide and 18 inches (0.5m) high. Crawling on rubbish for 15ft (4.5m). Archaeologically excavated.
References: Pennington, R. 1875. Quart. Journ. Geol. Soc. 31, p.238. Pennington, R. 1877. Barrows and Bone Caves of Derbyshire. p.53.

CAVE DALE CAVE No 3 NGR 1493 8251 Grade I (Arch)
(Creep Hole?)
Alt. 850ft (255m) Length: 6ft (2m)

Below and to the west of cave No.2. Halfway down the slope, close to old water pipe.
Small rock shelter ending in collapsed boulders. Reputed to have extended further at one time, and to have been dug archaeologically. This may be the Creep Hole noted by Pennington as connecting with a cave in the top of the Peak Cavern Gorge, probably Peveril Castle Cave.
Reference: Pennington, R. 1877. Barrows and Bone Caves of Derbyshire. p.57.

CAVE DALE CAVE No 4 NGR 1488 8240 Grade I
Alt. 850ft (255m) Depth: 100ft (30m)

In cleft to west of footpath up dale, where the dale narrows and steepens.
Narrow fissure descended by Puttrell into the roof of the Orchestra Chamber of Peak Cavern. Fitted with steel gate.

CAVE DALE CAVE No 5   NGR 1488 8259   Grade I
(Peveril Castle Cave)
Alt. 900ft (270m)   Length: 20ft (6m)

20ft (6m) higher and to left of caves 2 & 3. Below the west wall of the Castle Keep in the top of the Peak Cavern Gorge.
    Low chamber sloping down to the north east for 20ft (6m) mostly 2ft 6in (0.8m) high. Reputed to connect with cave No.3.

CAVE DALE CAVE No 6   NGR 1487 8257   Grade I
(Gorge Top Cave)
Alt. 900ft (274m)

A rock shelter in the trees by Peveril Castle Keep directly above Peak Cavern entrance.

CAVE DALE CAVE No 7 NGR 1504 8247 Grade I (Mine)
(Cave Dale Pipe)
Alt. 1000ft (305m)   Length: 200ft (60m)

High on the east side of Cave Dale. A dig entered a pipe cavern enlarged by the miners.
    Reference: Penney, D. 1974. Bull. B.C.R.A. No.3. Survey.

CAVE DALE CAVE No 8   NGR 1485 8225   Grade I
(Path Cave)
Alt. 925ft (282m)

Close to the path.
    A dig revealed a small cave with stalagmite floor and bone deposits.

CHRISTMAS HOLE   NGR 110 816   Dig. Lost
Alt. 1180ft (360m)   Depth: 100ft (30m)

In shallow dry valley 656 yards (600m) approx. south east of P8 and nearer the Sparrowpit-Castleton road. Now covered and exact location uncertain. No access allowed.
    A fissure cave dug by B.S.A. in Dec. 1947 to an impenetrable choke about 60ft (18m) down.
    Reference: Salmon, L.B. & Boldock, G. 1950. B.S.A. Cave Science Vol.2. No.11. pp. 122-123.

CHRISTMAS SWALLET   NGR 112 822   Grade V
(Swallet P9)
Alt. 1112ft (339m)   Length: 230ft (70m)   Depth: 230ft (70m)

Warning: The stream is present throughout the cave, and does not have to be very high to cause problems. The catchment area is as large as P8 and Giants together. All the pitches become impassable very easily, and the entrance section sumps in flood. Rescue of an injured caver from the bottom would be almost impossible.

Access controlled by Peakshill Farm. No access at present.

On the shale margin between Jackpot P8 and Snelslow Swallet.

A sporting little stream cave with four pitches after the capped artificial entrance shaft (23ft/7m). Climbable, but bolt belay available on left wall. Enlarged rift passage leads via two small drops to a low crawl with a pool (the old sump). The crawl is 20ft (6m) long, and must not be attempted in high water or threatening weather.

Beyond the pool is short drop into 10ft (3m) high chamber, then stooping narrow passage for 90ft (27m) to First Pitch. The passage becomes walking height, but still narrow and awkward.

First Pitch (26ft (8m) deep with bolt belay) is constricted at the top. Leads immediately to Second Pitch (33ft/10m). The two can be rigged as one 62ft (19m) pitch. Natural eyehole belay on second pitch, or bolt. A short obvious traverse 10ft (3m) down this pitch avoids a wet descent.

The passage is now the largest in the cave, and swings to the right. Third Pitch is quickly reached (30ft (9m) deep with bolt belays). Passage at bottom descends with a 6ft (2m) climb back under the pitch, and meets a rift turning 90 degrees to the right. This is the narrow blasted Ochre Rift, 13ft (4m) long, with a small ochre-coloured inlet, and is a crawl in the stream, emerging at a steeply descending and slightly larger passage.

This leads to a pool in a low passage, and drains out over the Fourth Pitch (25ft/8m) with a bolt belay. The pitch has been enlarged, but is still constricted, and dangerous in high water. A 10ft (3m) climb at the bottom reaches a sump which was dived to a blockage at -30ft (-9m).

Tackle:

Entrance Shaft:	25ft (8m) ladder; 35ft (11m) lifeline
SRT:	35ft (11m) rope. Bolt belay.
First Pitch:	30ft (10m) ladder; 40ft (12m) lifeline.
SRT:	50ft (15m) rope. Bolt belay.
Second Pitch:	35ft (11m) ladder; 46ft (14m) lifeline.
SRT:	60ft (18m) rope. Eyehole or bolt belay.
Second Pitch (dry traverse):	16ft (5m) ladder; 23ft (7m) lifeline.
SRT:	65ft (20m) rope.
Third Pitch:	30ft (9m) ladder; 40ft (12m) lifeline.
SRT:	50ft (15m) rope. Bolt belays.
Fourth Pitch:	30ft (9m) ladder (or 40ft/12m to include final climb). 50ft (15m) lifeline.
SRT:	50ft (15m) rope. Bolt belay.

References: Arveschoug, D. 1987. B.C.R.A. Caves & Caving No.35. pp.10-12. Survey. Salmon, L.B. & Boldock, G. 1950. B.S.A. Cave Science No.11.p.121. Whitehouse, R.H. 1967. Eldon P.C. Jour. Vol.7. No.2. pp.41-42

COALPITHOLE RAKE
NGR 104 809   Grade II-III (Mines)
Shaft No.1   Lost
Alt. 1060ft (323m)   **Length: 200ft (60m) approx.**   **Depth: 220ft (67m)**
Permission from Mine Cottage.

Three shafts in Perry Dale close to Mine Cottage, all now blocked.

Most westerly shaft is the hauling shaft, probably blocked for most of its depth. The other two, blocked at surface, were 100ft (30m) deep, connected at the bottom by a short level where a 35ft (11m) shaft led to a second level ending in a boulder choke close to the hauling shaft. From this level a 40ft (12m) shaft led to bottom level blocked to east and west, close to bottom of hauling shaft.

The 'lost' swallow which drained the rake was at 870ft (265.2m) A.O.D., 100 yards (91m) west of No.1. shaft. Water reappears at Russet Well, taking 3-4 days to flow through.

RAKE SHAFT   **NGR 101 810**   Grade III (Mine)
Alt. 1225ft (373m)   **Length: 500ft (152m)**   **Depth:320ft (97m)**
Permission from Gautries Side Farm.

On Gautries Hill, south of Perryfoot Farm. Covered with concrete slabs.

Entrance shaft 310ft (94m) deep. Beware of loose ginging for the first 50ft (15.2m). Blocked at the bottom, but with five cross cuts connecting to the vein and probable old climbing shaft. The lowest cross cut at about 285ft (87m) enters level to west blocked after 150ft (45m), and to east is 35ft (11m) shaft to bottom level. Thread entrance shaft ladder down. Across shaft a level can be entered, blocked after 50ft (15m). At bottom of shaft stream flows from west to east. Immediately west of foot of shaft, water rises from a sump which has been dived for 40ft (12m) to air space with level continuing. To east (downstream), narrow level ends after 150ft (45m) at a boulder choke where the stream sinks. Stream has been dye tested from No.8. shaft and might also be the water from Perryfoot Swallets, although this has not been confirmed. Stream probably goes to "Lost Swallow" in no 1 shaft, and from there to Russett Well.

Tackle – 325ft (99m) ladder; 350ft (107m) lifeline. (Long belay to tree.)
SRT: 350ft (107m) rope. Scaffold bar for belay.

VEER SHAFT   **NGR 100 810**   Grade III
Alt. 1060ft (323m)   **Length: 200ft (61m) approx.**   **Depth: 220ft (67m)**
Permission from Gautries Side Farm.

On Gautries Hill above Gautries Hill Pot.

Shaft is 120ft (36ft) deep (beware of stacked deads). Get off ladder 10ft (3m) above bottom, and thread ladder down unstable slope to the west, and down 2nd pitch 25ft (8m) deep. At bottom steeply descending passage with false floor soon leads to 40ft (12m) pitch. Traverse over pitch and rig hand line on 3rd pitch of 20ft (6m) with large chamber at the bottom. The 40ft shaft is visible in the roof. At end of chamber 10ft (3m) climb down with short blocked crawl. Awkward 20ft (6m) traverse across the climb leads to 4th pitch of 30ft (9m) with minor workings at the bottom, well above the presumed natural water course.

Tackle:

Main Shaft & 2nd Pitch:	150ft (46m) ladder; 200ft (61m) lifeline.
SRT:	150ft (46m) rope.
3rd Pitch:	30ft (9m) handline.
4th Pitch:	30ft (9m) ladder; 50ft (15m) lifeline.
SRT:	40ft (12m) rope.

HILLTOP SHAFT   NGR 099 811   **Grade II (Mine)**
Alt. 1225ft (373m)   **Length: 100ft (30m)**   **Depth: 100ft (30m)**

Permission from Gautries Side Farm.

On the north side of Gautries Hill.

Three minor levels at 50ft (15m), 60ft (18m) and 90ft (27m). Shaft blocked at bottom, well short of natural water course.

Tackle – 100ft (30m) ladder; 120ft (37m) lifeline. (Long belay to tree).
SRT: 120ft (37m) rope. Scaffold bar for belay.

NO. 8 SHAFT   NGR 096 812   **Grade II**
Alt. 1100ft (335m)   **Depth: 185ft (56m)**

Permission from Gautries Side Farm.

100 yards (91m) north of the road.

Large shaft 12ft (4m) across through the shales. 185ft (56m) to water with no levels going off. Water has been dye tested to Rake Shaft, taking two days.

Tackle – 185ft (56m) ladder; 200ft (61m) lifeline.
SRT: 200ft (61m) rope. Scaffold bar for belay.

NO. 10 SHAFT   NGR 092 812   **Grade II**
Alt. 1200ft (366m)   **Depth: 250ft (76m)**

Permission from Rushup Edge Farm.

Close to Rushup Edge Farm.

12ft (4m) diameter shaft through shales. 250ft (76m) to water. Only one level known at 20ft (6m) depth. Water enters through the brick lining, and can be heard at surface.

Tackle – 250ft (76m) ladder; 280ft (85m) lifeline.
SRT: 280ft (85m) rope.

References: Crabtree, P.W. 1966. Jour. B.S.A. Vol.6. No.42. pp.43-61. Elliot, D. 1975. Caves of Northern Derbyshire. Part 3. Ford, T.D. 1966. B.S.A. Cave Science Vol.5. No.39. p.379. Salmon, L. 1963. B.S.A. Cave Science Vol.5. No.33. pp.36-52. Survey. Salmon, L.B. & Boldock, G. 1949. B.S.A. Cave Science Vol.2. No.9. pp.15-20. Salmon, L.B. & Boldock, G. 1956. Trans. C.R.G. Vol.4. No.2.

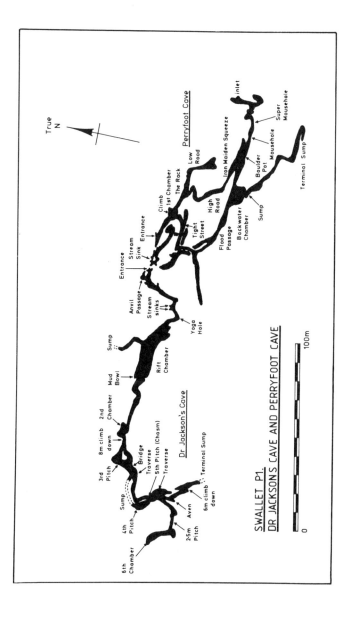

True N

Perryfoot Cave

inlet

Super
Mousehole

Low
Road

The Rack

1st Chamber

Climb

Mousehole

Boulder
Pot

Iron Maiden Squeeze

Stream
Sink Entrance

Entrance

High
Road

Tight
Street

Flood
Passage

Backwater
Chamber

Sump

Terminal Sump

Anvil
Passage

Stream
sinks

Yoga
Hole

Sump

Mud
Bowl

Rift
Chamber

2nd
Chamber

8m climb
down

3rd
Pitch

Bridge

Traverse

5th Pitch (Chasm)

Traverse

Dr Jackson's Cave

Sump

4th
Pitch

Aven

6m climb
down

Terminal Sump

6th
Chamber

2·5m
Pitch

SWALLET P1.
DR JACKSON'S CAVE AND PERRYFOOT CAVE

0   100m

COCKSHEAD MINE NGR 107 813 Grade III (Mine. Lost)
(S-P Hole)
Alt. 1230ft (375m)   Depth: 165ft (50m)

Through gate on right coming up hill from Perryfoot. Second shaft to the east, 50ft (15m) from the wall. The first shaft from the road also led into the mine. Both entrances now blocked.

Narrow entrance shaft. East from the base led to cavern and passages. Westwards from the shaft bottom led to 30ft (9m) pitch with loose boulders. Small passage led off, across second shaft to join up in lower levels by 35ft (11m) shaft. Lower levels flooded in wet weather. Water was believed to come from swallets to the north.

Reference: Chandler, B. 1953. British Caver Vol.24. pp.73-75. Survey.

CONIES DALE POT
NGR 131 808 to 131 811   Grade I (Digs)
Alt. 1300ft (390m)   Depth: 50ft (15m)

On the slopes north of the head of Conies Dale. A series of choked fissures and potholes. Most have been dug at some time or other, but were abandoned before reaching rock bottom. Still a promising site.

Reference: Workman, G. 1954. C.R.G. N/L No.49/50. pp. 7-8

COVE HOLE   NGR 115 822   Grade II (Dig)
(Snelslow Dry Valley Cave)
Alt. 1215ft (370m)   Length: 75ft (23m)   Depth: 92ft (28m)

Owned by Peakshill Farm. Access not normally granted.

In dry valley on left of track down to Peakshill Farm between Middle Hill and Snelslow.

Originally referred to as a short tight rift cave about 10ft (3m) deep. Dug to reveal a narrow twisting vertical tube, which has been enlarged. 15ft (5m) down leads to a small chamber excavated through in 1986 to a tight crawl. This reaches a pitch of 20ft (8m), which is broken and climbable with care. This is followed by a slope of calcited boulders to a tight choked rift. Blasting in this rift revealed a hole on the left wall, which has led to a tight pitch of 25ft (8m) into a choked calcited chamber. Digging is in progress.

Reference: Kitchen, G. 1965. B.S.A. digging report.

DIELASMA CAVE   NGR 135 832   Grade I
Alt. 1000ft (305m)   Length: 50ft (15m)

On Treak Cliff, north west of the show cave, near the crest of the ridge.

A small cave enlarged by mining, and easily explored by stooping. Named after the fossil abundant in the adjacent rocks.

DR. JACKSON'S CAVE   NGR 0989 8127   Grade V
Alt. 1033ft (310m)   Length: 1000 ft (300m) approx

Permission from Mr. Bagshawe, Torr Top Farm, Perryfoot.

Warning: Passage beyond Yoga Hole sumps in wet weather, and rescue from beyond would be exceptionally difficult.

A few yards west of Perryfoot Cave and the stream sink.

Dug into and explored by D.C.C. in 1969/70. Extended by E.P.C. 1972.

20ft (6m) entrance climb to small stream passage, left blocked with boulders where stream enters in wet weather. Right through short squeeze eventually leads to Yoga Hole after passing a few small inlets on the left, all blocked after a few feet. Stream sinks down 1 inch wide cracks where water backs up, forming a short canal, duck, or sump depending on weather. Through canal, an upward crawl leads to Yoga Hole, which must be entered feet first.

Narrow slippery tube descends 10ft (3m) (difficult to reverse) to small chamber. Upward crawl on left leads to large inclined rift passage to first pitch (25ft / 8m). Short crawl on right of rift passage ends in a small static sump. From first pitch large passage leads to short traverse and second pitch (25ft / 8m). At the bottom the chamber appears to be a dead end but the far wall is a rock bridge which can be climbed by a good climber. One alternative is a very dangerous and greasy traverse over from the top of the second pitch to Rock Bridge. Second alternative is to throw 50ft (15m) of ladder from top of second pitch to other side of Rock Bridge, which again is a difficult manoeuvre and ladder climb. Other side of Rock Bridge can be descended with the aid of 25ft (8m) of ladder to a static sump.

From top of Rock Bridge a very dangerous traverse out over the top of the final chamber leads to a passage in the right wall. Short walking size passage leads to hole in floor to 25ft (8m) pitch into The Chasm. Right to static sump, left to high passage which soon descends to low crawl blocked with boulders and very narrow. At top of hole leading to The Chasm the passage continues, breaking into The Chasm at a higher level. Very greasy and dangerous traverse across The Chasm to the continuation of the passage. After a few feet, very narrow passage on left leads to 25ft (8m) climb down rift. At bottom, left is too narrow while right soon ends in a static sump which has been dived for 10ft (3m) but is silted up. Back in the main passage, straight on leads to an interesting series of muddy crawls and chambers.

Tackle:

1st Pitch:	25ft (8m) ladder; 30ft (9m) lifeline. Short sling for belay.
2nd Pitch:	25ft (8m) ladder; 30ft (9m) lifeline. 10ft belay.
or Pitch to Bridge:	50ft (15m) ladder; 60ft (18m) lifeline. 10ft (3m) belay.
Rock Bridge:	50ft (15m) fixed line; 50ft (15m) lifeline.
Traverse Chasm Pitch (lower):	25ft (8m) ladder; 30ft (9m) lifeline. 20ft (6m) belay.
Chasm Pitch (upper):	45ft (14m) ladder; 50ft (15m) lifeline. Short sling for belay.
Chasm Traverse:	30ft (9m) fixed line. 50ft (15m) lifeline.
Terminal Rift:	30ft (9m) hand line.

References: Poole, C., Darroch, C., and Borthwick, P. 1970. D.C.A. N/L No.8. pp.3-4. Gill, D.W. 1973. D.C.A. N/L No.16.

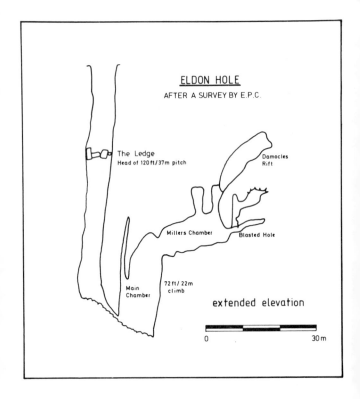

ELDON HOLE
NGR 1161 8039
Grade III

Alt. 1383ft (415m)
Depth: 245ft (82m)

Call on Mr. Harry Furness at Laneside Farm, Peak Forest (on main A623 at east end of village). Approach from Perry Dale up Eldon Lane and park at top end, just beyond Sweetknowle House. Recognisable footpath from here. Avoid using fence posts as belays.

On southern slopes of Eldon Hill.

The largest open pothole in Derbyshire, 110ft (34m) long and 20ft (6m) wide at the surface. Upper end of hole is most used for descent. Rope assisted scramble for 70ft (21m) ends at an outward sloping ledge. Pitch from here is 120ft (37m). From south end of the hole a free hang of 200ft (61m) can be obtained.

From bottom of shaft, cavern is reached through timbered shaft and crawl. Wide cavern 90ft (27m) high with good formations. Good light required! Climb on left leads to crawl passage, a possible dig. Fissure on right has been dug out for 60ft (18m) but has run in since. Lloyd (1780) reports a lower shaft with a stream in the bottom, but this has not been seen since.

New Eldon Series has been reached by Eldon Pothole Club climbing 80ft (24m) up the north wall of the Main Chamber. A series of well decorated rifts lead upwards to Millers Chamber, where a further 42ft (13m) climb leads to Damocles Rift, choked with flowstone at the top. This section is generally rigged, but contact Eldon Pothole Club to make sure.

Tackle:

N. End 1st Pitch:	100ft (30m) handline plus lifeline.	
Main Pitch:	130ft (40m) ladder; 150ft (46m) lifeline.	
	60ft (18m) belay.	
SRT:	150ft (46m) rope. Bolt belays.	
South End:	180ft (55m) ladder; 200ft (31m) lifeline.	
	40ft (12m) belay.	
SRT:	240ft (73m) rope.	
	Bolt belays.	
East Side:	200ft (61m) ladder; 220ft (67m) lifeline.	
	30ft (9m) belay.	
SRT:	240ft (73m) rope. Bolt belays.	
New Eldon Series:	80ft (24m) ladder & 42ft (13m) ladder and lifelines, or equivalent SRT ropes, plus bolts etc. Contact Eldon Pothole Club before attempting this section.	

References: Adam, W. 1840. The Gem of the Peak. Atkinson, F. 1949. B.S.A. Cave Science No.8. Survey. Kinsman, J. & Westlake, C.D. 1966. B.S.A. Cave Science No.38. pp.298-303. Survey. Lloyd, J. & King, E. 1780. Phil. Trans. Roy. Soc. Vol.61. pp,250-265. Survey. Simpson, E. 1949. B.S.A. Cave Science Nos. 7 & 8. Workman, G. 1953. The Speleologist Vol.1. Nos.2 & 3. Wright, A. 1971. Jour. S.U.S.S. Vol.2. No.1. pp.8-11.

ELDON QUARRY CAVES

ELDON QUARRY CAVE 1   **NGR 114 814**   **Lost**
Alt. 1350ft (405m)

An enlarged joint type of cave some 50ft (15m) deep intersected by quarrying during the War and since completely removed. It was well decorated with stalactites. There were rumours some years ago about blasting smoke appearing in Eldon Hole, 1/4 mile (400m) to the south.

NERVOUS BREAKDOWN   **NGR 113 811**   **Lost**
Alt. 1250ft (381m)

Possibly another section of Eldon Quarry Cave. Entered in 1977. A phreatic passage 4ft (1.2m) high and wide petered out after 70ft (21m) to an unstable bedding crawl. At the start of this crawl, a squeeze to the south was excavated, leading to a fine free-climbable pitch of 60ft (18m) choked at the bottom.

The whole cave was well decorated, but has either been destroyed or buried by further quarrying.

References: Phipps, M. 1981. The Lyre No.5. p.8. Survey. O.C.C. N/L Vol.13. No.6.

FROG HOLE   **NGR 121 823**   **Dig**
Alt. 1380ft (420m)

No access normally allowed.

In old quarry north of the road from Castleton to Perryfoot, west of Oxlow Farm. Digging over several years revealed a narrow fissure dropping 6ft (1.8m) into a passage at the head of a mud-filled pot. Now filled almost to the surface with rubbish, but was dug to a depth of 27ft (8m).

GAUTRIES HILL POT   **NGR 101 812**   **Grade I**
(Coalpithole Pot)
Alt. 1150ft (350m)   **Depth: 25ft (7m)**

Walled open pot on the hillside south of Perryfoot.

Scramble down into the pot at the east end. The way is open westwards, but choked immediately. A possible dig.

Reference: Elliott, D. Caves of Northern Derbyshire.

GAUTRIES HOLE   **NGR 1015 8145**   **Grade III**
(Jackdaw Pit, Swallet P.3)
Alt. 1040ft (312m)   Length: 800ft (240m)

Permission from Perryfoot Farm.

Entrance in tree-lined shakehole 200 yards north of the road at Perryfoot. Right entrance to short dry passage only. Left entrance is to stream passage. Upstream it can be followed for only a few yards. Downstream crawl through water until it disappears down an eye-hole supported with concrete. Turn right up into chamber. Climbing a muddy chute lead into partly flooded muddy rift and back to stream and terminal sump. Back at the chamber, two holes in the middle lead to small passage which increases in size after a few feet. Continue along passage to Angle Chamber and syphon with concrete

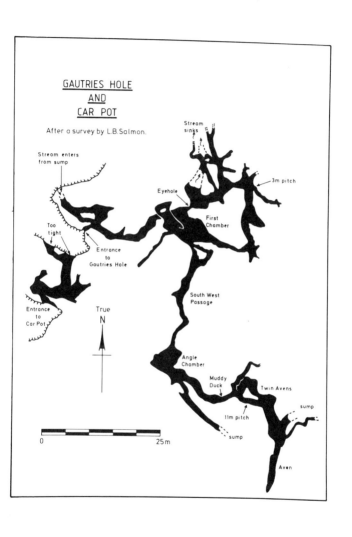

GAUTRIES HOLE
AND
CAR POT

After a survey by L.B.Salmon.

Stream enters from sump

Too tight

Entrance to Gautries Hole

Entrance to Car Pot

Stream sinks

Eyehole

First Chamber

3m pitch

South West Passage

True N

Angle Chamber

Muddy Duck

Twin Avens

11m pitch

sump

sump

sump

Aven

0   25m

dam. Return and climb up muddy slope on right (care–rope useful). After climb and muddy duck, passage leads to twin eyeholes and 30ft (9m) pitch into chamber, with sump pool at the bottom containing concrete dams. Pumping and diving by B.S.A. were unsuccessful. Stream liable to back up at the eyehole.

Tackle – 30ft (9m) ladder; 40ft (12m) lifeline; 20ft (6m) belay.

References: Anon. Undated. E.P.C.Jour Vol.6. No.1. p.19. Salmon, L. and Boldock, G. 1948. B.S.A. Cave Science Vol.1. No.6. pp.186-190. Survey.

GIANTS CAVE   NGR 116 826   Grade II
(UPPER CAVE   NGR 118 827)
(Peakshill Cave, P.11 & P.13)
Alt. 1215ft (370m)   Upper Cave 1245ft (380m)
Length: 295ft (90m)   **Depth: 33ft (10m)**

Permission from Peakshill Farm.

The resurgence cave is situated approximately halfway between the farm track and Giant's Hole, on the north flank of Peakshill.

The Upper Cave is a small swallet, but with another entrance as a concealed sloping rift close by, and the only way in. This is an awkward muddy drop of 15ft (5m) into a small streamway that can be followed westwards, mainly crawling, to an impenetrable sump after about 100ft (30m) The water re-emerges about 50ft (15m) west at the start of Giant's Cave, to go immediately underground again into this small system, which consists of 110ft (24m) crawl downstream to a sump (not free-diveable).

The stream re-emerges from the upstream sump in the Giant's Cave resurgence, which consists of an 80ft (24m) flat out crawl to the sump.

The stream flows past the Giant's Hole car park, and sinks again at P9–P10.

References: Elliott, D. Caves of Northern Derbyshire. Salmon, L.B. & Boldock, G. 1950. B.S.A. Cave Science No.11.p.121.

GIANTS HOLE   NGR 1194 8268   Grade II-V
(Swallet P.12)
Alt. 1224ft (373m)   Length: 10,231ft (3.13km)   Depth: 420ft (128m)

Permission from Peakshill Farm. Through trips using Giants as exit are not allowed.

Large swallet cave entrance in valley between Middle Hill and Peakshill. Reached from the Peakshill Farm track.

Extended by B.S.A. 1953–1957. Connected to Oxlow Caverns in 1966 by Eldon Pothole Club.

Warning: Stream passages below Garlands Pot may become impassable in flood conditions. The cave should not be descended by novices during heavy rain.

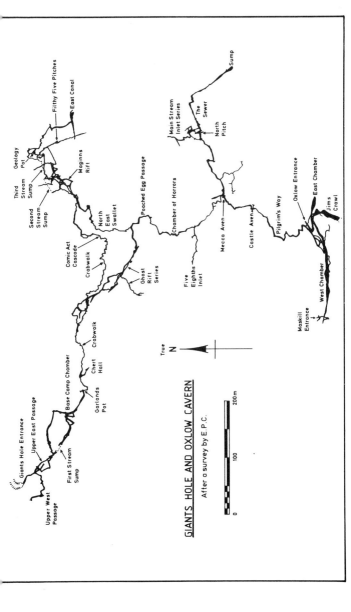

GIANTS HOLE AND OXLOW CAVERN

After a survey by E.P.C.

0   100   200m

A. Entrance to Eating House and Upper Series   Grade III
Length 8524ft (2.6km)

Large stream passage leads after 100ft (30m) to a short climb into the roof where Upper West Passage can be followed to the right, walking and crawling for 329ft (100m) blocked at the end. Also to left Upper East Passage is a crawl for 310ft (94m) to blockage, a grade 2 sporting trip for beginners. Back in stream, artificially enlarged walking passage, passing the former obstacle of "The Curtain", can be followed for a further 300ft (91m) to First Stream Sump. Large blasted tunnel on left leads past other former obstacles, "Pillar Crawl" and "Backwash Pool" to Base Camp Chamber, with the stream entering from the right.

Stream can be followed upstream in a high narrow passage to the outlet of the First Stream Sump. Climb in roof leads to decorated passage leading back above streamway to small chamber above Base Camp Chamber. Ahead is passage to High Level Sump, which has been baled but is blocked with flowstone.

From Base Camp Chamber a fine high passage leads downstream past Boss Aven to Garlands Pot, a 15ft (4.5m) pitch. A crawl on the left at the pitch top leads to October Aven, climbed for 30ft (9m) to a short choked passage. At bottom of Garlands Pot, high and narrow Crabwalk can be followed for just over 2000ft (610m) to Second Stream Sump. After first 120ft (37m) Chert Hall can be reached by a crawl at roof level on the right. After a further 380ft (116m) the 46ft (14m) climb to the Upper Series is reached. Crabwalk continues high and narrow for further 842ft (257m) to a squeeze, The Vice, followed after 25ft (8m) by the aptly named free-climbable Razor Edge Cascade. A further 110ft (34m) leads to Comic Act Cascade, 10ft (3m) deep. Great Relief passage which follows is larger, and leads to the Second Stream Sump after a further 575ft (175m). 50ft (15m) before the Second Stream Sump a passage on the right leads to the Eating House, where a small inlet stream enters from above. Left leads to St. Valentine's Sump and the Lower Syphon Complex, while a 10ft (3m) climb up by the inlet leads to Maggin's Rift and the Upper Series. A short crawl enters Maggin's Rift, actually a large vadose inlet passage rising steeply over boulders for 464 ft (141m). At the top the passage has been dug and can be followed past two squeezes to a 30ft (9m) aven. Beware of loose rubble.

At bottom of Maggin's Rift just beyond the entrance crawl muddy passage on the right leads to North East Swallet containing a small stream. A fine high passage can be followed upstream for 611ft (166m), free-climbing a 26ft (8m) cascade. A high level tube above the cascade has been dug by Crewe C.P.C., and is about 200ft (61m) long before it oxbows back into North East Swallet downstream. At end of North East Swallet is a junction. Left is Poached Egg Passage, 144ft (44m) long to Sardine Chamber, choked at the end. Just before the end a low opening on the right is the Chamber of Horrors (connection to Oxlow), a 728ft (222m) long flat out crawl with ducks, passing Five Eighths Inlet on the right. This is 250ft (76m) long, too tight for further progress. Stream sink on left (also too tight) dye tested to Main Stream Inlet in Oxlow Caverns. At end of Chamber of Horrors, just before the really tight section (original EPC dig) is Oxlow Aven on the right emitting a small stream.

Back at junction with Poached Egg Passage, on the right is Letter Box Passage leading to Ghost Rift, a 46ft (14m) scaling pole climb to the Ghost Rift Series, 816ft (214m) long. The main passage leads to a choke, but before the end a tight awkward passage on the left can be followed to pitches of 26ft (8m), 7ft (2m), 10ft (3m) where the way on is too tight but takes a small stream which probably goes to Five Eighths Inlet. Digging in the choke in 1990 led to a very dangerous route up through boulders (The Earth Leakage Trip) to a chamber and an upward continuation of the choke. A passage continues westwards to a further choke and short blocked pitch.

From Ghost Rift at far end is a small hole in hollow which is Giant's Windpipe, a wet low crawl with ducks to a junction. Left is Handshake Crawl which oxbows back into the passage after 176ft (54m) but is too tight in one place. To the right a larger passage continues, passing the other end of Handshake Crawl on the left and No Way Passage which is a high level passage blocked with calcite to right and left. Passage eventually breaks into the roof of Crabwalk. From here 46ft (14m) careful traverse/climb down into Crabwalk (rope or ladder useful for novices). Alternatively high level traverse in roof of Crabwalk, descending near Chert Hall.

B. East Canal via Geology Pot

Grade IV

Length (from entrance) 4513ft (1.38km)
Depth 420ft (128m) to normal East Canal surface level.

From Eating House small hole in the floor is a crawl to Lower Syphon Complex, but best way is forward under small waterfall to junction with climb up to Maggin's Rift, and left to a further junction. Right is East Overflow Passage to St Valentine's Sump while left is a crawl to a further junction. Left leads back to Eating House, straight on to North Rift (100ft/30m long), and right to the roof of the streamway between the Second and Third Stream Sumps. Obvious roof traverse downstream to gain a high level passage above the Third Stream Sump.

Walking passage to The Plughole, an awkward 13ft (4m) climb down (hand line useful) into chamber with 2ft of water. In roof is Cork Screw Shaft, a steep climb for about 200ft (61m) to a choke. Inlet also enters from St. Valentines Sump. A short passage leads to the head of Geology Pot, 40ft (12m) deep. Climb and traverse above Geology Pot to alternative route via Carnival Aven, which enters stream passage just before Far Curtain.

Short crawl from bottom of Geology Pot to the stream. Upstream for 117ft (36m) to 18ft (5.5m) cascade, with outlet of Third Stream Sump at the top. Downstream to a 13ft (4m) cascade, soon followed by Far Curtain, a wet crawl or duck. Spout Hall, a wet 8ft (2.5m) climb down into a deep pool, follows shortly. The route continues with short climbs, or a swim depending on water levels, to the deep East Canal. The Filthy Five pitches enter on the right, and the sump is to the left. It has been dived for 450ft (137m) to a depth of 100ft (30m) passing two air bells, first of which can be reached by non-divers in low water. In high water East Canal has been known to back up to bottom of Geology Pot. Far end of East Canal has been climbed for 50ft (15m) to 40ft (12m) of passage ending in blind avens, one of which has been climbed for 120ft (37m). Water has been dye tested to Russet Well via Speedwell Caverns.

Tackle:

Garlands Pot and Comic Act Cascade as under section D.

Geology Pot SRT	40ft (12m) ladder. 60ft (18m) lifeline. 80ft (25m) rope.
Cascade SRT	15ft (5m) ladder. 25ft (8m) lifeline. 30ft (9m) rope.
Spout Hall: SRT	10ft (3m) ladder. 20ft (6m) lifeline. 20ft (6m) rope.

C. East Canal via Filthy Five   **Grade IV**
Length (from entrance) 4011ft (1.2km)
Depth 420ft (128m) to normal East Canal surface level.

Warning: St. Valentine's Sump rapidly fills, and is difficult to bale from the other side. Baling outlet frequently blocked now. Make sure Far Curtain is accessible before abseiling Filthy Five for a round trip via Geology Pot!

Turn left at junction after Eating House and right to East Overflow Passage, a hands and knees crawl to St. Valentine's Sump. Small concrete dams enable sump to be baled into hole in floor until air space appears. Right turn after sump leads to Filthy Five Pitches of 13ft (4m), 8ft (2.5m), 16ft (5m), 8ft (2.5m), and 15ft (4.5m), one after the other, and very muddy. Dog Kennel follows, a crawl in glutinous mud which can require excavating. Junction follows. Straight on is South Rift, 100ft (30m) long, left is a short passage to the final pitch of 26ft (8m) into East Canal.

Tackle:

Garlands Pot:	15ft (4.5m) ladder; 25ft (8m) lifeline. 10ft (3m) belay.
Comic Act Cascade:	10ft (3m) ladder; 20ft (8m) lifeline. 20ft (6m) belay.
Filthy Five Pitches:	15ft (4.5m) ladder; 25ft (8m) lifeline. 10ft (3m) belay. 10ft (3m) ladder; 20ft (6m) lifeline. 2ft (0.6m) belay. 15ft (4.5m) ladder; 25ft (8m) lifeline. 12ft (4m) belay. 10ft (3m) ladder; 20ft (6m) lifeline. 2ft (0.6m) belay. 15ft (4.5m) ladder; 25ft (8m) lifeline. 2ft (0.6m) belay.
Dog Kennel Pitch:	25ft (8m) ladder; 30ft (9m) lifeline. 12ft (4m) belay.

D. The Giants-Oxlow System   Grade III – V
Total length 15,513ft (4.8km)
Max. Depth 693ft (211m)

The deepest system in Derbyshire. A fine system with everything for the sporting caver. The through trip from either Maskhill or Oxlow Caverns into Giants Hole is one of Britain's classics but is quite a serious undertaking. Cavers making through trips from Oxlow or Maskhill must leave the same way. The connection between Oxlow and Giants is very tight, and the ducks in the Chamber of Horrors may become impassable. Also the owner of Giants does not allow through trips using Giants as exit.

Interesting trips are:

Giants Hole to Oxlow Caverns (Pool Chamber), Depth 224ft (68m). Giants Hole to New Oxlow (Terminal Sump), Depth 256ft (78m). Oxlow Caverns to Giants Hole (East Canal), Depth 640ft (195m). Maskhill Mine to Giants Hole (East Canal), Depth 693ft (211m).

References: Atkinson, F. 1948. B.S.A. Cave Science Vol.1. No.5. pp.132-140. Survey. Deakin, P.R. 1966. E.P.C. Jour. Vol.7. No.1. pp.60-62. Salmon, L.B. 1956. B.S.A. Cave Science Vol.4. No.25. pp.1-33. Survey, and No.29. pp.230-241. Survey. Salmon, L.B. 1965. B.S.A. Cave Science Vol.5. No.38. pp.287-297. Survey. Westlake, C.D. 1967. Proc. B.S.A. No.5. pp.1-11. Westlake, C.D. 1972. E.P.C. Jour. Vol.8. No.1. pp.39-42. Whitehouse, R.H. 1966. E.P.C. Jour. Vol.7 No.1. pp.58-59. Yonge, C. Undated. Jour. S.U.S.S. Vol.2. p.31.

GOOSEHILL CAVE   NGR 1476 8269   Grade I
Alt. 670ft (204m)   Length: 15ft (5m)

In the last garden on the left on the footpath behind Goosehill Hall towards Cowlow and the Winnats.

A low arch 4ft (1.2m) wide, and 3ft (0.9m) high. Soon ends in a silt choke. Could have been an old resurgence.

HIATT CAVE   NGR 137 825   Grade I
Alt. 1200ft (360m)   Length: 50ft (15m)

In Shining Tor cliff high on the south side of the Winnats Pass.

A tube extending for approx. 50ft (15m), entered by digging. Several other small holes nearby.

HOLLANDTWINE MINE
NGR 1396 8125   Grade IV (Mine. Lost)
Alt. 1410ft (430m)   Length: 1500ft (457m)   Depth: 420ft (128m)

On Dirtlow Rake. Shaft recently obliterated by opencast mining. May be possible to re-open the shaft later.

Recorded as intersecting a "great swallow" at a depth of 600ft (183m). Hauling shaft was 375ft (114m) entrance pitch. The entrance shaft could also be descended for 150ft (46m) to a side level which allowed descent to be continued through a series of climbing shafts with fixed ladders to the bottom level.

After 200ft (61m) a dug out rift on the left leads to the natural series. Upstream leads to 40ft (12m) aven with 250ft (76m) of tight passage at the top. Downstream water can be followed to a 70ft (21m) pitch. At the bottom water sinks down an impenetrable fissure, and has been positively dye tested to Ink Sump in Peak Cavern.

At the top of the pitch 400ft of dry passage can be followed to a bedding plane collapse. A small hole, Dysentry Crawl, leads after 40ft (12m) of very tight and muddy passage to a further 350ft (107m) of passage terminating in a collapse.

Tackle:

Entrance Pitch:	375ft (114m) ladder; 400ft (122m) lifeline.
SRT:	390ft (119m) rope.
Alternative via	150ft (46m) ladder; 175ft (53m) lifeline.
climbing shafts:	70ft (21m) ladder; 100ft (30m) lifeline.
Aven:	40ft (12m) ladder; 100ft (30m) lifeline.
	+ scaling poles.

References: Anon. 1972. Descent No.22. p.13. Jarratt, A & Sulonen, S. 1972. D.C.A. N/L No.14. pp.2-3. Kinsman, J. 1966. Jour. E.P.C. Vol.7. No.1. p.12.

HURDLOW STILE PIPE
NGR 141 822 (approx)   Mine. Lost
(Hourdlo Steel Pipe)

In the vicinity of Hurdlow Barn.

Three mine shafts on an old plan and section lead to a natural swallow passage. The shafts are approximately 110ft (34m) deep.

Reference: Ford, T.D. 1965. Bull. P.Đ.M.H.S. Vol.2. No.4. pp.230-233.

LITTLE BULL PIT   NGR 1038 8167   Grade I. Dig
(Swallet P6)
Alt. 1100ft (330m)   **Length: 40ft (12m)**   **Depth: 25ft (8m)**

Permission from Perryfoot Farm. Small fee to be paid.

Pit adjacent to swallet P6.

The pit itself is an open pot (10m handline useful) floored with boulders and mud. Leads to chamber 15ft (5m) high. Several old digs under the walls.

The swallet nearby is a walking sized passage which has been dug, silted up, and redug several times. Some 10m of passage have been gained, with avens rising upwards. Mine shaft in field to west reaches a narrow vein. Crawl under stacked deads leads to silted natural passage which takes a small stream in wet weather.

References: Hatherley, P. 1978. Jour. S.U.S.S. Vol.2. No.6. pp.34-37. Survey. Hatherley, P. 1980. Jour. S.U.S.S. Vol.3. No.1. p.60. Salmon, L.B. & Boldock, G. 1950. B.S.A. Cave Science Vol.2. No.11. p.120. Worsencroft, K. 1963. E.P.C. Jour. Vol.5. No.4. pp.14-16.

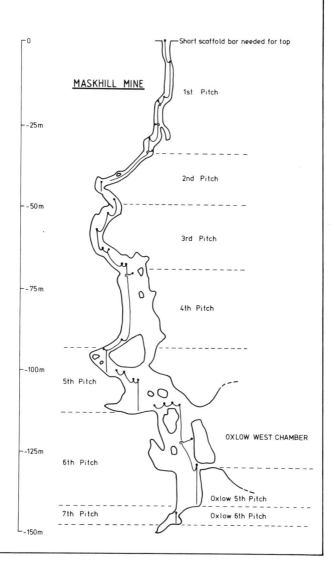

MASKHILL MINE

Short scaffold bar needed for top

1st Pitch

2nd Pitch

3rd Pitch

4th Pitch

5th Pitch

6th Pitch

7th Pitch

OXLOW WEST CHAMBER

Oxlow 5th Pitch

Oxlow 6th Pitch

0

-25m

-50m

-75m

-100m

-125m

-150m

LONGCLIFF MINE AND POT
NGR 141 825   **Grade II (Mine)**
Alt. 1000ft (305m)   Depth: 150ft (45m)

Shaft on highest prominent hillock behind Speedwell Cavern.

A mineshaft leads through the roof of a natural pot. Workings and a short second pitch extend some 200ft (61m) eastwards. Main shaft at present blocked by collapse of the hillock, and the ginging is unstable at the top.

Tackle:

Entrance Pitch:	130ft (40m) ladder; 150ft (46m) lifeline. Beam for belay.
2nd Pitch & traverse:	30ft (9m) rope.

Reference: Ford, T.D. 1962. Bull. P.D.M.H.S. Vol.1. No.7. pp.1-4. Survey.

MAM TOR SWALLET   NGR 1284 8313   Grade II
Alt. 1250ft (381m)   Length: 80ft (24m)   Depth: 30ft (9m)

Large entrance in shakehole by the roadside at the junction of the Chapel-en-le-Frith to Castleton and Sparrowpit roads where a small stream sinks.

Small chamber and low passage lead to the head of a 10ft (3m) pitch with a tight take-off. The chamber at the bottom contains much rubbish and bones, a choked aven in the roof, and the small surface stream which sinks in the floor. From the chamber a dug out crawl leads to a further 10ft (3m) drop where a tight crawl can be followed which takes a trickle of water, intersecting a small passage at right angles. Left is choked, and right becomes too low. The final 10ft drop has been buried by collapse. It has been said that the water reappears in Blue John Caverns, but this is unlikely.

Reference: Saville, B. 1959. The Lyre No.3. pp.56-58. Survey.

MASKHILL MINE   NGR 1224 8216   Grade V (Mine)
Alt. 1497ft (456m)   Length: 650ft (198m)   Depth: 500ft (152m)
(693ft/211m to East Canal of Giants Hole).

Important: Permission must be gained from Oxlow House Farm before descending, and the access route followed as for Oxlow Caverns. A plate on Oxlow Entrance indicates the direction of Maskhill.

Warning: The mine is now in a dangerous state of collapse, and great care is needed.

200 yards (183m) west of Oxlow entrance, and 52ft (16m) higher, near a dry stone wall.

A narrow mineshaft capped with concrete and covered with a steel lid. Entrance pitch 100ft (30m) deep, belay to rings on lid. Second pitch follows immediately to a large natural passage. A 7ft (2m) climb down leads to a steep slope arriving at the head of the third pitch, 36ft (11m) deep. A further steep slope follows to the head of the fourth pitch, Murmuring Churn. To the east is a 180ft (55m) drop which should not be laddered due to loose deads.

Descend in stages. The 82ft (25m) fourth pitch lands on a steep unstable slope, which drops for 13ft (4m) to the fifth pitch, 26ft (8m) deep. This can be free climbed with a hand line, or ladder belayed on far side of pitch.

At the bottom is a further pitch. Do not approach the edge as it is very loose. Descend via a walled shaft in the floor which can be free climbed in stages for about 50ft (15m). The bottom is the base of Murmuring Churn, where an impenetrable stream inlet enters and water flows down the pitch into Waterfall Chamber of Oxlow Caverns. Traverse over pitch to a bridge of debris where the sixth pitch can be laddered dry and is 141ft (43m) deep. At the bottom is Pearl Chamber, and the fifth pitch of Oxlow Caverns (not free-climbable) enters at the east end. The final wet pitch, the sixth of Oxlow or seventh of Maskhill, can be descended for 13ft (4m) to Pool Chamber and the terminal sump. The sump has been dived but is blocked with rubble after a short distance.

Tackle should be left in situ as through trips using Giants Hole as exit are not permitted. The mine is suitable for an SRT descent as numerous bolts have been placed for re-belays and deviations.

Tackle:

Entrance Pitch:	100ft (30m) ladder; 120ft (36m) lifeline. Short sling for belay.
SRT:	180ft (55m) rope; 3 re-belays. 2 deviations.
Second Pitch:	50ft (15m) handline; 50ft (15m) lifeline.
SRT:	16ft (5m) rope.
Third Pitch:	40ft (12m) ladder; 60ft (18m) lifeline. 20ft belay.
SRT:	85ft (25m) rope; 4 re-belays.
Fourth Pitch:	85ft (26m) ladder; 100ft (30m) lifeline. (Murmuring Churn).
SRT:	150ft (45m) rope; 3 re-belays. 1 deviation.
Fifth Pitch:	25ft (8m) ladder; 40ft (12m) lifeline. or 30ft (9m) handline.
SRT:	65ft (20m) rope; 1 re-belay. + 85ft (25m) rope. 4 re-belays.
Sixth Pitch:	140ft (43m) ladder; 150ft (46m) lifeline; Bolt belay.
SRT:	110ft (34m) rope; 7 re-belays; 1 deviation.
Seventh Pitch:	15ft (4.5m) ladder; 25ft (8m) lifeline. (Pool Chamber) 20ft (6m) belay.
SRT:	32ft (10m) rope.

References: Salmon, L.B. and Boldock, G. 1951. B.S.A. Cave Science Vol.3. No.17. pp.13-20. Survey. Westlake, C.D. 1972. E.P.C. Jour. Vol.8. No.1. pp.39-42. Survey.

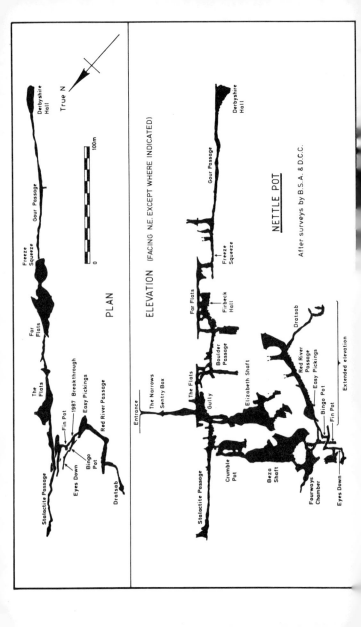

PLAN

ELEVATION (FACING N.E. EXCEPT WHERE INDICATED)

NETTLE POT

After surveys by B.S.A. & D.C.C.

True N

100m

0

MIDDLE BANK CAVE
NGR 144 824   **Grade I**
Alt. 1050ft (320m)   Length: 50ft (15m)

Above and to the east of Middle Bank Pot.

A small bedding cave completely excavated by the Technical Projects Unit of the B.S.A. in 1971, and found to end in a small chamber with no way on.

MIDDLE BANK POT
NGR 143 824   **Dig**
Alt. 1000ft (305m)   Depth: 50ft (15m) (now run-in)

On the east side of Middle Bank Gully on the hillside west of Peak Cavern.

A large open pothole, which was excavated to a depth of 50ft (15m). The shaft started to run back under the choke, and further excavation would have been too dangerous. The shaft has since run-in.

MOUNTBATTEN POT
NGR 125 816   **Grade II**
(Nettle Shaft Pot)
Alt. 1480ft (451m)   Depth: 137ft (42m)

Permission from Oxlow House Farm.

1/4 mile south of Nettle Pot.

A narrow natural fissure with a metal lid on top. Has been dug out to a small calcited chamber. Very tight.

Tackle – 137ft (42m) ladder; 150ft (46m) lifeline.

NETTLE POT
NGR 126 819   **Grade III-V**
Alt. 1515 ft (461m)   Length: 2100ft (640m) approx   Depth: 590ft (180m)

Permission must be gained from Oxlow House Farm before descending. Cavers must approach exactly as for Oxlow Caverns, then follow the direction marker on Oxlow entrance uphill to a gate. One gatepost has a fluorescent marker. Another marker can be seen on a distant post beyond Nettle entrance, or use the waymarker as a pointer and pace out 75 yards. The shaft is fitted with a steel lid.

Dug out by D.P.C. 1934. Extended D.C.C. 1987.

Entrance & Stalactite Passage   Grade III

Entrance pitch (160ft/49m) is tight in parts for the first 60ft (18m) through The Narrows. Rig the ladder or rope from the rings on the lid. Now best rigged for SRT via a rebelay, using a bolt at The Narrows and a Y-hang 30ft (10m) further down. On ladders best lifelined as two pitches as communication is difficult.

At bottom of pitch is The Flats, a washed out lava bed. There are short choked shafts in the floor, but to the east is the Gulley and Grand Canyon Pitch, 20ft (6m) deep. Traverse past the top of Elizabeth Shaft with care (handline or lifeline needed, or use 50ft ladder on Grand Canyon and lifeline from the top). Stalactite Passage is reached by crossing Elizabeth Shaft to a short climb down into a boulder strewn chamber. Small hole beyond is the top of Crumble Pot, while straight on is Stalactite Passage, becoming low, and floored with flowstone. Passage ends at 20ft (6m) aven with a tight crawl at the top heading for Jim's Crawl in Oxlow Caverns, 300ft (91m) away.

Elizabeth Shaft   **Grade IV**
From the bottom of the Grand Canyon, Elizabeth Shaft can be descended via
the first large hole in two pitches of 70ft (21m) and 100ft (30m). Not
recommended due to loose boulders. Best descent is via a small hole at the far
end, which is a 170ft (52m) fine direct descent, the longest natural
underground pitch in Derbyshire. The pitch lands on a rubble floor. A climb
up a slope leads to a short free-climbable pitch with a small stream entering
from Firbeck Hall and sinking into an impenetrable crack. From the foot of
Elizabeth to the east a further 40ft (12m) pitch in two sections can be
descended. Same stream enters and can be followed through EPC dig, The
Sting, 30ft (9m) of crawling through a tight duck and a boulder choke,
entering the bottom of Beza Pot at The Shakes.

Crumble and Beza Pots
Crumble Pot is 95ft (29m) deep, but only requires a 75ft (23m) ladder. Belay
to boulders at head of pitch. At bottom a climb up of 20ft (6m) leads to a
small hole where a 12ft (4m) rope pitch can be descended to the head of Beza
Pot, 150ft (46m) deep. Belay to calcited boulders. From the bottom a steep
boulder slope (50ft/15m handline useful) leads to The Shakes, where the
crawl enters from the bottom of Elizabeth Shaft. At the far end of The Shakes
a 20ft (6m) deep pot is blind. From the foot of the Beza Pot ladder, to the left
facing the ladder, a crawl leads to a tight 50ft (15m) rope pitch into a very
unstable area. Digging here revealed a further 30ft (9m) climbable pitch (Fin
Pot), but the way on is too tight for further progress.

   Digging in the area of Fin Pot in 1987 led to two extensions. One crawl was
followed to Bingo Pot, and a further crawl to another climb, Eyes Down, to
the lowest point 580ft (177m) below the entrance where work continues.
Further digging at Fin Pot revealed another crawl into a chamber, Easy
Pickings. The ascending Red River Passage continues, leading away from the
main joint, passing beneath avens to the base of a further aven. An awkward
descending crawl (Dratsab) ends at another climb, choked at the bottom.

Far Flats
The Flats at the bottom of the entrance pitch can be followed to the southeast
alongside the Gulley. 100ft (30m) of flat out crawling passes two choked
shafts in the floor, but the third can be descended for 35ft (11m) to a landing
on boulders opposite the entrance to Boulder Passage. This pitch can be
descended for a further 70ft (21m) where a small stream appears briefly on its
way from Firbeck Hall to Elizabeth. 100ft (30m) along Boulder Passage is
Suicide Pot, choked at the bottom after 60ft (18m). Ahead is Firbeck Hall
where an obvious aven can be climbed with the aid of a scaling pole and
ladder to Far Flats. Far Flats extends to the south east along the same washed
out lava bed as The Flats.

   After 150ft (46m) a 40ft (12m) pitch leads to the very tight Freeze Squeeze,
leading in turn to Gour Passage, generally walking size, and leading after
approximately 400ft (122m) to Derbyshire Hall. This chamber is 70ft (21m)
long, 20ft (6m) wide, with a flat roof and a floor consisting of a funnel of
boulders from which a draught issues. Three avens near the start of Gour
Passage were climbed, but were blind. A small inlet passage was pushed for
10ft (3m).

Tackle:

Entrance Pitch:	160ft (49m) ladder; 75ft (23m) & 120ft (36m) lifelines.
SRT:	200ft (61m) rope (rebelay at Sentry Box).
Grand Canyon:	25ft (8m) ladder; 60ft (18m) lifeline.
SRT:	80ft (24m) rope (including traverse).
Traverse:	Handline 60ft (18m)
Elizabeth Shaft:	170ft (52m) ladder; 200ft (61m) lifeline.
SRT:	200ft (61m) rope.
Bottom Pitches:	40ft (12m) ladder; 50ft (15m) lifeline.
SRT:	50ft (15m) rope.
Crumble Pot:	75ft (23m) ladder; 100ft (30m) lifeline.
SRT:	100ft (31m) rope.
Rope Pitch:	Handline 20ft (6m)
Beza Pot:	150ft (46m) ladder; 175ft (53m) lifeline.
SRT:	220ft (67m) rope (including Shakes).
The Shakes etc:	Handline 50ft (15m)
Suicide Pot:	25ft (8m) ladder; 50ft (15m) lifeline.
Firbeck Hall to	25ft (8m) ladder + scaling pole/bolts.
Far Flats:	60ft (18m) lifeline or 30ft (9m) SRT rope.
Far Flats Pitch:	40ft (12m) ladder; 50ft (15m) lifeline.
SRT:	50ft (15m) rope.

References: Chantry, M.H. 1937. Caves and Caving (pre-war series) No.1. p.34-37. Survey. Gill, D.W. 1970. E.P.C. Jour. Vol.7. No.3. pp.43-47. Survey. O'Neill, P. 1987. D.C.A. N/L No.65. pp.2-4. Survey. Salmon, L.B. and Boldock, G. 1951. B.S.A. Cave Science Vol.2. No.16. pp.331-338. Survey.

ODIN CAVE   NGR 135 834   Grade I
Alt. 850ft (255m)   Length: 140ft (42m)

No known access restrictions.
On the west side of the Mam Tor road close to Odin Mine.
Nice cave entrance. Very muddy. One chamber. 40ft (12m) shaft on hillside above leads into mud-filled continuation.

ODIN MINE   NGR 133 834   Grade III-IV (Mine)
Alt. 950ft (290m)   Depth: 450ft (137m)

Approach from west side of Mam Tor road to top of impressive fissure.
Warning: Much of this old mine is highly unstable and best avoided.
Belay handline round tree on north side and descend into first crack. Along passage 25ft (8m) chimney is climbed (rope handy) and leads to second shaft 35ft (11m) deep to lower workings. Facing ladder at bottom of shaft two ways

lead off: to left is 125ft (38m) pitch into a series of levels and stopes (**great care – lower levels very unstable**). To the right down steep slope, along a level containing dressed stone stemples in roof, to a climb down into the impressive Cartgate Chamber with stone arching in the roof. The chamber ends in a major collapse. Obvious arched passage entered by a short climb leads to two further pitches (tackle required).

Tackle:

Entrance:	60ft (18m) handline belayed to tree.		
Chimney climb:	40ft (12m) handline.		
	Ladder	**Belay**	**Lifeline**
Second Pitch:	35ft (11m)	30ft (9m)	55ft (17m)
Third Pitch:	125ft (38m)	Short belay	140ft (43m)

Various ladders, belays etc. required if other pitches in the mine are to be attempted.

References: Adam, W. 1838. Gem of the Peak. (Moorland Publishing reprint 1973 p.355). Anon. 1975. S.U.S.S. Jour. Vol.2. No.4. p.9. Bartrop, R. Undated. S.U.S.S. Jour. Vol.3. No.2. pp.16-17. Drury, D. 1980. Descent No.46. p.20. Ford, T.D. and Rieuwerts, J.H. 1976. P.D.M.H.S. Vol.6. No.4. Special publication. Survey. Smith, M.E. 1962. Bull. P.D.M.H.S. Vol.1. No.6. pp.18-23.

OLD MOOR DIG   NGR 145 811   Dig
Alt. 1350ft (411m)

An abortive dig in a shakehole, which was afterwards filled in.
Reference: Drakeley, K. 1981. The Lyre No.5. p.1

OLD TOR MINE   NGR 134 828   Grade II (Mine)
(Triangle Cave)
Alt. 1246ft (380m)   Length: 300ft (91m)   Depth: 70ft (21m)

Adit entrance high on the north side of the Winnats Pass at the end of the path. Gated. Permission required from National Trust.
Short adit leads into main chamber with a blocked shaft to surface. Pipe vein workings for Blue John stone extend north westwards to a 10ft (3m) pitch into lower passage. Muddy sump at end leads only to short passage. Beware infection from generations of cavers litter and dead sheep.

Tackle – 10ft (3m) ladder; 20ft (6m) lifeline.

OXLOW CAVERNS NGR 1241 8218 Grade III-V (Mine)
(Rackety Mine, Rickety Mine, Opens Mine)
Altitude: 1445ft (440m)
Length: 4632ft (1.4km) (Including Maskhill 5282ft/1.6km)
Depth: 477ft (145m) (To East Canal in Giants Hole 640ft/195m)

Permission must be sought from Oxlow House Farm, and an access fee paid. Access is via the lowered section of wall and wooden stile just before the third gate towards Perryfoot. Follow the wall uphill, and cross into the Oxlow Field by a stone stile in the wall. Proceed round the hillside, climbing up over the brow to Oxlow entrance.

Extended 1964 by B.S.A. and connected to Giants Hole by E.P.C. in 1966.

Oxlow to bottom of Maskhill Grade IV
Length: 1502ft (458m) **Depth: 445ft (135m)**
Entrance is mine shaft capped with concrete and fitted with an iron lid. First pitch is 53ft (16m) deep. Belay to bolts in concrete. Bottom of shaft is narrow to head of a steep slope of miners deads (beware of rotting timber supports). At bottom straight into is choked but low passage to left leads to head of Second Pitch, 36ft (11m) deep. At bottom, a slope and a short climb down where stream enters on right leads to Third Pitch, 46ft (14m) deep.

This is a good vantage point, with a fine view of East Chamber. At the bottom, a slope to the east and a short climb down lead to East Chamber, of impressive dimensions. At the far end is a short choked shaft in the floor. The north wall has been climbed by E.P.C. for 180ft (55m) to a 30ft (9m) passage ending at a tight aven, and a large rock bridge. From the bottom of the Third Pitch to the west, West Swirl Passage can be followed down a steep slope over deads to the head of the Fourth Pitch, where timbers are jammed across the passage. The Fourth Pitch consists of a very steep slope to the head of a 40ft (12m) pitch. Can be rigged with 80ft of ladder, or in two sections with a handline to the head of the pitch and a 40ft (12m) ladder to the bottom.

From the foot of the Fourth Pitch a steep slope leads down into West Antechamber. To the right (north) a 30ft (9m) ladder leads up to Pilgrim's Way and New Oxlow Series, but straight on is a low arch. An inlet enters on the right, and can be followed for 115ft (35m) to a sump which has been dived for 140ft (43m).

Stream has been tested from Black's Folly, the Rocky Tube before Castle Aven in New Oxlow Series. The low arch leads into West Chamber, of impressive proportions. At the far end a climb up a boulder slope leads to a short mined passage to the head of the Fifth Pitch, 46m (14m) deep. At the bottom is Pearl Chamber where a small waterfall enters from Maskhill Mine. This spot is the base of Maskhill's Sixth Pitch. The Sixth Pitch of Oxlow immediately follows, being 13ft (4m) deep to Pool Chamber and the terminal sump, which has been dived but is blocked with rubble.

Oxford Aven and Coconut Airways Grade V
Explored 1976 by E.P.C. Oxford Aven can be reached by turning left at the first junction in Pilgrim's Way. The passage leads via a tight squeeze to The Flue, dug in 1976 by T.S.G., which oxbows back into the wall of West Chamber at an aven. This has been climbed up 8 pitches to a height of 300ft (91m), choked at the top. The roof of West Chamber was traversed by bolting starting from the top of the Sixth Pitch in Maskhill. The three Coconut Avens were found, and the Great Aven was climbed to a height of 270ft (82m).

Passage opposite Pilgrim's Way
Reached with scaling poles, this tube can be followed as a crawl for 96ft (29m) to a voice connection with a similar tube off Suicide Chamber in the New Oxlow Series.

Jim's Crawl   Grade IV
Discovered 1968 by E.P.C.
   Above the Third Pitch is a 30ft (9m) bolt climb up to a crumbling rock
bridge. A further 30ft (9m) exposed climb leads to the top of East Chamber
where 166ft (51m) of very low but wide washed out lava bed can be followed
to a too-low section where water can be heard ahead. Four pitches in the
floor, all blocked at the bottom. Three can be free climbed. The fourth
requires 36ft (11m) of ladder. The passage is formed on the same bedding
plane as The Flats of Nettle Pot, and is roughly 300ft (91m) away from a
passage at the top of the aven in Stalactite Passage in Nettle.

New Oxlow Series   Grade IV
Length: 3034ft (925m)   Depth: 477ft (145m)
Discovered by the B.S.A. in 1964.
   Entered by climbing the 30ft (9m) fixed iron ladder from West
Antechamber to a high level phreatic tube leading after a short distance to a
junction. Left leads to The Flue and an eyehole into the roof of West
Antechamber. Right is Pilgrim's Way, 1010ft (308m) of hands and knees
crawling. A short distance along, two crawls on the right unite and lead to
Suicide Chamber, very unstable, and situated almost below East Chamber.
The tube continues to voice connection with the tube opposite Pilgrim's Way.
   Further along Pilgrim's Way on the left is the low arch to Castle Aven,
climbed for 50ft (15m) to a passage which is soon too tight. Castle Aven emits
a small stream which crosses Pilgrim's Way and enters Rocky Tube on the
right, which can be followed for 51ft (15m) to Black's Folly, a pitch of 26ft
(8m). The stream has been dye tested to the inlet in West Antechamber.
Pilgrim's Way continues to Mecca Aven, climbed for 130ft (40m) to a 6ft (2m)
long tube too tight for further progress. Just beyond Mecca Aven a passage
on the left leads to the Water Rift, 65ft (20m) high with no passages at the
top. Crawl on the left can be followed to a small stream which sinks and has
been dye tested to Main Stream Inlet. Upstream is a low crawl and very tight
section to Oxlow Aven and the connection with Giant's Hole via the
Chamber of Horrors, 728ft (222m) of flat out crawling with ducks.
   Back in Pilgrim's Way, the hands and knees crawl continues beyond Mecca
aven to Rainbow Aven. Walking size passage beyond passes low tube on right
after short distance. This is Icarus's Crawl, flat out for 225ft (69m) to a small
stream inlet. Downstream is too tight after a short distance. Halfway along
Icarus's Crawl is Henry Mares' Crawl on the right, 133ft (41m) of tight
crawling to a 20ft (6m) pitch with 5ft (1.5m) of water at the bottom. Passage
just before the pitch can be followed for about 20ft (6m), very tight. Another
low passage about halfway along can be followed for about 30ft (9m) before
becoming too low.
   The main passage continues at walking size to Jacob's Ladder, where a
small stream enters from an aven. Beyond is North Chamber leading to North
Pitch, 17ft (5m) deep (belay to boulders). At the bottom a low crawl, the
Portcullis, can be followed to Main Stream Inlet entering on the left from a
fissure. This tight fissure can be followed upstream to a 26ft (8m) cascade
which can be free climbed up two different routes. At the top is the Main
stream Inlet Series, consisting of 300ft (91m) of hands and knees crawling.

Main stream comes from small crack, while side passages are either too tight or break into avens. One passage branches back into roof of North Chamber and another into the top of North Pitch.

Downstream from the Portcullis a low wet crawl, The Sewer, leads to Boulder Chamber, where a high stream passage can be followed down to a sump and concrete dams. The sump has been passed by baling to P.B. Chamber and the terminal sump, which backs up and does not look hopeful.

Note: Cavers undertaking a trip from Oxlow to Giants must leave tackle in situ as exit is not allowed via Giants.

Tackle:

Old Oxlow

	Ladder	Belay	Lifeline
Entrance Pitch:	55ft (17m)	2ft (0.6m)	60ft (18m)
Second Pitch:	40ft (12m)	6ft (2m)	50ft (15m)
Third Pitch:	45ft (14m)	6ft (2m)	50ft (15m)
Fourth Pitch:	40ft (12m)	2ft (0.6m)	50ft (15m)
	plus 40ft (12m) handline		
Fifth Pitch:	45ft (14m)	2ft (0.6m)	50ft (15m)
Sixth Pitch:	15ft (4.5m)	20ft (6m)	20ft (6m)
East Chamber:	30ft (9m) handline.		
Rock Bridge above Third Pitch:	30ft (9m) + scaling pole		75ft (23m)
Bridge to Jim's Crawl:	30ft (9m) + scaling pole		75ft (23m)
Jim's Crawl Pitch:	35ft (11m)	10ft (3m)	40ft (12m)

New Oxlow
First to Fourth Pitches of Oxlow plus:-

Black's Folly Pitch:	25ft (8m)		30ft (9m)
Henry Mares' Pitch:	20ft (6m)		25ft (8m)
North Pitch:	20ft (6m)	15ft (4.5m)	30ft (9m)

References: Banner, C. 1972. E.P.C. Jour. Vol.8. No.1. pp.11-12; Bentham, K. 1978. D.C.A. N/L No.35. pp.1-2. Chantry, M.H. 1937. Oxlow Caverns Survey; Crabtree, P.W. 1965. B.S.A. Cave Science Vol.5. No.37. pp.229-238. Survey; Deakin, P.R. 1966. E.P.C. Jour. Vol.7. No.1. pp.60-62; Gill, D.W. 1970. E.P.C. Jour. Vol.7. No.3. pp.43-47. Mort, J. (Barmaster). B.S.A. Records; Pill, A.L. B.S.A. Cave Science Vol.1. No.5. pp.152-155; Salmon, L.B. & Boldock, G. 1951. B.S.A. Cave Science Vol.3. No.17. pp.13-20. Survey; Smith, P.B. 1966. B.S.A. Bull. No.72. pp.12-13; Westlake, C.D. 1966. B.S.A. Bull. No.71. pp.10-13; Westlake, C.D. 1967. Proc. B.S.A. No.5. pp.1-11; Westlake, C.D. 1972. E.P.C. Jour. Vol.8. No.1. pp.39-42. Survey; Westlake, C.D. 1967. E.P.C. Jour. Vol.7. No.2. pp.1-4; Winder, F.A. 1938. Unconventional Guide to the Caverns of Castleton. pp.48-56.

P0 SWALLET   **NGR 092 811**   **Grade II dig**
Alt. 1150ft (350m)   Length: 120ft (36m)   Depth: 60ft (18m).

A swallet taking a small stream.

Loose descent using handline (80ft/24m needed) to 40ft (12m) of walking passage to a diminutive sump. Care needed.

Reference: Bentham, K. 1988. T.S.G. Jour. No.13. pp.19-20.

P1 SWALLET   **NGR 0989 8127**   **Dig**
Alt. 1033ft (315)

Warning: Dangerous in all but dry weather.

Permission from Torr Top Farm.

At foot of blind valley between Dr. Jackson's and Perryfoot Caves.

A large stream sinks into a rift passage. This was forced in 1986 down some short cascades to a very wet duck to enter Perryfoot Cave. In wet weather the stream overflows to flood both Dr. Jackson's and Perryfoot Caves. Some of the water enters Dr. Jackson's Cave through tight inlets.

References: Gibson, R. 1986. Caves & Caving No.32. pp.22-23. Salmon, L.B. 1963. B.S.A. Cave Science Vol.5. No.33. pp.36-52. Salmon, L.B. & Boldock, G. 1949. B.S.A. Cave Science Vol.2. No.9. pp.15-20. Survey.

P4 SWALLET   **NGR 1016 8154**   **Dig**
(Sludge Pit)
Alt. 1050ft (320m)

Permission from Perryfoot Farm.

Wet weather stream sinking in small blind valley 100 yards (91m) north east of Gautries Hole. Attempts at excavation foiled by black mud.

Reference: D.C.C. Bulletin 1969.

P5 SWALLET   **NGR 1029 8163**   **Grade I (Dig)**
Alt. 1050ft (320m)   Length: 150ft (46m)   Depth: 70ft (21m)

Permission from Perryfoot Farm.

Excavated D.C.C. 1969 and E.P.C. 1980-83.

Small stream sinks in shakehole 240 yds (219m) north east of Gautries Hole.

A short passage leads to hauling shaft 43ft (13m) deep, best descended by a free-climbable pitch just beyond into Kaiser 1, a chamber now filled with excavated material. Rope Passage on left ends after 30ft (9m) and is formed in mud and boulders. Straight on is Dark Lane leading to Kaiser II amd III and Fingers Choke with no possibility of further extension. Majority of cave has been excavated.

References: Bentham, K. 1983. D.C.A. N/L No.52. pp.1-8. Survey. D.C.C. Bulletin 1969. Salmon, L.B. & Boldock, G. 1950. B.S.A. Cave Science Vol.2. No.11. pp.118-122.

P7 SWALLET   **NGR 1051 8173**   **Dig**
Alt. 1020ft (311m)

Permission from Perryfoot Farm.

Stream sinking in large shakehole and approximately 450ft (137m) north east of Little Bull Pit. Has been dug in vain. Water has been dye tested to the upstream inlet sump in the Lower Streamway of P8.

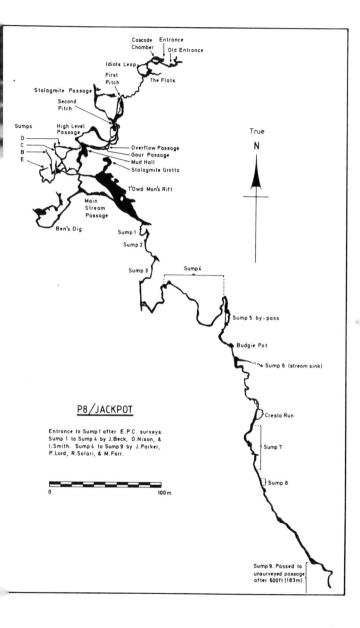

Cascade Chamber

Entrance
Old Entrance

Idiots Leap

First Pitch

The Flats

Stalagmite Passage

Second Pitch

High Level Passage

Sumps

D
C
B
E

Overflow Passage
Gour Passage
Mud Hall
Stalagmite Grotto

T'Owd Man's Rift

Main Stream Passage

Ben's Dig

True N

Sump 1

Sump 2

Sump 3

Sump 4

Sump 5 by-pass

Budgie Pot

Sump 6 (stream sink)

Cresta Run

Sump 7

Sump 8

P8/JACKPOT

Entrance to Sump 1 after E.P.C. surveys.
Sump 1 to Sump 4 by J.Beck, D.Nixon, &
I.Smith. Sump 4 to Sump 9 by J.Parker,
P.Lord, R.Solari, & M.Farr.

0 ————————————— 100 m

Sump 9. Passed to
unsurveyed passage
after 600ft (183m)

P8   **NGR 1079 8179**   **Grade III**
(Jack Pot)
Alt. 1068ft (326m)
Length: 3340ft (1018m) (+2000ft/600m approx beyond the sumps)
Depth: 230ft (70m)

Permission from Perryfoot Farm.
Explored B.S.A. 1964. Extended C.D.G. and E.P.C.
Approach from Perryfoot Farm where permission must be sought and a small fee paid. Entrances are in an irregular depression where a small stream sinks, 1000 yards (915m) north east of the farm, beyond Little Bull Pit. Please follow the way-markers.

Warning: This cave is not suitable for novices in wet weather when the First Pitch becomes very wet.

Old entrance leads to a muddy chamber with short crawls, a rift, and tight crawl to Cascade Chamber. 8ft (2.5m) concrete shaft down which the stream sinks leads quickly to the same place. Crawl over boulders to a clean-washed streamway. Above the first chute is a high level route along a mineral vein. The stream can be rejoined beyond Idiot's Leap by descending a 30ft (9m) climb. The streamway can be followed down several small cascades to Idiot's Leap, an 8ft (2.5m) climb. Narrow streamway with chutes and pools to the wet First Pitch of 25ft (8m), 270ft (82m) from entrance. Belay high on left wall.

Two routes below the pitch. Streamway continues for 100ft (30m) to the Second Pitch, 25ft (8m) with bolt belay into spectacular little chamber.

The other route is a 10ft (3m) climb to the Upper Series, opposite the First Pitch ladder. Short hands and knees crawl and easy traverse above the stream to a sharp left hand bend. Step over to the right leads to Stalactite Passage, 194ft (59m) long with a small stream, ending in a calcite choke. 20ft (6m) above the entrance to Stalactite Passage on the right is Steve's Passage leading back to a point high above the First Pitch. Main route is round left hand bend, and traverse over holes above the Second Pitch. Eyehole through flowstone leads to Upper Series Pitch, with an iron ladder. A further climb down leads to the foot of the Second Pitch.

From the bottom of the Second Pitch, a series of wet crawls lead via Overflow Passage to Sump D. Left just before Sump D leads to the Main Stream Passage, passing Sump C on the right.

Possible to leave Second Pitch ladder partway down, and climb round to bottom of Upper Series ladder. The route contracts to the smaller Gour Passage on the left. 75ft (23m) on is Mud Hall with High Level Passage on right, 200ft (61m) of roomy passage to a point opposite the top of the iron ladder. Across Mud Hall a dirty passage leads to the Main Stream Passage, which usually takes more water than the P8 stream.

Upstream is 100ft (30m) to the inlet sump, where the combined streams from P2 to P7 reappear. On the left are two openings to Sand Passage, mostly crawling with a tight duck and sump which must be bailed. Ends in static sump at the bottom of a slope. It is said that bad air has been met here. Just beyond Sand Passage on the right is the opening of Overflow Passage.

Downstream the passage is 30ft (9m) high with chutes and pools. A bouldery region follows, then a fine flowstone cascade and a final 100ft (30m) in a big hading rift (T'Owd Man's Rift) to Sump 1. A slippery climb up to the left leads to the vandalised Stalagmite Grotto and a low crawl to Christmas Aven.

A handline climb up the right wall of the Main Streamway before T'Owd Man's Rift leads into Ben's Dig, 600ft of walking passage leading to four chambers.

The upstream sump has been dived for 150ft (46m) to a depth of 90ft (27m) too tight for further progress. Only one air filled chamber below a boulder choke has been found.

Sand Passage has been dived in static water to a dead end after 15ft (4.5m).

Downstream Sump 1 is 105ft (32m) long and 15ft (4.6m) deep to an air bell. Sump 2 (12ft/4m deep and 100ft/30m long) leads to a further air bell 30ft (9m) across. Sump 3 (75ft/23m long) enters 130ft (40m) of stream passage to Sump 4. 300ft (91m) of constricted sump leads to a short stretch of streamway to Sump 5, 50ft (15m) long, and bypassed via an aven. A short stream passage leads to Budgie Pot, 15ft (4.5m) deep. After a further 100ft (30m) a small inlet enters, and the combined streams flow into Sump 6 which is blocked with pebbles and backs up. A rising phreatic tube, the Cresta Run, can be followed to Sump 7, which emits a trickle of water flowing to Sump 6. A passage continues to a 50ft (15m) pitch leading back into the Cresta Run. Sump 7 is 200ft (60m) long with a 20ft (6m) vertical pot. A short canal leads to the shallow Sump 8. 350ft (107m) of passage leads to Sump 9, passed in 1987 after a dive of 600ft (183m) to a short streamway and two unexplored 40ft (12m) pitches. Sumps 7 and 8 are currently (1990) blocked by heavy gravel depositon.

Tackle:

	Ladder	Belay	Lifeline
Idiots Leap:	20ft (6m) handline useful in high water.		
First Pitch:	25ft (8m)	5ft (1.5m)	40ft (12m)
Second Pitch:	20ft (6m)	2ft (0.6m)	40ft (12m)
Upper Series Pitch:	20ft (6m)	8ft (2m)	30ft (9m)
	(Fixed ladder in place at present).		

References: Bentham, K. 1984. E.P.C. Jour. Vol.9. No.4. pp.4-8. Survey. Also 1986. Vol.9. No.5. pp.6-18. Smith, P.B. & Waltham, A.C. 1973. B.S.A. Cave Science No.50. pp.21-28. Survey. Westlake, C.D. & Cobbett, J.S. 1972. E.P.C. Jour. Vol.8. No.1. pp.15-31. Survey.

PEAK CAVERN   NGR 1486 8259   Grade I-V (Part Show)
(The Devil's Arse)
Alt. 625ft (188m)   Length: 5.5 miles (8.9km)
                                Vertical Range: 560ft (170m) approx.
                Length incl. Speedwell: 9 miles (14.5km)

Warning: Frequent flooding occurs during the winter months, resulting in long stretches of the show cave being sumped, sometimes for several days.

Owned by the Duchy of Lancaster. Visiting clubs must be B.C.R.A. members. Individuals must sign an indemnity form, and must be at least 18 years of age. Access (Sundays only, November to March) controlled by B.C.R.A. Send S.A.E. with suggested date to J.S.Beck, Glebe Cottage, The Hillock, Eyam, Derbys.

Immense entrance at the head of the Peak Cavern Gorge below Peveril Castle.

A fine cave which with Speedwell Cavern forms a major system of considerable sporting and scientific interest. The following description should be regarded as a brief summary, and is intended to be read with reference to the large scale survey which is kept up to date by the T.S.G.

The Show Cave

Entrance chamber is 330ft x 102ft x 60ft high (101m x 31m x 18m). The terraces were used for rope making. Low down in the left wall is the Swine Hole, a large passage leading to a series of crawls, and to a 330ft (100m) sump which connects with the Outer Styx, the resurgence below the main entrance.

Several avens in the Vestibule roof have been climbed to reveal high level passages. Most extensive is the Krypton Series, above the Swine Hole, a series of joint-oriented passages almost reaching the surface in Cave Dale. The large aven above the bend in the top rope walk was climbed for 100ft (30m) to a large well decorated ascending passage (The Mendip Beer Monster's Secret Tap Room), ending at a calcite choke after 200ft (60m).

The visitors path descends to the inner gate, and via Lumbago Walk to the Inner Styx, a shallow pool. Then through a short low passage to two more large chambers, the Great Cave and Roger Rains House. The former is 150ft x 90ft x 60ft high (46m x 27m x 18m), and has several high level digs, a 150ft (45m) aven (with blocked connection to Cave Dale Cave No.4) and the high level Orchestra Passage, which leads to the Balcony overlooking Roger Rains House. Roger Rains Aven here is 130ft (40m) high, with a waterfall entering from the Cave Dale sink.

The route continues through Pluto's Dining Room, with inlet passages to right and left. That on the left is the Devil's Cellar, and is 395ft (120m) long. The show cave now ends at the top of the Devil's Staircase.

Down the steps is the Peak Cavern stream, flowing into Halfway House, which can be followed downstream for 120ft (37m) to a sump, where it flows to the Swine Hole and Outer Styx. (Sump dived to a slot after 130ft (40m)). The large main passage continues along the Five Arches for 500ft (152m), passing several avens. The show cave used to end here at the junction of Buxton and Speedwell Water passages.

The Far Reaches

The Buxton Water can be followed upstream to the left to Buxton Water Sump, a 330ft (100m) dive via a high aven into the Main Stream Passage. The right hand passage, or Speedwell Water, leads under the 250ft (76m) high Victoria Aven, with high level passages at both ends of the shaft still in the course of exploration.

A series of pools and canals leads past a narrow muddy passage on the right (eventually leading via an awkward climb and crawl to the high choked aven of Perseverance Pot) to a short stretch of large passage. A right hand branch leads to Speedwell Pot where floodwater used to enter the cave. The pot is now capped with concrete. A crawl to the huge choke in the bottom of Perseverance Pot follows, and one descends into Mucky Ducks, first passed by the B.S.A. in 1949 after a long dig.

The large Upper Gallery follows. After about 390ft (119m) a hands and knees crawl on the right is B-Cubed, a short dig. After a further 100ft (30m) a similar passage emitting a small stream is Pickering's Passage (see below).

Upper Gallery continues for 230ft (70m) to the junction with Treasury Passage on the right. The next right hand branch leads directly into Watershed Aven, and Upper Gallery continues, developing a narrow vadose trench, to the head of Surprise View. A 20ft (6m) climb with a fixed iron ladder descends into the lofty Main Stream Passage. At the top of Surprise View a passage on the right leads into the Main Stream Inlet Series.

Below Surprise View the Main Stream Passage can be followed downstream for 1080ft (329m). The last 500ft (152m) is a fine large phreatic tube, which gradually degenerates towards the upstream end of Buxton Water Sump. Upstream one reaches the waterfall at Squaw's Junction after 560ft (171m). Climbing this again leads into the Main Stream Inlet Series.

The next inlet on the left is Lake Passage with the by-passable Lake Sump (free-dive or by pass via a muddy crawl) to Ink Sump. A 630ft (192m) dive surfaces beneath a 75ft (23m) aven at the top of which is Doom's Retreat, an extensive dig amongst huge boulders close to Dirtlow Rake. Above the near end of Ink Sump, a slippery climb up a large phreatic ramp leads to two possible digs.

Beyond Lake Passage the main cave assumes very impressive proportions and passes a high level tube on the right connecting once again with the Main Stream Inlet Series. The next feature is a 40ft (12m) fixed iron ladderway into Maypole Inlet, an ambitious dig in a large phreatic roof tunnel.

Shortly after this, the main route ascends a boulder pile, with the Picnic Dig (and emergency food dump) higher still on the left. The large main passage continues, and the stream is regained just after the 250ft (75m) approx. of avens (not normally rigged) leading up on the left into Crystal Inlet. Easy walking, broken by one final boulder pile, soon leads to Far Sump, the limit of the cave for non-divers.

Far Sump Extension

Far Sump is a serious dive of 1265ft (385m) into Far Sump Extension. Two climbs up just past the end of Far Sump lead to large boulder choked passages, whilst the main way soon enlarges (after a careful squeeze through boulders) into a pleasant stroll for 1500ft (460m) to the large static Major Sump, choked at 33ft (10m) depth. A passage to the left approx. 500ft (150m) before Major Sump leads to Minor Sump, and a difficult crawl to a small stream passage, often completely flooded, The Rasp.

A low inlet crawl on the right 300ft (90m) beyond Far Sump enters Stemple Highway, a large complex phreatic rift. To the right, pitches up and down enter Salmon's Cavern, with no way on. To the left are 40ft (12m) and 20ft (6m) pitches up into 460ft (140m) of easy going (past small inlet sump) to the 150ft (46m) high Calcite Aven.

At the top of Calcite Aven is a large passage. A short distance along here is the 100ft (30m) high Cascade Aven on the left. At the top is Donatella's Aven, with various crawls leading off its base. The aven is 50ft (15m) high and leads to 100ft (30m) of passage via a final 13ft (4m) aven ending at a mud sump. This is 425ft (130m) above Far Sump level, about 200ft (60m) below surface, the highest known point in Peak Cavern.

Below the base of Cascade Aven, a dry passage leads to a scramble up into Fingernail Chamber. Here a 40ft (12m) pitch in the floor enters the impressive Balcombe's Way. Descending a loose boulder climb leads to the brink of a spectacular 200ft (60m) pitch back down into the roof of Salmon's Cavern, The Ride of the Valkyries. Partway along Balcombe's Way is a loose boulder slope up to the 100ft (30m) high Balcombe's Way Aven, entering an extensive bedding complex called The Total Perspective Vortex. To the right a crawl becomes too tight close to Donatella's Aven. To the left another crawl leads to three separate big shafts down. Vortex 1 is a 150ft (45m) pitch connecting with an aven in Balcombe's Way. Vortex 2 is a 33ft (10m) pitch, reached by a 50ft (15m) traverse, dropping into the roof of Western Highway. Vortex 3 is a loose wet shaft choked at 100ft (30m) depth.

The Main Stream Inlet Series
A short distance downstream from the Maypole Inlet ladder, a climb up (fixed rope normally in place) leads to a tube which immediately forks. Left is Window Dig, and to the right a slippery crawl leads to a further junction. To the right is a dangerous window into the roof of the Main Stream Passage, while ahead, crawling and stooping leads to the Main Stream Inlet, where the stream emerges from the bedding slot in the left wall. This is now largely concreted, and pipes lead the water away for use in various digs.

A right turn leads downstream to the top of the Squaw's Junction waterfalls, while straight on leads to a T-junction. Right leads to Squaw's Junction again, while left leads to Wigwam Aven, 90ft (27m) high with a tight passage at the top to the large Disappointment Rift.

Emerging in the bottom of Wigwam Aven, to the left and 10ft (3m) up is Cadbury Crawl, a 130ft (40m) long dig, and opposite is the main route.

The crawl soon enlarges at a junction. Left is a dig, while right soon develops a vadose trench and emerges into Galena Chamber. Climb down via the floor trench. Above the climb down into Galena Chamber is the entrance to the gated Wind Tunnel, 1250ft (381m) of arduous crawling to the top of Egnaro Aven in Speedwell Cavern. From Galena Chamber, an obvious rather muddy passage leads back to the top of Surprise View.

Pickering's Passage
An obvious hands and knees crawl on the north side of Upper Gallery, discharging a small stream. After 300ft (91m) a letter-box squeeze is followed by a left turn. A hole on the right is the way to Moss Chamber (see below) while straight on is Cohesion Crawl, leading to a large sump which overflows down the crawl. Climbing the boulder slope above the sump leads to Toadstool Aven, and a short side passage blocked with flowstone.

The hole on the right of the crawl leads to the base of a long slippery mud slope. At the top a narrow canyon passage leads via The Eyehole, a squeeze at roof level, to the top of a flowstone slope in a large chamber. Climb down to a pool, and up the far side (fixed rope usually in place). A short crawl and canal lead to the bottom of Moss Chamber, with its fine beehive slope of flowstone. On the right is the vertical tube in which Neil Moss died in 1959. At the top of the slope the passage continues through crawls and squeezes to the Balcony in Anniversary Hall. The boulder choke beyond here is extremely dangerous and should not be entered.

Treasury

From the junction in Upper Gallery, a keyhole shaped passage leads after 215ft (66m) to Treasury Chamber. On the far side of the chamber a gated crawl leads to Fawlty Tower, where an iron ladder leads to the long crawl to Egnaro Aven in Speedwell Cavern. Access is not allowed at the request of the owners of Speedwell Cavern.

On the left in Treasury Chamber is a low bouldery crawl to S.E.P. Sump. The main route out of the chamber is a boulder slope which leads down to a short pitch (fixed handline) and down a gravel slope to Treasury Sump, 80ft (24m) long and connecting (when it is not choked) with the Lower Bung Hole Series in Speedwell Cavern. In extreme floods, water rises up the slopes until it flows out to Upper Gallery, and on to join the main Peak Stream at the end of the Show Cave. Halfway House then backs right up the Devil's Staircase, and water flows out through the rest of the show cave to the Vestibule.

The White River Series – *see Addendum page 108*

References: Adam, W. 1838. Gem of the Peak. Reprinted Moorland Publishing 1973. pp.343-346. Anon. 1981. The Lyre No.5. pp.14-15. Brown, T. 1970. B.S.A. Bull. No.85. pp.1-4. Survey. C.D.G. Newsletters. (esp. 54 onwards). C.D.G. Derbyshire Sump Index. Cordingley, J.N. & Farr, M. 1981. B.C.R.A. Caves & Caving No.12. pp.10-12. Cordingley, J.N. 1986. The Peak Cavern System – a Caver's Guide. Vitagraph, Didsbury, Manchester. D.C.A. Newsletters. (No. 62 onwards). Gilbert, J.C. 1949. B.S.A. Cave Science Vol.2. No.10. pp.53-62. Survey. Gill, D.W. 1972. E.P.C. Jour. Vol.8. No.1. pp.36-38. Kitchen, G. 1971. Bull. B.S.A. No.4. pp.21-22. Kitchen, G. 1972. Bull. B.S.A. No.6. pp.8-9. Kitchen, G. 1971. Bull. B.S.A. No.3. pp.6-9. Nash, D.A. & Beck, J.S. 1989. The Peak Cavern Bibliography. Published by B.C.R.A. Salmon, L.B. 1962. B.S.A. Cave Science Vol.4. No.31. pp. 288-317. Survey. Salmon, L.B. 1952. B.S.A. Cave Science Vol.3. No.20. pp.177-181. Survey. Simpson, E, 1948. B.S.A. Cave Science Vol.1. No.3. pp.74-81. Survey.

PERRYFOOT CAVE   NGR 0989 8127   Grade III
(Manifold Cave)

Alt. 1033ft (315m)	**Length: 600ft (183m)**	**Depth: 97ft (30m)**

Permission from Torr Top Farm, Perryfoot.

In hollow immediately north of the road, close to stream sink P1 and Dr. Jackson's Cave. Obvious dry entrance to left of sink.

After short crawl and walk, small chamber has a choice of two ways on, which link up. At floor level a tight crawl in a passage with small pools leads to Iron Maiden Squeeze, which is very tight and must not be attempted by large persons. Beyond, the passage leads on to the final chamber. Alternative route is by delicate climb of 15ft (4.5m) out of the main passage, followed by very tight crawl for 10ft (3m), then series of crawls or walking. Turn sharp left at bottom of very muddy slope. Stream can be heard at bottom of very narrow shaft but cannot be reached. Continue along muddy passage to final chamber with concrete dams. Bailing by B.S.A. led to 200ft (61m) of passage with 25ft (8m) climb down to flooded rift chamber at 940ft (287m) O.D. The sump in the final chamber is at 970ft (296m) O.D. some 180 yards (165m) short of Coalpithole Rake, and about 100ft (30m) above the "Lost Swallet". Water reappears at Russet Well, Castleton.

References: Salmon, L.B. 1963. B.S.A. Cave Science Vol.5. No.33. pp.36-52. Salmon, L.B. & Boldock, G. 1950. B.S.A.Cave Science Vol.2. No.11. pp.118-123. Salmon, L.B. & Boldock, G. 1949. B.S.A. Cave Science Vol.2. No.9. pp.15-20. Survey.

PINDALE CAVE   NGR 157 823   Grade I
Alt. 800ft (240m)   Length: 50ft (15m)

Entrance at the uphill end of Pindale Quarry, in the opposite face to Black Rabbit Cave.

A crawl passage running under the dale for 50ft (15m), ending in a possible but difficult dig.

ROWTER HOLE   NGR 133 823   Grade III-IV (Mine)
(Longcliffe Caverns)
Alt. 1450ft (442m)   Length: 400ft (122m)   Depth: 270ft (82m).

Permission from Rowter Farm.

800ft (244m) north east of Rowter Farm. Approach through farm yard.

Entrance capped by platform and steel lid. Belay to lid. Fine 225ft (69m) deep mine shaft driven through solid rock for the first 170ft (52m), then entering a large chamber 60ft (18m) high, 20ft (6m) wide, and 100ft (30m) long. To the west, a steep rubble floored slope leads to a descending crawl into a mine level. This enters a large chamber leading up into the Abyss, a high natural aven with a short level 20ft (6m) up on one wall. Other openings can be seen 50ft (15m) up and at roof level, but as far as is known they have not been explored by cavers.

To the east from the entrance shaft a natural passage can be followed up a scree slope to where a stream enters from a bedding plane 30ft (9m) up in the north wall, Hypothermia Passage. This was dug out in 1976 to 80ft (24m) of very tight wet crawling to a larger passage where the stream enters from a boulder choke on the right. To the left a crawl leads to a small decorated chamber containing a blind aven.

From the entrance of the bedding plane a traverse leads upwards to a choke. Above, a chimney can be climbed for 20ft (6m) (beware of loose deads) into the Upper Chamber with unstable workings and shafts in the roof to east and west. 100ft (30m) rope useful for climb back down.

Back in the main chamber near the inlet are two shafts 25ft (8m) deep. The first is unstable but the second can be descended into a chamber with the stream entering. A further 25ft (8m) pitch follows down a rift. At the bottom an upward slope leads to a short climbable pitch with a short flooded working at the bottom. This has in the past been wrongly referred to as a sump.

At the foot of the second 25ft (8m) pitch a further short climb down enters a crawl containing the stream which sinks in the floor. The crawl is eventually blocked with gravel. Passage at the foot of the entrance shaft was dug by D.C.C. in 1984.

Tackle:

	Ladder	Lifeline
Main Shaft:	225ft (69m)	250ft (76m)
Upper Chamber:	–	100ft (30m) handline
2nd & 3rd Pitches:	50ft (15m)	75ft (23m)

References: Bentham, K. 1977. D.C.A. N/L No.32. Rucksack Club Journal 1938. Randles, J. 1953. The Speleologist (first series) No.1. pp.26-28. Survey.

RUSSET WELL   NGR 1482 8270   Dive
Alt. 615ft (187m).

In private garden on east side of entrance to Peak Cavern Gorge.

Main resurgence for the Castleton area. Water rises from a hole in a mineral vein some 10ft (3m) below the surface of a pool. Pumping into water mains during drought has failed to lower the level more than an inch or so, but clearing of Slop Moll resulted in a cessation of flow for a time. Diving has reached a depth of 90ft (27m), progress being halted by a tight slot.

References: Cave Diving Group Newsletter nos. 50, 53, 54, 56, 57, 59, 60, 61, 63, 64, 67, 68, 74, 84. Wright, M. undated. S.U.S.S. Jour. Vol.3. No.2. p.18.

SHEEPWASH CAVE   NGR 1007 8133   Grade II
(P2 Swallet)
Alt. 1064ft (324m)   Length: 100ft (30m)   Depth: 30ft (9m)

Permission from Perryfoot Farm.

In hollow 200ft (61m) north west of road junction at Perryfoot.

Inconspicuous entrance which takes a stream partly culverted. Entrance passage is a short crawl to an enlarged joint where the stream sinks. Can be descended for 15ft (5m) before it becomes too narrow for further progress. Across the joint a crawl leads to an aven which can be climbed for about 20ft (6m) blocked at the top. Tight high rift follows sloping downwards steeply to an awkward thrutch, immediately followed by a 15ft (4.5m) pitch into the main chamber. Pool at the north end is fed from surface stream re-appearing from tight inlet passage. To the left of the pool a descending tube leads to the terminal sump dived by CDG for 35ft (11m) blocked with silt. Inlet enters above the sump, and can be followed for a short distance before it becomes too tight. Perryfoot stream was diverted into Sheepwash Cave during the working of Coalpithole Mine.

References: Parker, J. 1971. C.D.G. N/L No.19. Salmon, L.B. 1963. B.S.A. Cave Science Vol.5. No.33. pp.38-39. Salmon, L.B. & Boldock, G. 1950. B.S.A. Cave Science Vol.2. No.11. pp.118-120. Survey.

SLITHERSTONES MINE No.1
NGR 125 815
Grade III (Mine)

Alt. 1470ft (448m)   Length: 140ft (43m)   Depth: 230ft (70m)

Permission from Oxlow House Farm.

South east of Nettle Pot, in the same field.

200ft (61m) deep engine shaft covered with concrete sleepers (please replace). Good ladder climb or prusik but communications difficult in shaft. Loose workings at bottom extend for a short distance to east and west. To west, slope leads down to pool which has been wrongly referred to in the past as a sump.

Tackle – 200ft (61m) ladder; 220ft (67m) lifeline.

References: Elliot, D. 1975. Caves of Northern Derbyshire Part 1. pp.23-25. Survey.

SLITHERSTONES MINE No.2
NGR 123 815
Grade II (Mine)

Alt. 1460ft (445m)   Length: 100ft (30m)   Depth: 180ft (55m)

Permission from Oxlow House Farm.

300 yards (274m) west of Shaft No.1.

Entrance covered with concrete sleepers please replace. 150ft (46m) deep shaft. Last 30ft (9m) contains rotten stemples which should be avoided. At bottom high narrow passage leads down to the east to 100ft (30m) of very unstable workings.

Tackle – 150ft (46m) ladder; 175ft (53m) lifeline.

References: Elliot, D. 1975. Caves of Northern Derbyshire Part 1. p.26. Survey.

SNELSLOW SWALLET   NGR 1125 8231   Grade III (Dig)
(P10)

Alt. 1154ft (351.7m)   Length: 140ft (43m)   Depth: Shaft: 187ft (57m)
                                                                    Swallet: 151ft (46m)

Owned by Peakshill Farm. Access not normally granted.

Southwest of Giants Hole, west of the farm track, 650ft (200m) NE of Christmas Swallet.

A series of parallel fissures. The stream is now diverted to Christmas Swallet. The largest fissure is the original rift entrance, dug via several short climbs to a hole leading westwards into an aven. An excavated rift chamber extends downwards for 65ft (20m), becoming wider at the bottom. On the west side at the bottom is a small passage leading to a further 33ft (10m) narrow pitch, which is choked. An artificial shaft from surface enters the aven, making it a 145ft (44m) pitch to the rift chamber floor. Digging is still in progress.

References: Clarke, J. Bull. B.S.A. No.85. p.4. Kitchen, G. Bull. B.S.A. Nos. 69-73. Survey in no.73. Mee, B. Bull. B.S.A. No.82. pp.9-10. Salmon, L.B. & Boldock, G. 1950. B.S.A. Cave Science Vol.2. No.11. p.121.

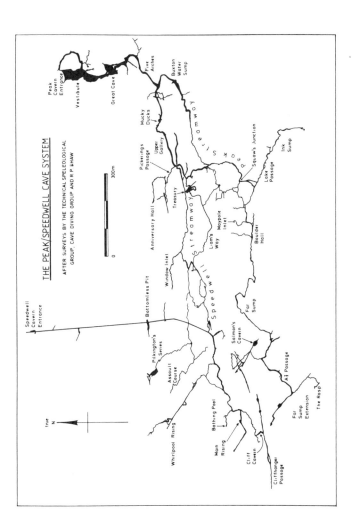

THE PEAK/SPEEDWELL CAVE SYSTEM

AFTER SURVEYS BY THE TECHNICAL SPELEOLOGICAL
GROUP, CAVE DIVING GROUP AND R P SHAW

0   300m

True N

Speedwell
Cavern
Entrance

Peak
Cavern
Entrance

Vestibule

Great Cave

Five
Arches

Buxton
Water
Sump

Mucky
Ducks

Pickerings Passage

Upper Gallery

Treasury

Peak Streamway

Squaw's Junction

Ink Sump

Lake Passage

Anniversary Hall

Maypole Inlet

Liam's Way

Boulder Hall

Window Inlet

Speedwell Streamway

Bottomless Pit

Pilkington's Series

Assault Course

Salmon's Cavern

Far Sump

A1 Passage

The Rasp

Far Sump Extension

Whirlpool Rising

Moon Rising

Bathing Pool

Cliff Cavern

Cliffhanger Passage

SPEEDWELL MINE AND CAVERN   NGR 1392 8274

(Navigation Mine)   **Grade IV (Part Show)**

Alt. 814ft (245m)   Length: 3.5 miles (5.7km)

Vertical Range: 522ft (159m)
Length: including Peak Cavern: 8.2 miles (13.2km)

Warning: The cave carries a large stream directly from the swallets of Rushup Edge to the resurgences of Russet Well and Slop Moll. It is seriously flood prone.

Access beyond the show cave not generally allowed.

Show Cave entrance at foot of Winnats Pass. Sealed shaft entrance by the toilets in the car park opposite.

Flight of steps down to the Canal. The 75ft (23m) shaft drops into the end of the level nearby. The Canal is a straight mine level with static water maintained at 3ft (1m) depth. The normal means of progression is now by electrically powered boat. Several veins are intersected, but the first passages of interest occur at Halfway House, where the level intersects Longcliffe Vein.

Passages to right and left are walled up, but another passage intersects the vein at loose and dangerous rising stopes. Natural passages have been described in the past, but not explored by modern cavers.

1500ft (460m) south from the entrance is the Bottomless Pit, a large phreatic cavity on Foreside Rake, which marks the end of the show cave. The aven here contains a short choked passage at about 130ft (40m) height, and a 40ft (12m) pitch down from the platform leads to a huge sump pool, choked underwater. It is believed that it received the spoil from the continuation of the main level. Water reappears at Russet Well in Castleton some 40ft (12m) lower and about ½ mile (800m) away. The Bottomless Pit cavern was referred to by Farey (1815) as "The Devil's Hall".

The mined passage continues beyond the Pit as wading in Far Canal. 500ft (150m) from the Pit is a low crawl on the right leading to Pilkington's Cavern. This, and the following five pitches have been scaled, and lead via a tortuous passage to Watricle Cavern, with a completely choked mineshaft leading on up. This point is about 400ft (120m) above the Far Canal.

A continuing crawl beyond the first pitch of Pilkington's Cavern leads to the Assault Course, a small streamway leading downstream to a small sump, and upstream via a very strenuous crawl to a blockage of boulders.

Other routes off the Far Canal are short downstream crawls, and must not be entered to avoid damage to dams maintaining the water level. At the end of Far Canal a large stream is met. Downstream is an 18ft (6m) pitch down a dubious iron ladder against the dam wall (The Bung Hole) into easy streamway. A large aven immediately on the right is Block Hall, climbed for 250ft (75m) approx. to a point with no obvious way on.

The Bung Hole streamway continues easily to a low duck, only passable in dry weather. The duck can be avoided by a dry oxbow 165ft (50m) further back on stream left to rejoin the main route just before Rift Cavern, where the 80ft (24m) high Egnaro Aven (fitted with iron ladders) marks the end of the Wind Tunnel connection with Peak Cavern.

Downstream is a deep pool (Puttrell's Pool), followed by an inlet cascade on the left. This is the Long By-pass, and can be followed, mainly crawling, to a dry passage connecting back to the Bung Hole Streamway.

The Lower Bung Streamway continues, and is very wet and difficult going except in drought conditions. It ends at the Downstream Sump, dived for 495ft (150m) to a depth of 16ft (5m). Three other passages lead off this streamway; the first is Window Inlet, 650ft (200m) of easy crawls including 53ft (16m) and 10ft (3m) sumps to a boulder blockage. The second passage is on the right, and is a deep canal soon ending at Treasury Sump, an unpleasant 80ft (24m) dive connecting with Treasury Chamber of Peak Cavern. The third passage is Overspill Passage, also on the right, 200ft (60m) from the Downstream Sump. It consists of 330ft (100m) of flood-liable crawl down to a sand choke and very low sump.

Upstream from the end of Far Canal is further wading to The Whirlpool, past a short mined passage on the left with natural chamber reached by dangerous boulder climbs. The Whirlpool is a short but turbulent swim if the pulsing stream is entering from Whirlpool Passage on the right.

This inlet can be followed by walking and crawling to the ebbing and flowing Whirlpool Rising, dived for 480ft (146m) to where the way on is too small. The first part of the sump can be by-passed via an awkward crawl to reach the first of two airbells.

The main route upstream across the Whirlpool is drier walking, past a roof level passage on the right connecting back to Whirlpool Passage, and past the Boulder Piles, with hanging chokes in the roof. Beyond here the route enlarges considerably. An iron ladder on the right (15ft/5m) leads to Bathing Pool Passage, ending at a large sump pool dived to 60ft (18m) with no way on.

Further upstream is Cliff Passage, shortly before Main Rising. This large sump has been dived past a deep area at -120ft (-36m) to a point where it rises to only 10ft (3m) depth. Beyond this point the sump descends to a large shaft which was still descending at the present limit of exploration, 610ft (185m) from base at 85ft (26m) depth.

Cliff Passage inlet passes ancient but vulnerable inscriptions on the wall (care!) to an easy crawl ending at a scramble up boulders to Cliff Cavern. At the head of the slope is a 160ft (50m) bolt climb into passages at both ends of the aven. To the west is Cliffhanger Passage, 660ft (200m) of large but very dangerous boulder strewn passage (including an oxbow) to a sump dived to an impossibly tight slot after 130ft (40m). To the east at the top of Cliff Cavern is Joint Effort, another large passage reached by a decidedly airy traverse. 500ft (150m) of varied going ends at avens (which close down at 30ft (9m) height, and two small sumps. The farthest of these sumps is a low 50ft (15m) dive to a climb emerging partway up the 40ft (12m) high Spidros Aven, too tight at the top.

References: Anon. 1981. The Lyre No.5. pp.14-15. Cave Diving Group reports. Various from 1970 onwards. Cordingley, J.N. 1986. The Peak Cavern System, a Caver's Guide. Vitagraph, Didsbury, Manchester. Ford, T.D. 1956. Trans C.R.G. Vol.4. No.2. pp.101-119. Survey. Pilkington, J. 1789. A View of the Present State of Derbyshire. pp.72-75. Puttrell, J.W. 1937. Caves and Caving (pre-war series) No.2. pp.44-47. Survey sketch. Puttrell, J.W. 1938. Caves and Caving (pre-war series) No.3. pp.85-88.

Survey (section) sketch. Puttrell, J.W. 1938. Caves and Caving (pre-war series) No.4. pp.125-126. Shaw, R.P. 1983. B.C.R.A. Cave Science Vol.10. No.1. pp.1-8. Survey. Simpson, E. 1954. B.S.A. Cave Science Vol.3. No.22. pp.267-273. T.S.G. Survey of the Peak/Speedwell Cave System. Warwick, G. 1947. British Caver No.17. pp.49-50.

SUICIDE CAVE   NGR 137 827   Grade II
(Horseshoe Cave)
Alt. 898ft (274m)   Length: 450ft (137m)
No known access restrictions.

Obvious entrance on the right near the foot of the Winnats Pass, with a second smaller entrance to the left.

First chamber has a boulder slope with a deceptive 15ft (4.5m) drop at the end. The route on is under the start of the slope. Left fork in second chamber leads to muddy crawls. Right to high third chamber. Back and foot traverse upwards at the end leads to rising passage with boulder choke at end, which has been dug upwards into a fissure to the surface.

Reference: Cordingley, J. 1976. S.U.S.S.Jour. Vol.2. No.5. p.9. Survey.

THISTLE POT   NGR 126 812   Grade I
Alt. 1430ft (436m)   Depth: 55ft (17m)
On the moor between Eldon Hole and the top of Conies Dale.

A 45ft (14m) water worn shaft dug by Pegasus Caving Club leads to two squeezes and an 8ft (2.5m) pitch into 80ft (24m) of well decorated rift passage. A 12ft (3.5m) pitch terminates in a flooded bedding plane. Extremely loose in parts.

Reference: Jarratt, A.R. 1973. D.C.A. N/L No. 17. p.2-3.

TREAK CLIFF CAVERN   NGR 136 832   Show
(Tray Cliff Cave, The Wonder Caves)
Alt. 950ft (290m)   Length: 1000ft (305m)
One mile west of Castleton on the Mam Tor Road. Entrance by footpath up Treak Cliff.

An outer series of caves much altered by mining for Blue John stone, with good examples easily seen. An inner series of grottoes with some of the best stalactites in Derbyshire, discovered in 1926.

References: Ford, T.D. 1954. Trans. Cave Research Group, Vol.3. No.2. pp.123-135. Survey. Guide Book. Story of Treak Cliff Cavern. Survey. Royce, S.J. 1945. Ancient Castleton Caves. pp.42-46. Survey.

TREAK CLIFF SEPULCHRAL CAVE   Lost
Immediately above Treak Cliff Cavern, but now quarried away. It contained a Bronze Age burial.

Reference: Armstrong, A.L. 1923. Jour. R.A.S. Vol.53.

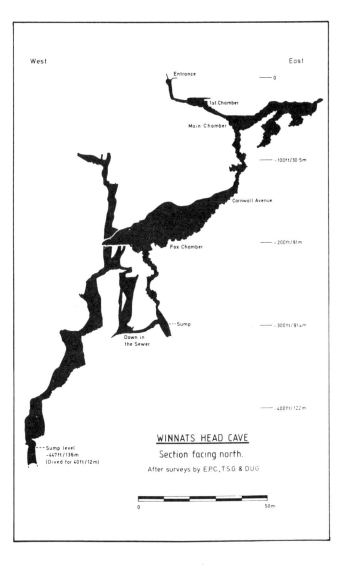

West   East

Entrance

— 0

1st Chamber

Main Chamber

— -100ft/30·5m

Cornwall Avenue

— -200ft/61m

Fox Chamber

- - - Sump

— -300ft/91·4m

Down in
the Sewer

— -400ft/122m

WINNATS HEAD CAVE

Section facing north.

After surveys by E.P.C., T.S.G. & D.U.G

- - Sump level
-447ft/136m
(Dived for 40ft/12m)

0   50m

TREE HOLE   NGR 135 832   Lost
Alt. 1000ft (305m)   Length: 300ft (91m)

On Treak Cliff, to the north west of the show cave and immediately north of the old quarries. Shaft in hollow close to lone tree, now filled in.

A narrow passage led through muddy crawls under stacked deads to two chambers with miners debris. A large collapsed choke formed a west (uphill) wall of the larger chamber, amd on the surface above a hollow suggests a former continuation to both the larger rock shelter visible from the valley, and to the small Dielasma Cave.

WINDY KNOLL CAVE   NGR 1263 8303   Grade I
Alt. 1344ft (410m)   Length: 120ft (37m)

In field between Chapel and Sparrowpit roads west of Mam Tor.

A broad entrance in an old quarry leads to a large cavern. Crawl on right at end leads to second chamber. Low crawl to third chamber and impenetrable fissure.

Windy Knoll Fissure, which yielded many thousands of animal bones, is now obliterated and is believed to have been backfilled immediately outside the present entrance. Remains in British Museum, and Buxton, Manchester, Derby and Cambridge Museums.

References: Dawkins, W.B. 1877. Quar. Jour. Geol. Soc. Vol.33. p.724. Heath, T. 1882. Derbys. Arch. Jour. Vol.4. pp.167-169. Survey of fissure. Pennington, R. & Dawkins, W.B. 1875. Quar. Jour. Geol. Soc. Vol.31.

WINNATS HEAD CAVE   NGR 1314 8282   Grade V
Alt. 1325ft (404m)   Length: 2000ft (610m)   Depth: 487ft (148.4m)

Permission from Winnats Head Farm.

In collapsed cave entrance in old quarry on south side of top of Winnats Pass.

Warning: The boulder choke below the Main Chamber is very dangerous, and rescue from beyond would be almost impossible.

Extended 1976 by T.S.G. & O.C.C., 1978 by E.P.C., and 1988 by D.U.G. and T.S.G.

Originally a 20ft (6m) long steeply sloping passage to a dig. Excavated in 1976 to reveal a low crawl leading to a small chamber. Further digging again in a low steeply sloping crawl through water entered the large Main Chamber, floored with boulders, 130ft (40m) from entrance. Large passage in roof to east exhibiting fine roof pendants can be followed for 130ft (40m) to clay choke. Holes in boulder floor can be descended for 50ft (15m) to blockages. 1978 E.P.C. dig in boulders in floor of Main Chamber can be descended through very loose and dangerous boulders to the top of Cornwall Avenue. This area is best avoided as the original pitches have collapsed.

From the bottom of the boulder choke a large passage, Cornwall Avenue, can be followed down a steep boulder slope for 60ft (18m) to emerge in Fox Chamber, 150ft (46m) long, 50ft (15m) wide, and 65ft (20m) high. Clay choke at end has been dug and holes in the floor can be descended through boulders to the top of a tight slot which drops down 15ft (5m) into a boulder chamber. From this chamber a passage round to the right (following a solid wall) leads through the 1988 dig (now a boulder squeeze) to a chamber with a steeply sloping boulder floor and solid roof and walls.

40ft (12m) down the slope is a 20ft (6m) diam. sump pool which has been dived. The water entering the sump from the boulder choke does not pass through the sump... it flows out to the left hand side into a passage which degenerates after 40ft (12m) into a hands and knees crawl half full of water for 30ft (9m) with the roof lowering for the last five.

Once out of the wet crawl, 20ft (6m) of rift passage puts one underneath a 40ft (12m) aven, the top of which is a rock bridge. A step across a parallel shaft and 15ft (5m) climb up leads to a standing height passage with two climbs of 10ft (3m) leading to crawling passage for 30ft (9m). Sharp left turn, then passage opens out beneath an aven. A stream enters from above, and cascades down the first shaft of 65ft (20m), with a ledge on the opposite side of the shaft away from the water.

The landing is in a chamber with a boulder floor, 30ft (9m) wide by 50ft (15m) long. At the far end it closes down to 6ft (2m) x 4ft (1.2m) on the lip of the next shaft, 45ft (14m) in a rift 10ft (3m) wide, 25ft (8m) long. The passage continues steeply sloping, walking size, at first with a boulder floor, then down two small climbs to the top of the final shaft. This shaft descends for 30ft (9m) to land on boulders wedged in the shaft, with the water dropping one side and the way on down the other side for a further 15ft (5m) drop. Small passage to sump after 15ft (5m). Water has been seen backed up as far as the wedged boulders.

The sump has been dived to a depth of 40ft (12m), where it is silted up.

Upstream

Upstream the aven divides into two. The dry one can be climbed between blocks to enter a chamber, with a small passage going off to a virtually static sump. By traversing around the left wall, the wet shaft is met again, and continues up for a further 20ft (6m) to a ledge, and a further 10ft (3m) to the base of another aven. The aven is 25ft (8m) high. From the top of the aven, step across the head of a parallel shaft (which takes the water), and climb up a small cascade and into 20ft (6m) of narrow passage with the stream, to the base of a wigwam shaped aven.

This aven is 15ft (5m) high, and at the top there are four small continuing avens, which all narrow with no obvious way on.

From the head of the 15ft (5m) aven a passage heads off, 15ft (5m) wide, 5ft (1.5m) high, with some fine stalactites. This gradually increases in height and continues for 60ft (18m) until the roof lowers to a choke with water entering. A small amount of water comes in from an immature side passage on the left, not passable.

Harpur Hill Series

can be entered by a traverse along a ledge on the right hand wall at the bottom of Cornwall Avenue. A flat out crawl leads to a chamber after 60ft (18m) of passage blocked at the end, but with voice connection to blocked passages at the top of Cornwall Avenue. Straight on is a narrow rift passage over a hole in the floor to a 7ft (2m) climb down, leading to a low passage 17ft (5m) long blocked with clay. Above the 7ft climb two passages can be climbed for about 40ft (12m). The first is blocked with boulders, the second rejoins the Harpur Hill entrance chamber at roof level. A third way on from the chamber is a walking passage on the left leading after 50ft (15m) to a 10ft (3m) climb down. Climb is followed by a further 55ft (17m) of passage containing a small stream to a mud sump, which has been dug.

Tackle:

40ft (12m) climb up to head of 1st Pitch may be rigged, but beware of old ropes of doubtful vintage.

1st Pitch downstream:	70ft (21m) ladder; 85ft (26m) lifeline.
SRT:	100ft (30m) rope; Belay to eyehole + bolt.
	35ft (11m) to ledge with 2 rebelays.
2nd Pitch downstream	50ft (15m) ladder; 60ft (18m) lifeline.
SRT:	70ft (22m) rope; Bolt behind head at pitch top.
	Rebelay on opposite wall.
3rd Pitch downstream:	35ft (11m) ladder; 45ft (14m) lifeline.
SRT:	65ft (20m) rope.
	Bolt at pitch head plus rebelay on opposite wall.
Final climb:	Handline, or thread third pitch tackle down below jammed boulders.

If upstream pitches are rigged, old tackle must be viewed with extreme caution. References: Gill, D.W. 1978. D.C.A. N/L No.36. p.9. Gill, D.W. 1978. B.C.R.A. Caves & Caving No.1. p.14. Skorupka, R. 1988. C.D.G. N/L No. 86. p.8

ADDENDUM

PEAK CAVERN – *continued from page 97*
The White River Series
Beyond the gated dig from Treasury, the route soon becomes flat crawling in mud. A tight squeeze leads to a fork. Right is Liam's Way, leading to Colostomy Crawl and Egnaro Aven. Left is a slippery climb of 10ft (3m) and a steeply ascending crawl (excavated in 1991) to a large chamber, The Ventilator. A pitch of 52ft (16m) leads up to the base of a loose boulder slope, The Terminator. A short pitch of 12ft (3.5m) and a short climb lead to Fever Pitch (50ft/15m), which emerges at the base of two flowstone ramps. To the right is the Fourth Pitch of 50ft (15m) to a small chamber.

A roomy crawl, Monday the Thirteenth Passage, leads to a T-junction with a large trunk passage, The Kingdom. Breakdown soon gives way to exceptional formations, including a 'white river' of calcite. A short pitch in the floor leads to the Moosetrap Series, five spectacular wet pitches to a sump roughly 300ft (91m) below The Kingdom. Beyond the Moosetrap The Kingdom continues, varied and impressive. A deep shaft (The Big Hole) is by-passed by an oxbow. The Kingdom ends at a blank flowstone wall, and a crawl at the top rejoins the vadose trench, which ends at a chamber 2010ft (613m) from the Ventilator.

The Big Hole, a fine free hang, leads down to a complex series of large chambers and mine workings still in the process of exploration.

A dangerous traverse round the rim of the Fourth Pitch leads to a flowstone ramp up to the base of a well decorated aven. To the left a large passage leads to White River Passage, very well decorated, and with an almost continuous flow of white calcite. All leads in this area end at complete flowstone chokes.

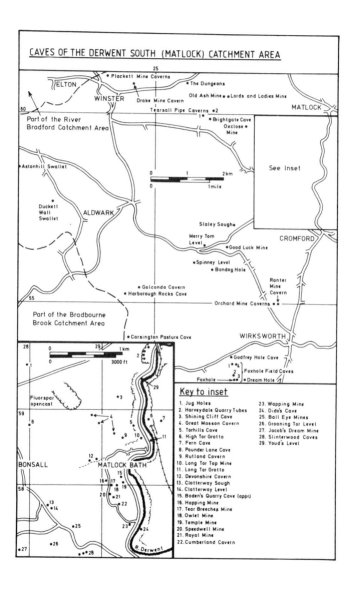

CAVES OF THE DERWENT SOUTH (MATLOCK) CATCHMENT AREA

ELTON

WINSTER

- Plackett Mine Caverns
- The Dungeons
- Drake Mine Cavern
- Old Ash Mine
- Lords and Ladies Mine

MATLOCK

Tearsall Pipe Caverns • 2
• 1
• Brightgate Cave
Oxclose Mine

Part of the River Bradford Catchment Area

See Inset

- Astonhill Swallet

Duckett Wall Swallet

ALDWARK

Slaley Sough
Merry Tom Level
• Good Luck Mine

CROMFORD

- Spinney Level
- Bondog Hole

Ranter Mine Cavern

- Golconda Cavern
- Harborough Rocks Cave

Orchard Mine Caverns • •

Part of the Bradbourne Brook Catchment Area

- Carsington Pasture Cave

WIRKSWORTH

- Godfrey Hole Cave
- Foxhole Field Caves
Foxhole • • Dream Hole

BONSALL

Fluorspar opencast

MATLOCK BATH

R. Derwent

Key to inset

1. Jug Holes
2. Harveydale Quarry Tubes
3. Shining Cliff Cave
4. Great Masson Cavern
5. Torhills Cave
6. High Tor Grotto
7. Fern Cave
8. Pounder Lane Cave
9. Rutland Cavern
10. Long Tor Top Mine
11. Long Tor Grotto
12. Devonshire Cavern
13. Clatterway Sough
14. Clatterway Level
15. Boden's Quarry Cave (appr)
16. Hopping Mine
17. Tear Breeches Mine
18. Owlet Mine
19. Temple Mine
20. Speedwell Mine
21. Royal Mine
22. Cumberland Cavern
23. Wapping Mine
24. Dido's Cave
25. Ball Eye Mines
26. Groaning Tor Level
27. Jacob's Dream Mine
28. Slinterwood Caves
29. Youd's Level

THE DERWENT SOUTH (MATLOCK) CATCHMENT AREA

The deeply incised River Derwent drops below the 100m contour in its course through the spectacular gorges at Matlock, while the limestones rise steeply up dip to over 300m to the west and south west.

Unfortunately large vadose caves and risings are unknown. Drainage and cave development are largely governed by lavas and mineral veins within the limestone, and possibly by the occurrence of dolomitic limestones.

The thermal springs constitute a proportion of the total drainage, along with surface streams and the few steeply dipping but immature stream caves. The greatest proportion of the drainage emerges from lead mine soughs, indicating the extent to which the natural drainage has been modified by mining.

The majority of the known caves have been intersected by the miners, and there are some classic examples of ancient mineralised solution caves.

Dolomitisation of the limestone probably took place during the Permian. This was followed by mineralisation when hydrothermal mineral fluids dissolved limestone along major joints, and deposited the well known range of Derbyshire minerals.

The Tertiary and Pleistocene saw the re-invasion of these cavities by streams flowing under phreatic or epiphreatic conditions, and many were filled with sediment during several glaciations. The source of these sediments is still in some doubt, but a lot of material was undoubtedly derived from the overlying gritstone.

The interesting story of the geological history of the area is not within the scope of this book. A great deal has been written about it elsewhere, and the reader is referred to the cited references for further information.

Many of the mines are still being systematically explored and surveyed, and much work remains to be done.

ASTONHILL SWALLET   NGR 213 586   Dig
Alt. 950ft (285m)

Old swallet in a hollow two fields east of Astonhill Farm.
　　Full of collapsed limestone blocks.
　　Reference: Mellors, P.T. 1969. The Speleologist Vol.3. No.19. p.17.

BALL EYE MINES   NGR 285 574   Grade IV (Mine)
Alt. 600ft (180m)
Length: More than 1 mile (1.6km)

On the hillside on the north of the Via Gellia, a few hundred yards down from the Pig of Lead pub. The quarry is currently being worked, and there is no access at present. Contact D.C.A. for up to date information.

A complex of mine workings and natural caverns mainly developed on two levels. At the top is the large open 'Hermitage' (also known as Rugs Hall), believed to be the chamber where a fossil elephant was found. Part of chamber is now dangerously unstable owing to adjacent quarrying. Crawl at rear leads to series of low pipe workings which have been intersected by the quarry face and are now very unstable. Danger from quarry blasting!

Main lower workings can be entered at several points from ledge about 100ft (30m) above the road. Westernmost entrance is Houghton Pipe, trending north westwards for some 400ft (120m) with two levels. Main entrance from terrace leads into complex of pipe workings and caverns with two blind shafts in the floor. Crawl on right leads to Van Traverse Cavern (see below). Climbing down incline and doubling back to the shaft leads to Foutrabbey Sough, over 1000ft (300m) long, with climbing shaft connection to upper series.

Immediately to the right and above Main Entrance is entrance to Ball Eye Rake, with high but partly collapsed stopes. The Rake is intersected by the quarry face just beyond the Hermitage, and can usually be seen to continue on the far side of the quarry. Eastern end of terrace has several short openings, and entrance to Van Traverse series, a single large cavern parallel to the hillside with much fluorspar and a shaft into toadstone in the floor. Several short branches lead off. Inner end of lower series, including Fountrabbey Sough, are under the quarry floor. Exploration at any time when the quarry is working is dangerous!

References: Buckland, W. 1823. Reliquiae Deluvianae. Dawkins, W. Boyd. 1874. Cave Hunting. pp.284-5. Heath, T. Derbys. Arch. Jour. Vol.4. p.162. Hurt, L. 1970. Bull. P.D.M.H.S. Vol.4. No.4. pp.289-305. S.

BODENS QUARRY CAVE   NGR 293 581   Lost

Exact site no longer known.

A bone cave intersected by quarrying "in a declivity about 20ft above the River Derwent on the east side of the Heights of Abraham". Finds include bones of rhinoceras, hyena, bear, and bison.

References: Law, R. 1878. Trans. Manch. Geol. Soc. Vol.15. pp.52-55.

BONDOG HOLE   NGR 266 559   Lost (Mine)
Alt. 1075ft (325m)

Listed by Farey (1811) "in 4th Lime-stalactites". Large single cavern at foot of 240ft (73m) deep mine shaft of Bondog Mine. Decorated level off at 150ft (46m). The chamber has now been intersected by Middleton Limestone Mine and largely destroyed.

References: Farey, J. 1811. A General View of the Agriculture and Minerals of Derbyshire. Vol.1. p.293. (London). Orpheus C.C. N/L Vol.10. No.1. 1974.

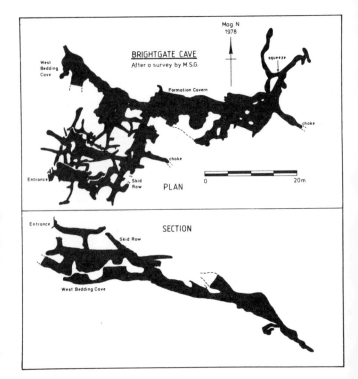

BRIGHTGATE CAVE
After a survey by M.S.G.

Mag. N
1978

West Bedding Cave

Formation Cavern

squeeze

choke

choke

Entrance

Skid Row

PLAN

0   20m

Entrance

SECTION

Skid Row

West Bedding Cave

BRIGHTGATE CAVE   NGR 265 599   Grade II
Alt. 950ft (290m)   **Length: 1080ft (329m)**   **Depth: 85ft (26m)**

Entrance on south side of head of dry valley below Brightgate Farm, amongst boulders below small outcrop.

An interesting system combining joint maze and bedding passages, unusual in this area in being unmodified by mining.

Drop down into entrance chamber with tight inlet on right. 10ft (3m) deep hole in floor drops to narrow descending rift into the Labyrinth, an intricate joint maze in dipping limestone. Various routes through this into 8ft (2.5m) high chamber or into Skid Row, and abandoned inlet with a smooth sloping calcite floor. Both routes rejoin in a sloping bedding chamber with some formations and 18th century miners' inscription. Descending bedding chambers continue on to a final smaller passage, squeeze, and choke. Just before the squeeze a draughting tube on the left leads through a tight squeeze to an aven.

Back in the first 8ft (2.5m) high chamber, opposite the main passage is the entrance to the Western Bedding Cave, 50ft (15m) of low bouldery crawl to an earthy draughting choke. One of the main rifts in the Labyrinth can be followed as a traverse at a higher level, and opens into a small chamber with some stumpy stalagmites.

References: Hurt, L. 1967. British Caver. Vol.47. p.74. Hurt, L. 1968. British Caver. Vol.48. pp.19-21. Ryder, P. 1979. Trans. B.C.R.A. Vol.6. No.1. Survey.

CARSINGTON PASTURE CAVE   NGR 243 541   Grade I
Alt. 1000ft (300m)   **Length: 25ft (8m)**

In the middle of the pasture.

A single chamber with a walk in entrance in a hollow. Soot on the roof, and a chimney shaft, suggest habitation at some time.

CLATTERWAY LEVELS   NGR 283 577 (Lower)   Grade II
                       NGR 282 578 (Upper)   (Mine)
(Ball Pie Mine, Brogdale Pipe)
Alt. 500ft (150m)   Length: 2000ft (600m) approx

Upper Entrance: Follow public footpath between stone cottages. Immediately beyond Burton Place Cottage climb up steep bankside and bear left through trees and undergrowth.

Lower Entrance: A low opening in the wood south of the first cottages going up the hill from the Pig O' Lead pub to Bonsall.

Narrow upper entrance, rediscovered by Masson Caving Group in 1988, leads after 75ft (23m) to 38ft (12m) deep shaft blocked at the bottom. Level off at 20ft (6m) leads after 50ft (15m) to 11ft (4m) deep free-climbable shaft. Level continues over shaft but is soon blind. The free-climb leads into fairly complex pipe workings which eventually lead through to the lower entrance.

Tackle – Upper Entrance: 40ft (12m) ladder; 60ft (18m) lifeline.

References: Chandler, P. 1988. Clatterway Level & Sough, Bonsall. D.C.A. N/L No.68.pp.6-8.

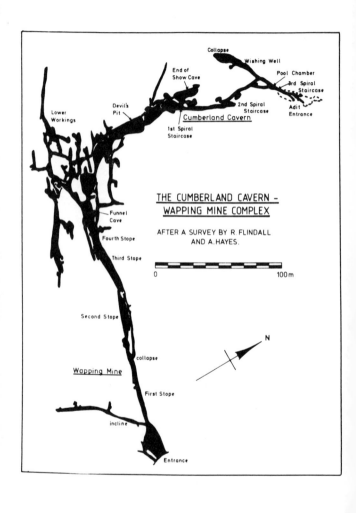

THE CUMBERLAND CAVERN – WAPPING MINE COMPLEX

AFTER A SURVEY BY R. FLINDALL AND A. HAYES.

0   100 m

N

Collapse
Wishing Well
Pool Chamber
End of Show Cave
3rd Spiral Staircase
Adit Entrance
2nd Spiral Staircase
Devil's Pit
Cumberland Cavern
1st Spiral Staircase
Lower Workings
Funnel Cave
Fourth Stope
Third Stope
Second Stope
collapse
Wapping Mine
First Stope
incline
Entrance

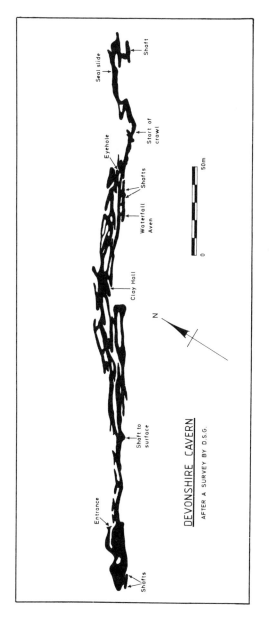

DEVONSHIRE CAVERN

AFTER A SURVEY BY D.S.G.

Shaft

Seal slide

Start of crawl

Eyehole

Shafts

Waterfall Aven

Clay Hall

N

Shaft to surface

Entrance

Shafts

0   50m

CLATTERWAY SOUGH   NGR 282 578   Grade II (Mine)
(Brogdale Sough)
Alt. 500ft (150m)   Length: 1000ft (300m) approx

Permission required from Mr D. White, Hollowbrook Cottage.

In garden immediately north of the first cottages going up the hill from the Pig O' Lead to Bonsall.

First 300ft (91m) is 4ft (1.2m) high with 3ft (.9m) of water. Then dry, totalling some 1000ft (300m) of levels with small solution cavities. There are a number of shafts going both up and down (difficult free-climbs, best laddered) in the dry section.

CUMBERLAND CAVERN   NGR 2923 5773   Grade II
                                                    (Formerly Show Mine)
Alt. 525ft (158m)   Length: 1/4 mile (400m)

Proceed up Wapping Lane or Clifton Road near the Church.

Mined level leads to pipe vein workings and natural caverns, which link with Wapping Mine. The Show Cave has been abandoned and the entrance has partly collapsed.

References: Adam, W. 1838. The Gem of the Peak. Derby. pp.60-61. (Moorland Publishing reprint 1973). Flindall, R. and Hayes, A. 1972. Bull. P.D.M.H.S. Vol.5. No.2. pp.114-127. Survey.

DEVONSHIRE CAVERN NGR 290 584 Grade III (Mine)
Alt. 700ft (213m)   Length: 1000ft (305m)   Depth: 260ft (80m)

All entrances now blocked except entrance just off the footpath to Bonsall off north end of Upperwood Road. This entrance is gated, and requires an adjustable spanner. Please keep the gate closed. Please park down in the valley rather than fill the turning space in the narrow road.

A former show cave at first going down the dip of the beds with lower levels, crawls to side, and mine galleries in upper parts. Extensive roof falls in places, partly blocking lower series.

References: Adam, W. 1838. The Gem of the Peak. Derby. p.62. (reprint Moorland Publishing 1973). Larson, J. 1954. The Speleologist Vol.1. No.3. pp.121-127. Survey.

DIDO'S CAVE   NGR 296 574   Grade I & Dive (Mine)
(Nether Hagg Mine)
Alt. 300ft (91m)   Length: 1400ft (426m)

Entrance is set back on the east bank of the Derwent near the weir at Masson Mill.

Totally mined except for short natural sections, its exploration has been the preserve of divers. 200ft (61m) of easy passage leads to a short climb down into The Lake. At the eastern end of The Lake Sump One (25ft/8m) leads to a short section of canal and then into Sump 2 (80ft/25m). There are two air bells in Sump 2, which terminates in a choke and access can be gained to further passage by crawling over boulders. From The Lake, going north, is the Coffin Level, 56ft (17m) long. This level joins two parallel rifts, surfacing in another "lake". To the west are Sumps 4 & 5 both 20ft (6m) in length, ending with a small airspace called The Teapot. To the east are Sumps 6 & 7, 20ft (6m) and 23ft (7m) long, and finally Sump 8, 218ft (66m) goes to the end of the rift. 110ft (33m) into Sump 8 a passage goes off to the right and surfaces after a short distance in Lord Nelson's Passage, choking after 100ft (30m).

There are numerous shafts in the floor in this cave which should be avoided.

References: Bentham, K. 1977. CDG N/L No.45. pp.21-22. Survey. Bentham, K. 1978. DCA N/L No.37,p.4., and CDG N/L's 37,38,46,57. Murland, J. 1978. CDG N/L No.49. p.25. Survey. Phipps, M. 1981. The Lyre No.5. pp.21-22. Survey.

DRAKE MINE CAVERN   NGR approx 244 608 Lost (Mine)

Listed by Farey (1811). Believed to be near the intersection of Shack Vein and Drake Vein.

Reference: Farey, J. 1811. A general view of the Agriculture and Minerals of Derbyshire. p.293

DREAM HOLE   NGR 275 530   Grade I (Mine/Arch)
Alt. 800ft (240m)   **Depth: 50ft (15m)**

North of Sprink Wood, south-west of Wirksworth, on the summit of the hill.

Large open fissure. Partly mined. Scramble down the west end. Crawl, and then climb. Among the remains found was an almost complete skeleton of a rhinoceros, now in Oxford University Museum. No modern excavation of deposits attempted.

References: Buckland, Rev. W. 1824. Reliquae Deluvianae (with section drawing). Dawkins, W.B. 1874. Cave Hunting. pp.284-285. Heath, T. 1882. Derbys. Arch. Jour. No.4. pp.163-165.

DUCKET WALL SWALLET   NGR 222 577   Dig
(Greenlow Swallet)
Alt. 980ft (299m)

A small stream sinks under stone troughs.

Shaft dug here in 1967 was refilled as too tight. A second shaft a short distance to the north was on the site of the former sink, among loose material, mostly clay. Only one solid wall. Dug to a depth of 30ft (9m) and refilled and abandoned in 1975.

References: Farey, J. 1811. A general view of the Agriculture and Minerals of Derbyshire. p.295. Mellors, P.T. 1976. D.C.A. N/L No.27. p.5. Mellors, P.T. 1969. The Speleologist Vol.3. No.19. p.17.

THE DUNGEONS   NGR 259 609   Grade I
Alt. 750ft (225m)   Length: 20ft (6m)

Landslips in the limestone south west of Wensley.

Short lengths of bedding and fissure cave exposed by landslip. One is a possible dig.

FERN CAVE   NGR 298 588   (Fern Cave)   Grade II
NGR 298 589   (Roman Mine)   Show Mine
Alt. 600ft (180m)   Length: 600ft (180m)

On summit of High Tor, Matlock.
   Very old open worked out lead vein. Connects with Roman Mine.
   References: Arnold, F.H. 1881. Science Gossip Vol.XVII, p.283.

FLUORSPAR CAVERN   NGR 291 581   Grade II (Mine)
(Jacob's Cavern)

Alt. 600ft (180m)

Adit close to Upperwood Road above Old Pavilion site.
   A series of old "pipe-vein" workings for lead and fluorspar, once a show
cave, but more recently mined. Parts are in a dangerous state. Links with the
Hopping, Royal and Tear Breeches Mines. Most entrances are now closed.
   References: Frost, R.V. 1953. The Speleologist, Vol.1. No.2. pp.63-67.
survey. Flindall, R. & Hayes, A. 1973. Bull.P.D.M.H.S. Vol.5. No.4.
pp.182-189. Survey.

FOX HOLES   NGR 2723 5300   Grade II
(Odin Cavern)
Alt. 800ft (240m)

Towards the east end of the low limestone outcrop above Sprink Wood, ¼
mile (0.4km) east of Pittywood Farm.
   Described by Buckland (1833). Reopened by the Odin Club. 60ft (18m)
crawl to circular domed chamber 30ft (9m) in diameter. Ochreous clayey fill
had been mind for ochre. Several small mined levels lead off from the
chamber.
   References: Buckland, W. 1833. Reliquiae Diluvianae. p.65. Kirkham, N.
1967. Bull. P.D.M.H.S. Vol.3. No.3. p.166. Potts, J. 1990. O.C.C. Jour.
No.6. (in preparation). Survey.

FOX HOLES FIELD CAVES   NGR 2717 5304   Grade I
NO.1 CAVE
Length: 15ft (4.5m)

210ft (64m) north west of Fox Holes. A short bedding plane cave on the west
facing slope.

NO.2 CAVE   NGR 2721 5301

60ft (18m) north west of Fox Holes. A rock shelter in the west end of the
same limestone outcrop.

NO.3 CAVE   NGR 2725 5300

60ft (18m) east of Fox Holes. A rock shelter in the east facing slope.

NO.4 CAVE   NGR 2727 5304

170ft (55m) north east of Fox Holes. A short rift cave in the south facing slope.
   Reference: Potts, J.E. 1990. O.C.C. Jour. No.6 (in preparation). Surveys.

GODFREY HOLE CAVE   NGR 271 536   Grade I
Alt. 750ft (225m)   Length: 70ft (21m)

Immediately behind cottages of Godfreyhole hamlet.

A short walk-in cave. Appears to have been used as a cowshed, and has had two "rooms" walled off. A trial archaeological dig was fruitless.

GOLCONDA CAVERN   NGR 246 554   Grade III (Mine)
Alt. 1160ft (348m)   Depth: 500ft (150m)

To the north east of Harborough Rocks.

400ft (122m) deep shaft. Not normally accessible. Lower Golconda shaft, ¼ mile (400m) to north west, is 290ft (88m) deep and contains a partly collapsed ladder way. The mine consists of a large series of solution cavities close to the junction of the limestone and dolomite. Farey (1811) referred to "A very large cavern in 4th lime".

References: Farey, J. 1811. A general view of the Agriculture and Minerals of Derbyshire. p.294. Ford, T.D. & King, R.J. 1966. Trans. C.R.G. Vol.7. No.2. pp.91-114. Survey. Ford, T.D. & King, R.J. 1965. Economic Geology Vol.60. Survey. Puttrell, J.W. 1960 (Reprint of article in Sheffield Telegraph). Bull.P.D.M.H.S. Vol.1. No.2. pp.8-12.

GOOD LUCK MINE   NGR 2700 5649   Grade II (Mine)
Alt. 675ft (206m)   Length: 3540ft (1079m)

Gated. Access by arrangement with R. Amner, 58 Foljambe Avenue, Walton, Chesterfield.

At top of an obvious spoil heap on the south side of the Via Gellia.

An extensive series of narrow adits, crosscuts, and small stopes of the early 19th century, which have intersected a number of small solution caverns.

Several other shorter levels lie in the immediate vicinity, and notes can be found in the references given.

References: Amner, R. & Naylor, P. 1973. Bull.P.D.M.H.S. Vol.5. No.4. Survey. Flindall, R. & Hayes, A. 1972. Bull.P.D.M.H.S. Vol.5. No.1. pp.61-80.

GREAT MASSON CAVERN
NGR 292 586   Grade III-V (Part Show)
Alt. 840ft (256m)   Length: 3 miles (5km)

Owner is Mr. Pugh, Heights of Abraham, Matlock Bath.

Show Cave entrance close to Victoria Tower on Heights of Abraham.

Entrance is via worked out Great Rake stopes, leading into a northward continuation of the Rutland (Old Nestus) Pipe, with numerous worked out pipe-vein cavities lined with calcite and fluorspar. Masson Cavern at end of Show Cave is large phreatic chamber, with former staircase leading to the "back door" at 291588.

The so-called "lake" is a flooded level. Branch galleries (now blocked off) led into workings and pipe veins of Black Ox, Carding's Nestus, and High Loft Mines with continuation into Crichman and Beck Mines. Former links with King Mine and Knowles Mine workings (now destroyed by opencast fluorspar workings on the summit of Masson Hill). Branch system near Beck Shaft once led ENE into Queen Mine workings, trending downhill towards Matlock, and linking with Youd's Level which discharges into the Derwent at 295594, making this one of the deepest cave-cum mine systems in the country.

References: Dunham, K.C. 1952. Memoir of the Geological Survey on "Fluorspar" p.99. Survey. Flindall, R. & Hayes, A. 1976. The Caverns and Mines of Matlock Bath. Part 1. Moorland, Hartington. Survey.

GROANING TOR LEVEL NGR 2830 5722 Grade I (Mine)
(Hallicar Wood Level)
Alt. 600ft (180m)   Length: 850ft (255m)

At top of field on south side of Via Gellia directly above car park near Pig O' Lead.

An easy walk in adit leads to two small chambers in decomposed toadstone. A small stream rises near the terminal choke and sinks in a small hole in the floor.

References: Smith, & Ford, T.D. 1971. Bull.P.D.M.H.S. Vol.4. No.5. pp.378-9. Survey. Flindall, R., Hayes, A. & Rieuwerts, J. 1977. Bull. P.D.M.H.S. Vol.6. No.6. pp.275-277. Survey.

HARBOROUGH ROCKS CAVE
NGR 2422 5523   Grade I (Arch)
(Harborough Cave)
Alt. 1165ft (355m)   Length: 50ft (15m)

Obvious entrance high in Harborough Rocks above Brassington.

Single chamber 6m x 10m (20ft x 30ft) with chimney to surface and narrowing fissures at back. Excavated Romano-British finds in Derby Museum. Second small cave nearby.

References: Armstrong, A.L. 1923. Jour. Roy. Anthrop. Trust. Vol.53. pp.402-16. Survey. Brailsford, J.W. 1957. Derbys. Arch. Jour. No.77. pp.54-55. Fox, W.Storrs. 1909. Derbys. Arch. Jour. No.31. pp.89-96. Jackson, J.W. 1929. Naturalist. pp.105-107. Potts, J. 1988. D.C.A. N/L No.67. pp.11-13. Survey. Smith, R.A. 1909. Derbys. Arch. Jour. No.31. pp.97-114.

HARVEYDALE QUARRY TUBES
NGR 296 598   Grade II-III
Alt. 350ft (105m)   Length: 2100ft (640m)

Access not normally allowed.

In disused quarry, variously known as Harveydale, Holt, or Hope Quarry. Four tubes, 30-50ft (9-15m) above the quarry floor.

A: Length 1500ft (457m). Long crawl in bedding tube with low meander channel often the only way through. At 375ft (114m) from the entrance is a cross passage. Right is a long wet crawl. Left is walking to another junction. Left (down dip) is dangerously tight and deceptive. Right leads into the side of a deep mine shaft on Seven Rakes Vein, with water some 65ft (20m) below.

B: Too tight for entry.

C: Hands and knees crawl for 300ft (92m) in a westerly direction to a small shaft 30ft (9m) deep. Cross this and a further 300ft (92m) crawl leads to the same shaft as tube A, but 30ft (9m) higher up.

D: A tight tube at the south end of the quarry which closes after a few feet.

Reference: Operation Mole reports for 1958-1959. Reprinted in British Caver Vol.31.

HIGH TOR GROTTO   NGR 296 588   Grade I
Alt. 350ft (106m)   **Length: 300ft (90m)**

Permission from the Paint Works.
    North of the Paint Works on the east bank of the Derwent.
    A former show cave with good calcite crystals.
    Reference: Adam, W. 1838. The Gem of the Peak. (Reprint by Moorland, Hartington, 1973) p.63

JACOB'S DREAM MINE   NGR 278 571   Grade I (Mine)
Alt. 700ft (210m)   **Length: 500ft (150m) approx**

In topmost crags on the south side of the Via Gellia directly above the works.
    Easy walk-in adit leads to small chamber with faulted wall of toadstone, some small solution features and a small stalactite grotto.

JUG HOLES   NGR 2797 5959   Grade II
Alt. 850ft (255m)   **Length: Over ½ mile (0.8km)**

No known access restrictions.
    In wood south of Leawood Farm and north of Salters Lane, on summit of Masson Hill.
    Large cave entrance in wood leads to workings ahead and to the left. On right near foot of slope is descent into series of muddy caverns, with branches to old workings, and finally out to the adit entrance lower down the hill. At back and to right 12ft (4m) shaft leads to Boulder Maze on left and roomy but dirty stalagmite caverns with limestone roof and floor of green clay (decomposed basalt lava). Once noted for its bats and for the "sound of a barking dog" caused by a small syphon pool no longer operative.
    References: Nash, D.A. 1957. Trans. C.R.G. Vol.5. No.1. pp.13-22. Worley, N.E. and Nash, D.A. 1977. Trans. B.C.R.A. Vol.4. No.3. pp.388-401. Survey.

LONG TOR GROTTO   NGR 297 586   Grade II (Mine)
Alt. 300ft (90m)   **Length: 300ft (90m)**

Entrance below wicket gate on river bank just north of the footbridge to the paint works. Entrance passage may contain sewage.
    Sough tunnel runs westwards under the main road. Series of old workings in Great Rake with solutional effects in bedding etc. Difficult to understand why it was called a Grotto, though it appears to have been open to visitors at some time.

LONG TOR TOP MINE   NGR 2955 5865   Grade II (Mine)
(Little Dish Mine)   **2945 5860 (shaft)**
Alt. 500ft (152m)   Length: 500ft (152m)

Permission required from nearby Derwent House.

At the top of Long Tor Quarry overlooking the main road, almost directly under the cable car wires.

A concealed low entrance. A through passage to the foot of a shaft in the wood above. A good sporting scramble popular with novice cavers.

LORDS AND LADIES MINE NGR 270 605 Grade II (Mine)
Alt. 600ft (180m)

On the east side of Northern Dale, between Wensley and Snitterton.

A series of old lead mine workings which have intersected several small solution caves.

References: Nash, D.A. 1957. Trans. C.R.A. Vol.5. No.1. p.22. Riley, P. 1977. Bull. P.D.M.H.S. Vol.6. No.5. p.244.

MERRY TOM LEVEL   NGR 264 565   Grade I
(Lower Nimblejack Level. Twenty Friend Vein)
Alt. 650ft (198m)   Length: 350ft

Immediately below the Middleton road, near Nimblejack Corner.

Small slabbed entrance soon enlarges to 5ft x 2.5ft (1.5 x 0.75m). After 270ft (82m) a square shaft in the roof discharges a trickle. The level ends at a handpicked stope in the vein.

Reference: Smith, A. & Ford, T.D. 1971. Bull. P.D.M.H.S. Vol.4. No.5. p.381. Survey.

MILLCLOSE MINE NGR Shaft – 259 625 Grade II (Mine)

Sough – 264 626

Watts Shaft – 257 618

Alt. Shaft 400ft (122m)   Length: over ½ mile (0.8km)

Access strictly by permission of the Works Manager, H.J. Enthoven and Sons Ltd. prior to visit.

Half a mile north west of Darley Bridge, in the outbuildings. Shaft boarded over and locked.

Entrance shaft has fixed iron ladders to the only accessible level at a depth a 60ft (18m). The shaft continues down for over 800ft (244m) but is full of water and boarded over. From the shaft a passage leads to a T-junction. Right leads to a water filled passage and old pumping shaft (which is not boarded over). Left at the T-junction leads to Yatestoop Sough, along which water rushes to the exit and into the River Derwent. Interesting ochreous deposits in the roof and on the sides of the sough.

Sough can be followed into the mine until roof fall prevents progress. Very strong current of water pours over the top of the fall. Digging here enabled some progress to be made, but divers reported the level reducing in size beyond, with little hope of further exploration. Flooded caverns below the water table contained a lining of lead ore etc.

Watts Shaft. Large open shaft 190ft (58m) deep to water. Level at 157ft (48m) heads south for 540ft (165m), and is the pumpway into Old Millclose Sough. It is driven in shale, ventilation is poor, and it is silted at the far end. A side passage leads east, then turns south, passing the Fire Engine Shaft (covered at the surface) with old ladders still in place. The silted end of the level is just beyond.

NEW SPEEDWELL MINE

Royal Mine and Pavilion Mine (qv) are names for workings dating from the 1950's on the site of New Speedwell. New Speedwell was obliterated.

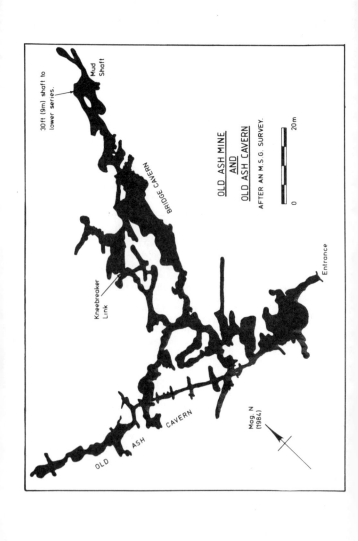

30ft (9m) shaft to lower series.

Mud Shaft

BRIDGE CAVERN

Kneebreaker Link

OLD ASH CAVERN

Entrance

Mag. N (1984)

OLD ASH MINE
AND
OLD ASH CAVERN

AFTER AN M.S.G. SURVEY.

0   20m

OLD ASH MINE   NGR 269 605   Grade II
Alt. 600ft (183m)   Length: 1150ft (350m) approx

On the west side of Northern Dale, opposite Lords and Ladies Mine, roughly midway between Wensley and Snitterton.

An adit leads into a complex system of mined and natural passages. A very tight squeeze was pushed in 1982 to discover a further 300ft (91m) of mostly natural passage with some fine formations, and further evidence of entry by miners via a now run-in shaft.

Mud shaft leads to short lower levels.

A 150ft (46m) shaft on the hill top at 268 605 enters the system at Bridge Cavern, where a pendulum is required to get onto the rock bridge 30ft (9m) above the bottom of the shaft.

Tackle:

	Ladder	Lifeline
Bridge Cavern shaft:	150ft (46m)	180ft (55m)
Mud Shaft:	30ft (9m)	40ft (12m)

References: Gibson, R. & Ryder, P. 1983. B.C.R.A. Caves & Caving No.20, p.16. Nash, D.A. 1957. Trans C.R.G. Vol.5. No.1, p.22.

ORCHARD MINE CAVERNS NGR 283 550 approx. Lost

No longer known. In one of many veins lying parallel to and on the east side of the Middleton–Wirksworth road. Farey's description appears to be confused with Orchard Pipe Caverns at Winster on page 264.

Reference: Farey, J. 1811. A general view of the agriculture and minerals of Derbyshire. p.294.

OWLET HOLE MINE   NGR 292 580 Grade I (Mine)
(Victoria Cavern)
Alt. 500ft (152m)   Length: 400ft (122m)

Gated. Owned by P.D.M.H.S. Keys obtainable from the Mining Museum.

High on the hillside just south of Matlock Bath. Shaft entrance is 200 yards down the footpath from the Upperwood Layby.

The shaft entrance is rigged with iron ladders, and enters the mine 50ft (15m) from the main passage. The system consists of a mined pipe vein.

Reference: Maddocks, C. 1957. The Lyre No.2. pp.42-43. Survey.

OXCLOSE MINE   NGR 275 597   Grade IV (Mine)
Alt. 730ft (223m)   Depth: 350ft (107m)

Access not normally granted.

Escape Route shaft in field behind Leawood Cottage, Snitterton. Main Shaft in next field downhill.

The first pitch of the Escape Route is a 60ft (18m) shaft, with ladder belayed to rail to avoid ginging. Short crawl to the second pitch of 25ft (8m), with ladder belayed to foot of the first. From the foot of the pitch proceed down dip for 700ft along a complex route. Take care to avoid an 80ft (24m) shaft in the floor. A mined area around the Engine Shaft is reached at the 200ft (61m) level. Shaft continues to 300ft (92m) level. Workings continue

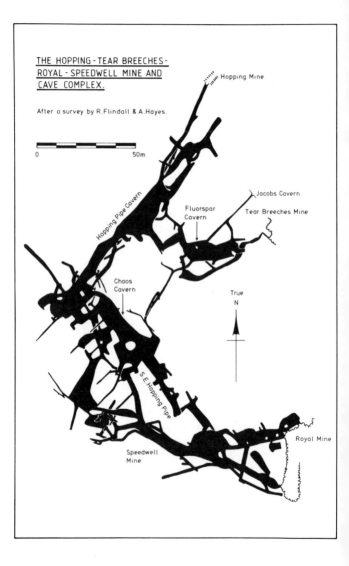

THE HOPPING-TEAR BREECHES-
ROYAL-SPEEDWELL MINE AND
CAVE COMPLEX.

After a survey by R.Flindall & A.Hayes.

0   50m

Hopping Mine

Hopping Pipe Cavern

Fluorspar Cavern

Jacobs Cavern

Tear Breeches Mine

Chaos Cavern

True N

S.E.Hopping Pipe

Speedwell Mine

Royal Mine

down dip, passing a 10ft (3m) pitch, and the Phosphorescent Pool shaft (reflecting daylight from surface). A large chamber, flooded at its lower end, can be reached, and another route leads to the Engine Shaft at the 300ft (92m) level.

Reference: Nash, D.A. 1957. Trans. C.R.G. Vol.5. No.1. pp.19-20.

PLACKETT MINE CAVERNS   NGR 237 610   Mines
Alt. 700ft (213m)   **Depth: over 300ft (91m**

Permission rarely given.

North west of Winster. Main Shaft at 237 610, another at 239 608.

A vast cavern 120 yards (110m) high was recorded by Farey (1811). Recent explorations have revealed an extensive series of pipe-vein workings.

Reference: Farey, J. 1811. A general view of the agriculture and minerals of Derbyshire. p.294.

POUNDER LANE CAVE   NGR 280 588   Grade I
(Pounder Cave)
Alt. 870ft (265m)   **Length: about 100ft (30m)**   **Depth: 30ft (9m)**

In crags east of Pounder Lane.

Small arch entrance enlarged by mining. Walking size passage for 20ft (6m) to Triang Pot, dug out to 28ft (9m) depth by Jackpot Caving Group with low bedding passage at the bottom. Artificially enlarged by Masson C.G. without success. East passage continues across top of pot for 30ft (9m) to 7ft (2.5m) blind pot, dug by Masson Caving Group in 1988.

Tackle – 30ft (10m) handline.

Reference: Chandler, P. 1977. Descent No.37.pp.14-15. Survey.

RANTER MINE CAVERN   NGR 284 550   Lost

Grid reference given is for Ranter Mine shaft.

A "lost" cavern listed by Farey, 1811. Probably in the vein running parallel to and east of the Middleton and Wirksworth road. Orchard Mine Cavern is probably close by.

Reference: Farey, J. 1811. A General view of the Agriculture and Minerals of Derbyshire. Vol.1. p.265.

ROYAL MINE   NGR 2915 5784   Show
(New Speedwell Mine. Pavilion Mine)
Alt. 600ft (183m)

A complex incorporating Tear Breeches Mine, Hopping Mine, and Speedwell Mine, Matlock. Old lead mine workings and 20th century fluorspar workings, intersecting sand filled caverns. Outer parts have been developed as a guided mine tour, with taped commentary and automatic lighting effects.

References: Adam, W. 1838. Gem of the Peak. 1973 reprint by Moorland Publishing, Hartington. pp.63-63. Flindall, R. & Hayes, A. 1973. Bull. P.D.M.H.S. Vol.5. No.4. pp.182-199. Survey.

RUTLAND CAVERN   NGR 2925 5858   Show (Mine)
(Old Nestus Grotto. Nestus Mine)
Alt. 675ft (206m)   Length: 560ft (171m)

On Heights of Abraham, approached through grounds off Upperwood Road.

Artificial passage for 240ft (73m) leads to chamber 300ft (91m) long. Branches into two near the end. On the left is Old Nestus Cavern, one of the oldest lead mines in Derbyshire, with good evidence of pick work. Good mineralisation features in upper galleries up Roman Stairs. Also various rare minerals found in the Lower Nestus workings down shaft (now blocked) below Tower House.

References: Flindall, R. & Hayes, A. 1976. The Caverns and Mines of Matlock Bath. Moorland, Hartington. Hurt, L. 1968. Bull. P.D.M.H.S. Vol.3. No.6. pp.369-379.

SHINING CLIFF CAVE   NGR 292 592   Grade II
Alt. 700ft (213m)   Length: 200ft (61m)

Difficult to find among crags and undergrowth, at the foot of a small bluff forming part of Shining Cliff.

An 8ft (2m) drop between boulders into a low passage trending north via small chambers to a terminal crawl. There is some evidence of mining at the far end. From the main passage one can enter high narrow rifts. The left hand one has a flowstone wall and leads via a climb to a short choked inlet passage, the right hand one is a blind traverse.

SLALEY SOUGH   NGR 2719 5710   Grade II (Mine)
Alt. 675ft (206m)   Length: 2269ft (691.6m)   Depth: 151ft (46m)

Adit entrance near the top of the North side of the Via Gellia, about 200ft (61m) above the A 5012 road about 50 yards east of the conspicuous entrance to Bonsall Leys Level.

From the 3ft (1m) square entrance a crosscut 6ft (2m) high and 3ft (1m) wide leads northwestwards. Initially the floor has a few inches of water, but soon becomes dry. After 150ft (46m) the level is 5ft (1.5m) high and 2ft (0.6m) wide, and continues to close until it is only 3ft (1m) square. Great Rake is intersected 460ft (140m) from the entrance.

Easy walking to the right for 40ft to the top of a winze 52ft (16m) deep and partly backfilled. A small level continues for 20ft (6m) to a forefield.

To the left of the T-junction is the foot of the First Raise, and the main level, 6ft (2m) high and 3.5ft (1m) wide, runs for 330ft (100m) to the Second Raise. Here the main level turns north west, and a crawl continues ahead into a larger passage which turns south east 145ft (44m) beyond the raise.

The main level soon turns west-north-west again, passing a zone of calcite strings and vugs after 180ft (55m). 40ft (12) further, a branch on the right leads to a 151ft (46m) blind pitch.

The main level continues past the base of the Third Raise as a crawl over fallen toadstone, and continues larger again for 445ft (136m) to Parson Rake. The Fourth Raise lies 150ft (46m) further, and the main level continues for a further 500ft (152m) to the Western Forefield.

Reference: Flindall, R.B. & Hayes, A.J. 1971. Bull. P.D.M.H.S. Vol.4. No.6. pp.431-437. Survey.

SLINTER WOOD CAVES   NGR 288 571   Grade I
Alt. 550ft (165m)   **Depth: 100ft (30m)**

In the cliff almost opposite Ball Eye Mine.

Three small caves. The floor of one collapsed to reveal a 100ft (30m) deep hole. Various mine levels in the same area have been described by Flindall et al, 1977.

Reference: Flindall, R.B., Hayes, A.J., & Rieuwerts, J.H. 1977. Bull. P.D.M.H.S. Vol.6. No.6. pp.263-279. Surveys.

SPEEDWELL MINE   NGR 2907 5788   Mine
Alt. 550ft (168m)

Adit entrance now partly concealed by rubbish in road fork at Upperwood.

Old lead mine, formerly a show cave. Parts more recently worked for fluorspar and calcite via adits, as Royal Mine from top of Old Pavilion grounds, and accessible via adits from there. Also known as New Speedwell Mine, or Angelina's Cavern, though that name more strictly applied to a chamber now mined away. Whole system is somewhat unstable, and parts are in a dangerous state. Link route to Fluorspar Cavern. All entrances blocked.

Reference: Flindall, R. & Hayes, A. 1973. Bull. P.D.M.H.S. Vol.5. No.4. pp.182-199. Survey.

SPINNEY LEVEL   NGR 261 561   Grade II (Mine)
(Anglo-Saxon Mine)
Alt. 700ft (210m)   Length: c.1000ft (305m)

Behind the only large hillock close to the road from Nimblejack corner in the Via Gellia south to Hopton.

Flooded entrance. The level trends westwards. The first hundred feet (30m) is low with 2ft (60cm) of water and a partial roof collapse, then a well decorated section leading to dry levels with a blind shaft in the floor and two short upper series. Also known as Anglo-Saxon Mine from the four letter inscriptions near the end!

Reference: Smith, A. & Ford, T.D. 1971. Bull. P.D.M.H.S. Vol.4. No.5. p.382.

TEAR BREECHES MINE NGR 2912 5800 Grade III (Mine)
Alt. 600ft (183m)

Most entrances except Royal Mine, which is a show cave, are blocked. No access at present.

Three main entrances.

1) Hopping Mine adit above Upperwood Road.

2) Jacob's (or Angelina's) Adit and steps immediately across and below the road (also known as Fluorspar Cavern).

3) Speedwell Mine (also known as New Speedwell, Royal or Pavilion Mine) in old opencast fluorspar pit at the top of the Pavilion grounds.

A complex system of mined out fluorspar deposits and old solution caves. Once a group of separate mines, there have been other adits and at least

8 shafts, though the mines were all finally linked in the course of mining operations in the 1950's. The names have all been variously applied to whole mines or individual chambers, but the original, according to mine records, was Tear Breeches Mine. Various parts have been show caves at times. Hopping Adit branches into an incline down into Jacob's Cavern, and a level straight ahead into a large muddy cavern. Levels from both meet in stopes at the foot of Jacob's entrance steps; a series of stopes leads on through the former Speedwell Cavern into the workings developed from the adit in the top of the Pavilion grounds. These contain a striking fault-bounded chamber with toadstone clays. The whole complex is rather unstable and sewage has leaked in at one point.

References: Frost, R.V. 1953. The Speleologist (Derbyshire) Vol.1. No.2. pp.63-67. Flindall, R. & Hayes, A. 1973. Bull. P.D.M.H.S. Vol.5. No 4. pp.182-199.

TEARSALL PIPE CAVERNS No.1   NGR 263 600   Lost
Length: Over 1000ft (305m)

The mine consisted of a series of sub-parallel levels connected by steep shutes down from the bedding, with buddle pools and sledge runs.

Most of the complex has now been quarried away.

Reference: Flindall, R. 1974. Bull.P.D.M.H.S. Vol.5. No.6. pp.373-382. Survey.

TEARSALL PIPE CAVERNS No.2
NGR 266 602   Grade III (Mine)
(Dalefield Mine (part)?
Alt. 800ft (244m)   Length: Sump Series: 1700ft (518m)
Pool Series: 1000ft (300m)

Pool and Sump shafts are both lidded and locked. A key and box spanner for both shafts are kept by Mr Walker at Brightgate Farm. Other shafts are covered with concrete sleepers.

15 shafts in a field downhill and north of Tearsall Farm.

Sump Series: Entered by Sump Shaft (60ft/18m) at the bottom extremity of the field, or by Wall Shaft (55ft/17m) adjacent to the dry stone wall at the top of the field. Sump Shaft leads to a large natural and mined passage 12ft (4m) high running north-south. Northerly leads to a meander passage with a stream sinking in the floor. The stream rises from an upstream sump which has been dived for 30ft (9m) and is believed to come from Pool Series. Near to where the stream sinks a tight rift gives access to Ridgeways Series and Rift Chamber, some 40ft (12m) high and rather dangerous. From the shaft bottom the passage south goes through the Gnasher Crawl to the Main Chamber, and thence up a wet crawl, Thrutchers Paradise, to the base of a small climbing shaft. This leads to the base of Wall Shaft and a series of mined passages continues westwards with at least three shafts to the surface, but all sealed.

Pool Series: Situated adjacent to Sump Series and entered by four shafts, Pool Shaft (47ft/14.4m), Line Shaft (44ft/13.5m), Fern Shaft (36ft/11m) and Short

Drop Shaft (15ft/4.6m). Pool shaft is now lidded and locked. From Pool Shaft, upstream is short series of mined/natural passages, which basically form a short round trip starting and ending at Stal Chamber. Downstream over miner's clay dam into Main Chamber. There are three ways off – a large obvious passage to the left, a rope climb to the left, and a short climb straight ahead.

The short climb is followed by a climb down into mined passage with stacked deads. There are two ways off – ahead is a crawl to a small chamber with small but pretty formations, or scramble over small boulders to a junction. Straight on down under deads (care) is T'Owd Man's Passage, which reaches a dead end after 80ft (24m). Near the end are two short branches to the left (Webb's Way) and right. Right at the junction leads to the bottom of Line Shaft and another choice. Left is soon blind. Right leads under small hole into passage containing cave pcarls, and after a short step up the passage gets tight and muddy. Up the small hole, left leads back to Line Shaft, right closes down after a very tight crawl, and a low crawl through a muddy pool leads past small stalactites to a junction. Left rises quite steeply to a dead end. The other route is a climb down a fixed rope back into Main Chamber.

Following the large obvious passage from Main Chamber, clamber over fallen deads to a collapse. Climb to a small narrow passage leading to the New Extension (1987). Shaft just beyond narrow section is Fern Shaft. Large walking sized passage closes down after short drop. Crawl on right near Fern Shaft leads to a boulder choke which draughts (possibly from a shaft nearby). A climb on the left leads to bottom of Short Drop Shaft.

Just before Short Drop Shaft, a narrow passage on the right is Mick's Amazement, which soon enlarges to walking size, and after a short stooping section reaches a fairly large cross passage with a few formations. Obvious passage straight on leads to an unstable area with rotten timbers, a blocked shaft to surface, and a shaft to a lower level. (Lower shaft can be free-climbed with care, or use 15ft (5m) ladder and belay). The other way on from the cross passage leads up to a boulder choke on the right, and a small rising passage to the left with drops back to Mick's Amazement.

References: Beeston Mines Research Group Report No.1. Derbyshire Caving Club N/L 1960,1961,1964,1965. Peakland Archaeological Society Journal No.21. 1966. Survey by Derbyshire Caving Club, W.2. Pool and Sump Series. Survey Pool Series & New Extensions 1987 by Phil Ingham & Masson Caving Group.

TEMPLE MINE   NGR 292 581   Show (Mine)
(Temple Pipe Cavern)
Alt. 400ft (122m)   Length: 500ft (152m) approx

Owned by P.D.M.H.S. Access controlled by the Mining Museum. Small charge made.

Entrance is an adit off Temple Road, opposite the Peak District Mining Museum.

A series of fluorspar workings with numerous small sand-filled caverns. One level was driven into a thick clay wayboard and into the top of a lava flow.

TORHILLS CAVE   NGR 2943 5879   Grade II (Mine)
(Dark Hole Mine. Primrose Mine)
Alt. 500ft (152m)   Length: 250ft (76m)

Two entrance at different levels in the crag opposite High Tor. Part cave, part mine, on the line of Great Rake. Bottom entrance leads to Clay Cavern, with climb into upper series of mined and natural passages and grottos reached from upper entrance. A small stream flows in wet weather and backs up in terminal chambers, which contain interesting sediments and rock formations. Draught connects to blocked surface workings on rake just below footpath from Matlock Bath.

Reference: Findall, R. & Hayes, A. 1976. The Caverns and Mines of Matlock Bath. pp.27,44,48.

WAPPING MINE   NGR 2939 5749   Grade II (Mine)
Alt. 400ft (122m)

No access at present.

In the wood close to the Wapping footpath.

The first section is a high mined out vein, with an unstable roof in places. Where the vein gives way to pillar and stall workings climb up to left into higher natural passages which link with Cumberland Cavern. Lower Mine workings continue under part of this and there used to be several link routes.

Reference: Flindall, R. & Hayes, A. 1972. Bull. P.D.M.H.S. Vol.5. No.2. pp.114-127. Survey.

YOUD'S LEVEL
NGR (Main entr.) 2955 5945   Grade III (Mine)
Alt. 295ft (90m)   Length: 1.2 miles (1.9km)

Main entrance lies at back of public toilets on Artists Corner. Key available from Peak District Mining Museum, Matlock Bath. Access to all shafts on the system is via Greenhills Farm (294 598), off Salters Lane on the way up to Masson Quarry. The farmer is Mr Frank Kirkum, from whom permission must be sought.

Railway Shaft, Greenhills Farm: NGR 29425956
Alt: 532.79ft (162.40m)
Day Shaft, Greenhills Farm: NGR 29215959
Alt: 576.31ft (175.66m)
Overseer Shaft, Greenhills Farm: NGR 28975928
Alt: 774.64ft (236.11m)

Railway Shaft – Large shaft mound surrounded by trees. Shaft is 6ft (2m) diameter & 150ft (46m) deep, where it is blocked. 80ft (24m) of fill between here and coffin level of main system. Level at 95ft (29m) going 400ft (122m). No connection with the sough.

Day Shaft – Large shaft mound surrounded by trees. 4ft 6ins x 2ft 6ins approx. (1.4 x 0.75m). 266ft (81m) deep to main system coffin level. Level at 90ft (27m), small opening, hard to get into. Driven in toadstone wayboard, low and wet for 400ft (122m), but not yet followed to a definite end.

Overseer Shaft – 2ft 6ins (0.75m) dia. air ducting for the first 16ft (4.9m), then into solid rock 4ft x 2ft (1.2 x 0.6m). 20ft of rubble was removed from the top of the shaft, and the ginging replaced by air ducting to leave a shaft 200ft (61m) deep. There are no side levels.

All the above shafts are covered with concrete railway sleepers.

Main Level – Entrance is a short shaft into the level, which goes north under the road. Size increases to walking height after 230ft (70m). Stream is met just beyond, flowing into a stope (pumped out and found to be blind). A short trial leads to a dog leg shaft blocked 82ft (25m) up. The passage then turns left into the longest coffin level in Derbyshire, 1200ft (365m). Shortly after the turn a shaft in the roof leads up to the Waterfall Series. The level is silted here, and is a low crawl in water for 65ft (20m). A short trial on the right leads to the bottom of the blocked Railway (Haslam) Shaft.

The coffin level now averages 4ft 6ins (1.4m) high by 1ft 8ins (0.5m) wide. A short trial is passed, and approx. 655ft (200m) beyond the Waterfall Series shaft, a further trial goes for 312ft (95m) to the south west.

A "Y" junction is reached. Right leads to the bottom of Day (Deep) Shaft. The sough continues in a south westerly direction, through a number of low crawls over miners' backfill, passing through an 80ft (25m) long chamber. Eventually the level splits at an area of workings known as Old Jant Mine.

Right follows the stream into a small area of ramifying workings. Left steps up and climbs steeply, passing a short shaft to higher workings on the right. At the top of the steep rise, a very low tight crawl is followed by a hands and knees section and another tight section. Just beyond is the Overseer Shaft Chamber (shaft also known as Upper Close Shaft).

The passage continues to rise steeply through old stopes to a forefield. A climb up into the stopes above leads on upwards and forwards to the bottom of Gentlewoman's Shaft, a stepped shaft blocked from surface to the step.

Beyond, large passages trend south westwards. It was possible to follow a crosscut and continue into the Masson Mine complex, but the connection has been severed by quarrying. A shaft a short distance back from this point, on the edge of the quarry, is open to surface but covered with a large rock.

Waterfall Series – A difficult 82ft (25m) climb up the Waterfall Shaft against the flow of water gives access to a level in a toadstone wayboard. A short distance into the level, a climb leads up into ramifying workings. Main level continues low and wet for 400ft (122m) to a fall with the stream flowing from one side of the level.

Reference: Warriner, D., Willies, L., & Flindall, R. 1981. Bull. P.D.M.H.S. Vol.8. No.2. pp.65-108.Surveys.

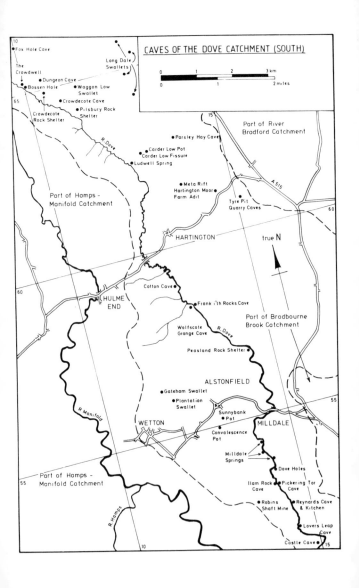

CAVES OF THE DOVE CATCHMENT (SOUTH)

Fox Hole Cave

Long Dale Swallets

The Crowdwell

Dungeon Cave

Bossen Hole

Waggon Low Swallet

Crowdecote Cave

Pilsbury Rock Shelter

Crowdecote Rock Shelter

R. Dove

Part of River Bradford Catchment

Parsley Hay Cave

Carder Low Pot
Carder Low Fissure
Ludwell Spring

A 515

Part of Hamps - Manifold Catchment

Meta Rift
Hartington Moor Farm Adit

Tyre Pit Quarry Caves

HARTINGTON

true N

HULME END

Cotton Cave

Frank i'th Rocks Cave

Part of Bradbourne Brook Catchment

Wolfscote Grange Cave

R. Dove

Peasland Rock Shelter

ALSTONFIELD

R. Manifold

Gateham Swallet

Plantation Swallet

Sunnybank Pot

WETTON

MILLDALE

Convalescence Pot

Milldale Springs

Dove Holes

Ilam Rock Cave

Pickering Tor Cave

Robins Shaft Mine

Reynards Cave & Kitchen

R. Hamps

Part of Hamps - Manifold Catchment

Lovers Leap Cave

Castle Cave

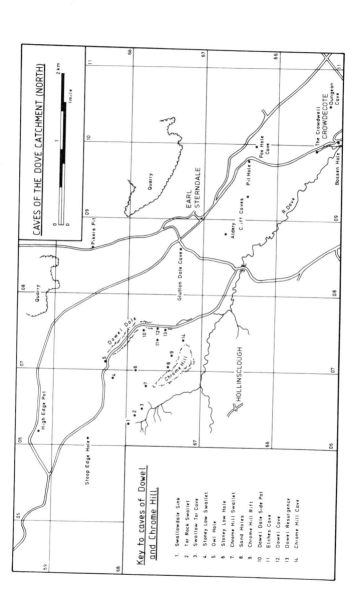

CAVES OF THE DOVE CATCHMENT (NORTH)

Key to caves of Dowel and Chrome Hill

1. Swallowdale Sink
2. Tor Rock Swallet
3. Swallow Tor Cave
4. Stoney Low Swallet
5. Owl Hole
6. Stoney Low Hole
7. Chrome Hill Swallet
8. Sand Holes
9. Chrome Hill Rift
10. Dowel Dale Side Pot
11. Etches Cave
12. Dowel Cave
13. Dowel Resurgence
14. Chrome Hill Cave

CROWDECOTE
The Crowdwell
Dungeon Cave
Bosson Hole
Fox Hole Cave
Pit Hole
Alderty
Cliff Caves
EARL STERNDALE
Glutton Dale Cave
Quarry
Pikers Pit
Quarry
R. Dove
HOLLINSCLOUGH
Dowel Dale
Chrome Hill
High Edge Pot
Stoop Edge Hole
Quarry

THE RIVER DOVE
CATCHMENT AREA

The River Dove can conveniently be divided into two areas, North and South. The upper 10kms of the river generally follows the strike along the shale/limestone boundary, the limestones dipping approximately 18 degrees to the south west.

At the northern end is Dowel Resurgence, fed by a group of sinks high in the reef limestone. Some have been inconclusively dug, but the system seems to be immature.

The two major risings further south, the Crowdwell and the Ludwell, both have high discharge figures of roughly 50 l/sec., but are not fed from any known sinks. No extensive digging has been carried out at these sites or in the numerous dolines in the Dove catchment as a whole.

North–south faulting and folding gives rise to some striking limestone scenery along the course of the Dove, and leakage seems to have been prevented by the building of wiers with clay-puddled floors to improve the fishing. This has effectively prevented the river from disappearing underground.

Incision of both the Dove and the Manifold took place during the Pleistocene, the pre-glacial river downcutting in a series of stages to preserve a number of river terraces. From Wolfscote Grange the river cuts through the upper reef limestones for the next 8 kms, doubling in size at the Milldale Risings. Although no dye tests have been carried out, it is suspected that these risings are partly fed from the sinks to the north west, Gateham and Plantation Swallets. It is possible that an extensive system awaits the determined digger here.

ALDERY CLIFF CAVES   NGR 088667 to 093664   Digs
Alt. 1000ft (300m)

On west slopes of Aldery cliff, half a mile south west of the village. One small cave above Underhill Farm; two badger lairs half a mile to S.E. and a fissure pot on the crest above.

One of the badger lairs has been dug out for 30 feet.

Reference: Tottle, P. 1959. The Lyre, Vol.1. No.3. p.60

BOSSEN HOLE (Crowdecote)   NGR 100 652   Grade I
Alt. 800ft (240m)   Length: 114ft (34m)

200ft (61m) south east of Crowdwell Spring.

A hands and knees crawl. Contains a small shattered chamber and ends at a

small hole in the floor. Liable to flooding.
   Reference: Crabtree, P.W. 1970. Jour.S.U.S.S. Vol.1. No.6. pp.238-9.
Survey.

CARDER LOW FISSURE   NGR 127 627   Dig
Alt. 1050ft (320m)

Above the Ludwell.
   A choked fissure apparently on a vein or fault, with a noticeable draught in
cold weather. A possible dig. Further down the hill are choked shafts, and on
a continuation is Carder Low Mine. Below is the Ludwell, a major
resurgence.

CARDER LOW POT   NGR 129 627   Dig
Alt. 1050ft (320m)

Adjacent to a boundary wall.
   A choked pot. Digging would involve removal of small boulders.

CASTLE CAVE   NGR 1491 5128   Grade I
Alt. 550ft (167m)   Length: 15ft (5m)

At top of scree in crags 200 yards (182m) south west of Dovedale stepping
stones.
   An inviting large cave entrance which closes completely 15ft (3m) in.

CHROME HILL CAVE   NGR 074 673   Grade I
Alt. 1150ft (349m)   Length: 20ft (6m)

On north side of Chrome Hill, visible from Dowell Farm.
   A stooping height entrance soon closes down. Corroded flowstone visible
on the walls.
   Reference: Smith, P. 1960. The Lyre No.3. p.61.

CHROME HILL RIFT   NGR 072 674   Grade I
Alt. 1175ft (358m)   Length: 25ft (8m)

Above and to the right (west) of Chrome Hill Cave.
   A tight sporting rift descends to a crawl blocked by dripstone.
   Reference: Smith, P. 1960. The Lyre No.3. p.61.

CHROME HILL SWALLET   NGR 068 678   Grade II
Alt. 1200ft (366m)   Length: 93ft (28m)   Depth: 30ft (9m)

Difficult to find.
   An active swallet with a tight letter-box entrance. A low crawl leads to a
narrow descending slot which is difficult to reverse. Progress is halted after
another drop by a large wall of mud 40ft (12m) along Magic Hammer
Passage, a promising streamway. Rabbit Inlet on the left can be climbed and
followed back close to the entrance.
   Reference: Phipps, M. 1981. The Lyre No.5. pp.4-5.

CONVALESCENCE POT   NGR 130 550   Grade I
Alt. 800ft (240m).

200ft (61m) south of Sunnybank Pot.
   Short pitch into earth-choked section of Sunnybank Pot.

COTTON CAVE   NGR 127 589   Grade I
Alt. 710ft (213m)

In the grounds of Beresford Estate, Hartington. Entrance well hidden.
   Contains one small chamber. Charles Cotton is said to have hidden there.
Three small rock shelters nearby.

CROWDECOTE CAVE   NGR 109 646   Dig
Alt. 850ft (255m)

A small rising on the limestone/shale junction at the base of a small outcrop
adjacent to the Crowdecote–Pilsbury bridle path. To gain access boulders
must be removed from a fissure. A very tight descending crawl which might
be forced further.

CROWDECOTE ROCK SHELTER   NGR 105 649   Dig
Alt. 790ft (237m)

At the foot of a limestone outcrop.
   A probable old resurgence cave, now blocked by silt.

THE CROWDWELL   NGR 100 653   Dig
Alt. 800ft (240m)

Large resurgence in Upper Dove Valley.
   Water emerges from buried culverts below growing rubbish heap.
   Reference: Smith, P. 1960. The Lyre No.3. p.60.

DOVE HOLES CAVES   NGR 1425 5353   Grade I
Alt. 700ft (210m)

On the left bank of the River Dove, south east of Hanson Grange, opposite
Hall Dale.
   Two large entrances 55ft (17m) and 30ft (9m) wide and high. Both close
almost immediately.

DOWEL CAVE   NGR 075 676   Grade I (Arch)
Alt. 1025ft (308m)   Length: 50ft (15m)

50 yards (45m) up the dale from the present rising.
   An old resurgence cave, consisting of a fissure descending inwards, choked
at the bottom. Archaeological excavation uncovered the remains of ten
Neolithic inhumations.
   References: Bramwell, D. 1957-60. P.A.S. N/L Nos.14-17. Bramwell, D.
1959. Derbys. Arch. Jour. No.79. pp.97-109. Survey. Bramwell, D. 1960. The
Lyre No.3. pp.13-15 & 67. Bramwell, D. 1977. P.A.S.Bull. No. 30. p.8. Hart,
C.R. 1984. North Derbyshire Archaeological Survey.

DOWEL DALE SIDE POT   NGR 075 678   Grade II
Alt. 1100ft (335m)   **Depth: 45ft (14m)**

20ft (6m) above the road.

   Discovered and dug in 1985. A series of short free-climbs in an excavated rift lead to a boulder floor. Two short passages at the bottom. Could still be a promising dig.

   Reference: Gibson, R. 1986. E.P.C. Jour. Vol.9. No.5. pp.4-5. Survey.

DOWEL RESURGENCE   NGR 075 675   Grade II
Alt. 950ft (290m)   **Length: 50ft (12m)**

At the foot of Dowel Dale opposite the farm.

   Main rising for the Dowel Area. Fissure entrance which has been enlarged soon degenerates to 30ft (9m) of very tight rift passage leading to a sump blocked with boulders! Only for thin people who like spiders!

   References: Gibson, R. 1981. D.C.A. N/L No.47. p.4. Smith, P. 1960. The Lyre No.3. p.67.

DUNGEON CAVE   NGR 105 653   Dig
Alt. 1200ft (365m)

High on the hill east of Crowdecote.

   Formerly dug by Orpheus Caving Club.

ETCHES CAVE   NGR 074 676   Grade I
Alt. 1025ft (308m)   **Length: 300ft (90m)**

100 yards (91m) west-north-west of Dowel Resurgence, and 75ft (23m) above it.

   A short rift cave was dug by Orpheus Caving Club into a series of well decorated rifts connected by muddy crawls.

   References: Smith, P. 1960. Lyre No.3. pp.65-66. Survey. Harrison, H.R. & Haskew, M.T. 1965. The Lyre No.4. pp.25-28. Survey (post-extension). Pernetta, J.C. 1966. P.A.S. N/L No.21. pp.11-16.

FOX HOLE CAVE   NGR 100 663   Grade I (Arch)
(High Wheeldon Cave)
Alt. 1360ft (408m)   **Length: 180ft (56m)**

In small outcrop on north west end of High Wheeldon on National Trust property.

   Drop 8ft (2.5m) into passage leading to chamber 20ft (6m) long where there is a branch to the right leading to a second chamber. Zigzag passages beyond. Excavated remains in Buxton Museum. Further digging in progress.

   References: Bramwell, D. 1962-1977. P.A.S. N/L No.18. pp.1-6 & 32. No.19. pp.10-12. No.20. pp.8-10 and 11-12. No.21. pp.6-7 & 10. No.22. pp.5-6. No.23. pp.5-6. No.24. pp.7-8. Bramwell, D. 1970-1977. P.A.S. Bull. No.25. p.8-10. No.26. pp.1-4. No.27. pp.1-3. No.29. pp.7-8. No.31. pp.5-6. No.30. pp.4-6. Bramwell, D. 1971. Derbys. Arch. Jour. No.91. pp.1-19. Survey. Gee, S. 1958-1960. P.A.S. N/L No.15. pp. 17-18. Survey. No. 16. p.25. No.17. pp.13-14. Jackson, J.W. 1951. Derbys. Arch. Jour. 71 (New Series Vol.24) pp.72-77. Jones, R.T. 1977. P.A.S. Bull. No.30. pp.2-3. Shimwell, D.W. 1971. P.A.S. Bull. No.26. pp.7-13.

FRANK 'ITH ROCKS CAVE   NGR 1317 5843   Grade I
                                                (Arch)
Alt. 765ft (233m)   Length: 150ft (46m)

South of the footbridge on the east side of Wolfscote Dale.

A large cave entrance leads to a chamber with a crawl on the right, which leads through the cliff to emerge close to the entrance of a second cave. This consists of a rising muddy rift passage blocked after 100ft (30m), which could be dug.

Archaeological remains in Buxton Museum.

References: Palmer, L.S. 1926. Proc. Univ. Bristol Spel. Soc. Vol.11. No.3. Jackson, J.W. 1926. N.W. Naturalist, p.193.

GATEHAM SWALLET   NGR 1170 5630   Dig
(Dumble Hole)
Alt. 830ft (253m)

Opposite Gateham Farm, near Wetton.

A large swallow hole. Partly excavated by Birmingham Cave and Crag Club, but abandoned owing to unstable walls.

References: Warwick, G.T. 1965. Geog. Journal Vol.131. No.1. p.49.

GLUTTON DALE CAVE   NGR 086 673   Dig
Alt. 1050ft (320m)

A road drain is channelled into a small cave mouth which was excavated for 30ft (9m) but has since been filled in.

Reference: Smith, P. 1960. The Lyre Vol.1. No.3. p.61.

HARTINGTON MOOR FARM ADIT
NGR 145 612   Grade II (Mine)
Alt. 985ft (300m)   Length: 975ft (297m)

Warning: Used by bats during the winter... take care not to disturb.

Entrance at end of obvious "cutting" in field.

Large mined passage is followed for 600ft (180m) approx. passing some small but pretty formations after 400ft (120m) approx, to reach an almost total blockage. Unpleasant flat out crawl over farm refuse on right for 8ft (2.4m) leads to more large mined passage. Two short branches – one on the right is walking size and contains formations, and leads through a shallow wet section to a forefield. Main level continues to a forefield.

HIGH EDGE POT   NGR 062 692   Dig
Alt. 1350ft (405m)   Depth: 8ft (3m)

A few yards south of the road.

A swallet taking a little water, dug out to a depth of 8ft (3m).

ILAM ROCK CAVE   NGR 1418 5311   Grade I
Alt. 525ft (158m)   Length: 30ft (9m)

Inside the detached Ilam Rock.

Entrance 4ft high rising to 30ft (9m) inside. Overhanging walls have much tufa inside.

LONG DALE SWALLETS

Digs

NGR 128649, 128658, 129643, and 131654
Alt. 1050–1100ft (320–335m)

In the floor of Long Dale.
A series of small inactive swallets. The first listed occasionally takes water from a dew pond. Little hope of extension as mineshafts nearby give no encouragement.

LOVERS LEAP CAVE   NGR 1448 5182   Grade I
Alt. 500ft (150m)   Length: 10ft (3m)

Just above river level below Lovers Leap.
A small resurgence cave, blocked at the end with calcite.
Reference: Potts, J. 1976. D.C.A. N/L No.27. p.6.

LUDWELL SPRING   NGR 124 625   Dig
Alt. 750ft (229m)

Water supply. Permission must be sought before interfering with the spring.
A large resurgence below the road. Water issues from an impenetrable slot. A short mine level is nearby, with good flowstone.

META RIFT   NGR 136 616   Grade I
Alt. 975ft (297m)   Length: 20ft (6m)

At the foot of one of the larger scars on the west side of Long Dale.
A narrow rift cave about 20ft long and 14ft high.
Reference: Phipps, M. 1974. O.C.C. N/L Vol.10. No.3. pp.20,22,23. Survey.

MILLDALE SPRINGS   NGR 141 541   Springs
Alt. 525ft (160m)

Both banks of the River Dove from 141 543 down to Doveholes.
A group of resurgences from both banks, responsible for a large part of the river's flow below Milldale.

OWL HOLE   NGR 071 683   Lost
(Dove Pit)
Alt. 1225ft (373m)   Depth: 50ft (15m).

Was a 50ft (15m) deep pothole by the roadside, with a short crawl to the north west. There was an easy scramble down the south side. The pothole is now completely filled with rubbish.
Reference: Smith, P. 1959. The Lyre No.3. pp.60-67.

PARSLEY HAY CAVE   NGR 137 629   Grade I
Alt. 1000ft (305m)   Length: 20ft (6m)

In Long Dale in disused quarry south of Vincent House.
Entrance high up in quarry. 12ft (4m) crawl then very tight into small chamber. No way on. Only to be attempted by thin men.

PEASLAND ROCK SHELTER   NGR 1434 5689   Grade I
(Iron Tors Cave)
Alt. 650ft (198m)

On the east bank of the River Dove, 15ft (4.5m) above the path, opposite Peasland Rocks, a few hundred yards downstream from Biggin Dale.

A large cave entrance which is little more than a rock shelter with a small blocked tube at the end.

PICKERING TOR CAVE   NGR 1424 5312   Grade I
Alt. 550ft (168m)

Opposite Ilam Rock, 100ft (30m) up Pickering Dale.
A small cave.

PIKERS PIT   NGR 086 685   Dig
Alt. 1225ft (373m)

525ft (160m) west of Greensides Farm.
A large collapsed swallet. Boulder ruckle penetrable for only a few feet. Water resurges at Dowel Resurgence.
Reference: Smith, P. 1959. The Lyre No.3. p.62.

PILSBURY ROCK SHELTER   NGR 113 643   Grade I
Alt. c.1000ft (c.300m)

Well above the Crowdecote to Pilsbury bridle path. Difficult to find, close to a small tree.
A rocky shelter. It might be extended by excavating among loose blocks.

THE PIT HOLE   NGR 098 664   Grade I
Alt. 1000ft (305m)

In south corner of quarry.
A choked tube. A grating in the road nearby covers a natural fissure.
Reference: Smith, P. 1959. The Lyre No.3. pp.60-61.

PLANTATION SWALLET   NGR 1195 5600   Grade V Dig
(Rakes Wood Swallet)
Alt. 900ft (274m)   **Depth: 180ft (55m)**

Situated in the centre of Rakes Wood Plantation.
A large swallet taking several streams in wet weather. Dug over a period of years to a depth of 40ft (12m) by Birmingham Cave and Crag Club and O.C.C. Dug by Eldon Pothole Club to reach a depth of 180ft through a lethal boulder choke. Now capped and locked.
Reference: Bentham, K. 1987. BCRA Caves and Caving No.38. p.2.

REYNARD'S CAVE   NGR 1452 5252   Grade I (Arch)
Alt. 360ft (110m)   Length: 40ft (12m)

High on the east side of Dovedale. Between Bostern Grange and Sharplow Dale.
A natural arch and cave. Two smaller caves behind. The larger is Reynard's Cave, the other Reynard's Kitchen (qv). Archaeologically excavated.

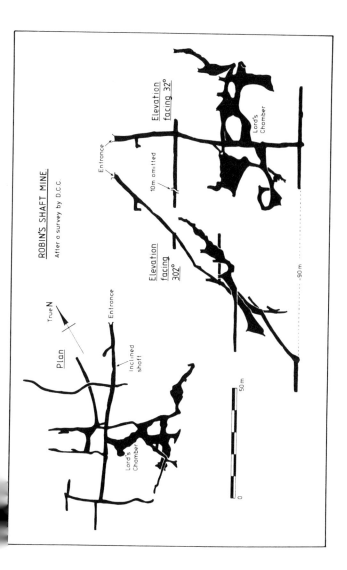

ROBIN'S SHAFT MINE

After a survey by D.C.C.

Plan

True N

Entrance

Inclined shaft

Lord's Chamber

50 m

0

Elevation facing 302°

Entrance

10m omitted

90 m

Elevation facing 32°

Lord's Chamber

Reference: Adam, W. 1838. Gem of the Peak. 1973 reprint by Moorland Publishing, Hartington. pp.215-216.

REYNARD'S KITCHEN   NGR 1452 5252   Grade I
Alt. 370ft (113m)

High on the east side of Dovedale, above and behind the large natural arch.
A small cave with a short climb in the roof.

ROBIN'S SHAFT MINE   NGR 1355 5276   Grade III
Alt. 1075 (328m)   **Depth: 295ft (90m)**

Permission from Miners Cottage Farm. Small fee.
Close to Miners Cottage Farm, Hamton Low.
Large mine shaft inclined at between 45 and 60 degrees. A short level is passed after 60ft (20m), with two further blind levels at 145ft (44m). Between 260ft (79m) and 295ft (90m) are various entrances to a system of impressive part-natural phreatic chambers and passages up to 60ft high, roughly inclined down from east to west. Several high avens have been climbed to a height of approximately 150ft (46m). There are possible digs in the floor at the lowest points.
The main shaft continues down to 400ft (122m) (300ft/91m depth) to end in partly flooded mine workings.
References: Boardman, P. 1982. B.C.R.A. Caves and Caving No.16. pp.2-4. Survey. Darroch, C. 1981. Descent No.48. pp.16-17. Darroch, C. 1981. D.C.A. N/L No.47. pp.2-3.

SANDHOLES SWALLET   NGR 071 675   Dig
Alt. 1200ft (366m)   **Depth: 30ft (9m)**

1000 yards (914m) west of Dowell Farm under the north face of Chrome Hill.
A dig in a choked swallet has been pushed to a depth of 30ft (9m) in very unstable ground. Water reappears at Dowell Resurgence.
References: Phipps, M. 1981. The Lyre No.5. p.4. Smith, P. 1960. Lyre No.3. pp.63 & 65.

STONEY LOW HOLE   NGR 070 679   Grade I
(Tor Rock Cave)
Alt. 1325ft (404m)   **Length: 50ft (15m)**   **Depth: 25ft (8m)**

A fissure in a scarp. Fissure leads to tight 25ft (8m) pitch. A constricted dig is possible at the bottom.
Tackle – 25ft (8m) ladder; 30ft (9m) lifeline.
References: Smith, P. 1960. The Lyre No.3. p.63. Phipps, M. 1981. The Lyre No.5. p.4.

STONEY LOW SWALLET   NGR 069 682   Dig
Alt. 1275ft (389m)

A swallet which has been unsuccessfully dug. Dye took 44 hours to reach Dowel Resurgence only 1000 yards (914m) away and 325ft (99m) lower.
Reference: Smith, P. 1960. The Lyre No.3. pp.63-64.

STOOP EDGE HOLE   NGR 061 685   Grade II
Alt. 1425ft (434m)   **Depth: 50ft (15m)**

A tight fissure dug in 1957. 50ft (15m) deep. No ladder required.
   Reference: Smith, P. 1960. The Lyre No.3. p.62. Sketch survey.

SUNNYBANK POT   NGR 132 552   Grade II
Alt. 800ft (244m)   **Length: 150ft (46m)**   **Depth: 20ft (6m)**

Vertical entrance under a small tree.
   A 20ft (6m) pitch leads to a very narrow rift where progress can only be made by traversing halfway up.

Tackle – 20ft (6m) ladder; 30ft (9m) lifeline.

SWALLOWDALE SINK   NGR 063 680   Grade II
Alt. 1150ft (350m)   **Length: 115ft (35m)**   **Depth: 40ft (12m)**

A letter box entrance below Stoop Farm. Slit entrance leads to a narrow passage where a small hole can be descended in the floor to a tiny chamber. A squeeze enters a short length of stream passage ending at a silted sump. A 10ft (3m) climb leads via an awkward vertical tube to a chamber close to the surface.
   References: Smith, P. 1959. The Lyre Vol.1. No.3. p.61. Phipps, M. 1981. The Lyre No.5. p.5. Survey.

SWALLOW TOR CAVE   NGR 065 678   Arch
Alt. 1000ft (305m)

A small cave excavated archaeologically.
   Reference: Smith, P. 1960. The Lyre No.3. p.61.

THORSWOOD SWALLET   NGR 117 473   Dig
Alt. 960ft (293m)

In a hollow on the north side of the road near Thorswood House.
   A choked sink taking a small stream.

TOR ROCK SWALLET   NGR 064 679   Grade I
Alt. 1250ft (381m)

South of Stoop Farm, a few hundred feet above and to the east of Swallow Brook.
   A small stream sinks down a very low bedding plane. Has been pushed by Eldon P.C., but too narrow for further progress. Resurges a few hundred feet lower down in valley floor.

TYRE PIT QUARRY Cave 1   NGR 151 609   Dig
Alt. 1100ft (335m)   **Length: 80ft (24m)**

A crawl for 50ft (15m) to a small chamber. Becomes too tight 20ft (6m) further.
   Reference: Allwright, P. 1972. O.C.C. N/L Vol.8. No.5. pp.1-2. Survey.

TYRE PIT QUARRY Cave 2   NGR 151 609   Dig
Alt. 1115ft (340m)   Length: 8ft (2.5m)

40ft (12m) along and 15ft (4.5m) up the face from cave no.1. A small cave only 8ft (2.5m) long.

WAGGON LOW SWALLET   NGR 114 649   Dig
Alt.c.1150ft (350m)

Permission from Cronkston Grange Farm.
    In small blind valley adjacent to a wall.
    A swallet blocked by easily removable boulders. Emits a draught in cold weather.

WOLFSCOTE GRANGE CAVE   NGR 131 584   Digs
Alt. 725ft (221m)

South of the footbridge, opposite Frank I'th Rocks Cave.
    Small blocked cave entrances.

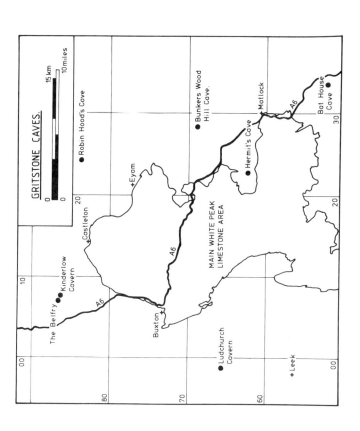

GRITSTONE CAVES.

- The Belfry
- Kinderlow Cavern
- Castleton +
- Eyam +
- Robin Hood's Cave
- Buxton
- Bunkers Wood Hill Cave.
- Hermit's Cave
- Matlock
- Bat House Cave
- Ludchurch Cavern
- Leek +

MAIN WHITE PEAK LIMESTONE AREA

A6

15 km
10miles

GRITSTONE CAVES

The White Peak limestone outcrop is almost completely surrounded by escarpments of the overlying Namurian gritstones. There are no known solution caves in the gritstone: most of the drainage, apart from local percolation down joints, remains on the surface.

All the caves listed here are formed either by wind erosion along major joints, by the partial detachment of huge blocks from the scarp faces, or have been artificially excavated. Most provide a useful shelter for climbers and walkers from the harsh conditions that can prevail on the high gritstone moorlands.

BAT HOUSE CAVE   NGR 335 523   Arch
Alt. 550ft (167m)

In Shining Cliff Woods, near Alderwasley.

A gritstone fissure which yielded a Roman brooch and pottery.

References: Haverfield, F. 1905. Victoria County History of Derbyshire. p.236. Ward, J. 1899. The Reliquary. Vol.V. S.

THE BELFRY   NGR 072 866   Lost
Alt. 1800ft (549m)

On the south edge of Kinderlow, just below the edge.

A maze caused by the splitting off of gritstone blocks.

BUNKERS HILL WOOD CAVE   NGR 284 690   Arch
Alt. 1050ft (320m)

In the gritstone scarp south east of Chatsworth.

An archaeological cave in gritstone. Middle Bronze Age remains have been found.

Reference: Radley, J. & Cooper, L. 1966. Derbys. Arch. Jour. Vol.86. pp.93-98. Survey.

HERMIT'S CAVE   NGR 227 623   Grade I
Alt. 800ft (240m)

In Cratcliffe Tor, near Birchover.

A semi-artificial enlarged joint in gritstone. Formerly used by a hermit who carved a Crucifixion in the wall. Now used by climbers as a shelter.

KINDERLOW CAVERN   NGR 072 867   Grade I
Alt. 1800ft (549m)

¼ mile (0.4km) east of shooting hut near top of Oaken Clough on Kinderscout.

In gritstone. Entrance among tumbled blocks, difficult to find. A series of fissures in the gritstone.

LUDCHURCH CAVERN   NGR SJ 987 657   Grade I
Alt. 1050ft (320m)

Near Wincle, Cheshire.

A partly open fissure in gritstone, of impressive size.

ROBIN HOOD'S CAVE   NGR 243 837   Grade I
Alt. 1350ft (411m)   Length: 50ft (15m)

In the gritstone scarp of Stanage Edge.

A series of wind eroded holes in the gritstone scarp. Used by climbers for camping.

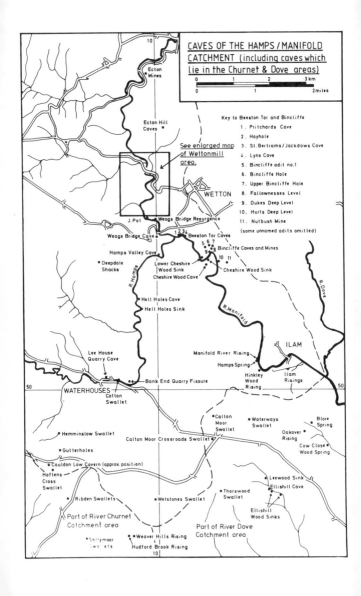

CAVES OF THE HAMPS / MANIFOLD CATCHMENT (including caves which lie in the Churnet & Dove areas)

Key to Beeston Tor and Bincliffe

1. Pritchards Cave
2. Hayhole
3. St.Bertrams / Jackdaws Cave
4. Lynx Cave
5. Bincliffe adit no.1
6. Bincliffe Hole
7. Upper Bincliffe Hole
8. Fallownesses Level
9. Dukes Deep Level
10. Hurts Deep Level
11. Nutbush Mine

(some unnamed adits omitted)

See enlarged map of Wettonmill area.

Ecton Mines

Ecton Hill Caves

WETTON

J.Pot

Weags Bridge Resurgence

Weags Bridge Cave

Beeston Tor Caves

Hamps Valley Cave

Bincliffe Caves and Mines

Deepdale Shacks

Lower Cheshire Wood Sink

Cheshire Wood Cave

Cheshire Wood Sink

R.Hamps

R.Manifold

R.Dove

Hell Holes Cave

Hell Holes Sink

ILAM

Lee House Quarry Cave

Manifold River Rising

Hamps Spring

Hinkley Wood Rising

Ilam Risings

Bank End Quarry Fissure

WATERHOUSES

Cotton Swallet

Calton Moor Swallet

Waterways Swallet

Blore Spring

Hemminslow Swallet

Calton Moor Crossroads Swallet

Oakover Rising

Cow Close Wood Spring

Gutterholes

Cauldon Low Cavern (approx.position)

Hoftens Cross Swallet

Leewood Sink

Ellishill Cave

Ribden Swallets

Wetstones Swallet

Thorswood Swallet

Ellishill Wood Sinks

Part of River Churnet Catchment area

Part of River Dove Catchment area

Saltymoor Swallets

Weaver Hills Rising

Hudford Brook Rising

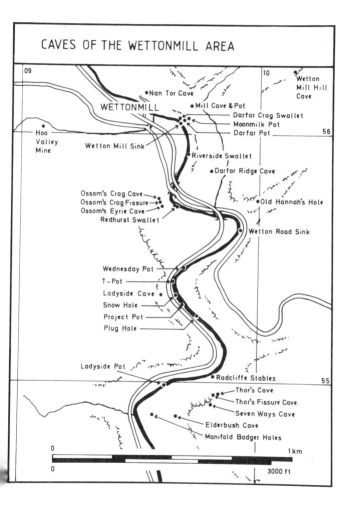

CAVES OF THE WETTONMILL AREA

THE HAMPS/MANIFOLD
CATCHMENT AREA

As in the case of the River Dove, the Rivers Manifold and Hamps accumulate on the Namurian Grits and Shales to the west. To the north of Wetton, adverse folding together with the shaly nature of the limestones keeps the Manifold on the surface. On reaching reef limestones at Wetton Mill, however, the river sinks underground, and during the summer months, the river bed is dry as far as the risings at Ilam. As water levels increase, the river migrates downstream, successively overpowering the various swallets. Thus for the majority of the year, the swallet caves in the river bed are inaccessible. The Wetton Mill sinks have been dye tested to the Main Rising at Ilam.

The river Hamps sinks in a similar manner at Waterhouses, and this water has been tested to the Hamps Spring and the Upper Rising, both near Ilam. The sinks along the limestone/shale boundary to the south west have been dye tested to the Hinkley Wood Risings, although there appeared to be a connection between these risings and the Upper Rising at Ilam.

The Wetton Mill–Ilam system is unlikely to be penetrable for great distances. The gradient is shallow, and the known caves are all terminated by sumps, although determined pushing in drought will undoubtedly reveal more open passage.

The Waterhouses–Ilam system is a rather better prospect. The straight line distance is roughly 4km (2.5 miles), and the fall is in the order of 70m (230ft). This gives a gradient of just under 100ft per mile, which suggests a significant length of vadose cave passage carrying the entire River Hamps. The intermediate Waterways Swallet may therefore one day present exciting discoveries.

The hydrology of the area is fascinating, and the reader is referred to the cited references for further information on the structural geology and geomorphology.

Included in this chapter is a small area of limestone which drains into the River Churnet. The stream found in the Ribden Mine probably drains to the Weaver Hills Rising, but this is not known to have been tested. Also included is the small area of limestone which drains south eastwards to the lower River Dove, where there are small sinks and risings about which little is known.

BANK END QUARRY FISSURE
NGR approx 092 502   Lost

Now largely quarried away.
Reference: Brown, E. 1865. Trans. Midland Scientific Association. pp.34-38.

BENT CHISEL POT   NGR 0977 5498   Dig
Alt. 560ft (171m)   **Depth: 10ft (3m)**

100ft (30m) downstream of Radcliffe Stables on the same side of the river at the foot of a small crag.

Filter gate on entrance. Please replace. Originally a thick concrete plug, a 1.5ft (0.3m) hole was made in this and a rift excavated for about 10ft (3m). Acts as a sink or resurgence when river is flowing.

References: Milner, M. 1985. D.C.A. N/L No.60. p.9. Milner, M. 1984. The Manifold Caver. p.32.

BINCLIFFE HOLE   NGR 114 538   Grade I
Alt. 900ft (274m)   **Length: 25ft (8m)**

In topmost outcrop above Bincliffe Mine Levels, on National Trust property.

A badger lair. Flat out crawling as far as possible (about 25ft/8m).

BINCLIFFE LEVELS   Grade II (Mines)
Alt. 550 – 1000ft (167 – 305m)

A group of eleven adits (two blocked) mostly well hidden in thick scrub vegetation on a steep hillside.

Adit 1:	NGR 11303 53786
	Length: 357ft (109m).
Adit 2:	NGR 11480 53756. Fallownesses Level, Fallows Level
	Length: 1425ft (434m).
Adit 3:	NGR 11464 53628. Dukes Deep Level.
	Length: 1300ft (396m).
Adit 4:	NGR 11571 53754
	Length: 300ft (91m).
Adit 5:	NGR 11574 53811
	Length: 105ft (32m).
Adit 6:	NGR 11594 53573
	Length: 18ft (5.5m).
Adit 7:	NGR 11630 53382. Hurts Deep Level.
	Length: 1099ft (335m).
Adit 8:	NGR 11548 53807
	Length: 108ft (33m).
Adit 9:	NGR 11833 53385. Nutbush Mine.
	Length: 216ft (66m).
Adit 10:	NGR 11535 53804
	Length: 10ft (3m).
Adit 11:	NGR 11525 53814
	Length: 52ft (16m).

Two entrances are close to river level and lead to long adits. The third long adit is high in the hillside between two miners' coes. Most of the adits are easy walking and some lead into natural solution cavities. Some penetrate old stempled workings with dangerously unstable stacked deads, and some go under choked shafts on the hilltop. Several of the levels contain good cave pearls, which should not be trodden on!

Reference: Pedrick, P.D. and Chapman, C.J. 1974. Bull. P.D.M.H.S. Vol.5. No.5. Survey.

BINCLIFFE MINE, UPPER
NGR 115 538   Grade III (Mine)
Alt. 975ft (292m)

The most northerly of three shafts near a sycamore tree.

A 40ft (12m) pitch with a chamber 25ft down containing large dog tooth spar. A further descent of 15ft (5m) to a scree heap with passages running north and south leading to several parallel passages with cave pearls and stalactites. Several short drops need care, and unstable deads require considerable caution.

Tackle – 40ft (12m) ladder; 100ft (30m) lifeline; Stake belay.

BREDON BROOK SINKS   NGR 08 51   Digs
Alt. 700ft (213m)

Brook loses water in its bed at a number of points between Back o' th' Brook and its confluence with the River Hamps near Lee House. In prolonged dry weather the bed progressively dries up as far as a point roughly one third of a mile (0.5km) below the ford at Back o' th' Brook. Stream was positively dye tested to Ilam in June 1990.

References: Harvey, F.A. 1977. Waterfall of Yesterday. p.40. Milner, M. 1984. The Manifold Caver. p.6. Mellors, P.T. 1989. D.C.A. N/L No.71. p.3.

CALTON MOOR SWALLET   NGR 115 493   Dig
Alt. 1035ft (315m)   Length: 12ft (4m)

Dug out by D.S.G. in inclined bedding passage. Possibilities are poor. Rising unknown.

Reference: Beasley, F. 1975. D.C.A. N/L No.24.

CALTON MOOR CROSSROADS SWALLET
NGR 116 487   Dig
Alt. 1000ft (305m)

Small swallet near crossroads. Poor possibilities.

Reference: Beasley, F. 1975. D.C.A. Newsletter No.24.

CAULDON LOW CAVE   NGR 07 48   Lost

Bone cave now completely quarried away. Exact position not known.

Reference: Trans. North. Staffs. Field Club Vol.XL p.85. & Vol.XLI p.92.

CHESHIRE WOOD CAVE   NGR 1132 5330   Grade I
Alt. 800ft (240m)   Length: 40ft (12m)

At top of wood in a crag half a mile (800m) below Beeston Tor. See also Lower Cheshire Wood Cave.

A bedding crawl with some formations.

Reference: North Staffs. Field Club Journal, Vol.4. 1964.

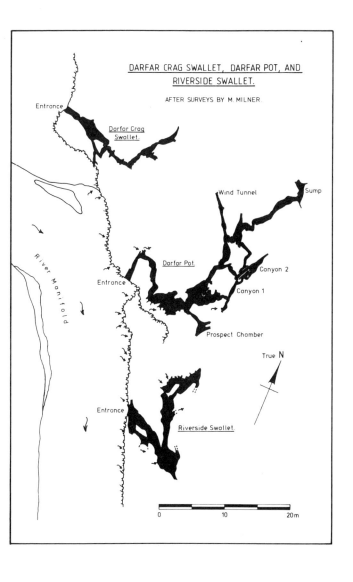

DARFAR CRAG SWALLET, DARFAR POT, AND
RIVERSIDE SWALLET.

AFTER SURVEYS BY M. MILNER.

Entrance

Darfar Crag
Swallet.

River Manifold

Wind Tunnel

Sump

Darfar Pot.

Entrance

Canyon 2

Canyon 1

Prospect Chamber

True N

Entrance

Riverside Swallet.

0   10   20m

COTTON SWALLET   NGR 089 502   Lost
Alt. 690ft (210m)   Length: 25ft (8m)

In bed of River Hamps, 450ft below the bridge.
   Had a solid rock roof and ran south under river and road. Ended in a
choke. Sink has been dye-tested to Hamps Spring and Ilam Upper Rising.
   Reference: Clark, 1917. Trans. North Staffs. Field Club Vol. 52. pp.25-33.

DARFAR CRAG CAVE   NGR 0971 5590   Grade I (Digs)
(Darfar Badger Caves)
Alt. 750ft (229m)   Length: 100ft (31m)   Depth: 10ft (3m)

Several badger holes (in use) in the trees halfway along the ridge.
   Entered in 1987. Left hand (northerly) entrance leads to short descending
phreatic passage. Immediately inside on the right a small muddy passage can
be followed via several small muddy chambers to second entrance, which is
gated and needs a spanner to open. Shaft in floor descends for 10ft (3m)
before becoming too low.

DARFAR CRAG SWALLET   Grade II
NGR 0967 5607   (Dig)
Alt. 625ft (191m)   Length: 130ft (40m)   Depth: 30ft (9m)
Warning: Lower sections flood prone with water rising from below.
   Large sloping entrance shaft 25ft (8m) deep (ladder & short belay) leads to
choke (dig). On right a way may be open to a continuation passage via a
crawl. Right leads to narrow rifts approaching the river, left leads for 40ft
(12m) to a mud choke, passing a dig on the right which draughts, and is less
than 30ft (9m) from the end of the Wind Tunnel in Darfar Pot.
   References: Milner, M. 1984. D.C.A. N/L No.56, p.13. Milner, M. 1984.
The Manifold Caver pp. 13-14. Survey.

DARFAR POT   NGR 0970 5603   Grade IV
Alt. 610ft (186m)   Length: 1200ft (366m)   Depth: 150ft (46m)
**Warning: The cave is very flood prone, and is the first cave to be affected if the
river floods. Only descend in settled conditions. The sump backs up to river
level (ie. fills the cave) and does so very quickly.**
   In the cliff face at river level in upstream corner of Wetton Mill Main Sink.
Filter gate on entrance. Please replace.
   Discovered 1979. Extended 1980 & 1983 by Trent Valley Caving Group.
   Awkward, steeply descending entrance passage leads after 54ft (17m) to
Water Chamber, with river visible on right. Left (downslope) leads to holes in
floor on left and right. Left is dead end, right is downward squeeze to river
entering from between boulders. Left leads under a flake (water sinks in
floor) into Glory Chamber, 16ft (5m) long, 30ft (9m) high, 7ft (2m) wide.
   Muddy climb up immediately right leads to two ways. Right spirals up for
20ft (6m), then too narrow. Eyehole on left is awkward squeeze and climb
down (handline useful) into Prospect Chamber, parallel to Glory Chamber
and very close to the end of Riverside Swallet. In floor at lowest point of
Prospect Chamber a narrow rift has been descended for 20ft (6m) to top of
Waterfall near Canyon 1.

From Glory Chamber hole in floor at far end leads down to Lower Glory Chamber and squeeze on left near bottom leads to top of Canyon 1, a narrow 25ft (8m) pitch. Tight squeeze on left (downstream) at bottom leads to bottom of Canyon 2, while to the right is the bottom of the waterfall. At top of Canyon 1, a very tight squeeze down to the right of the pitch leads to the top of the waterfall.

Above the hole down to Lower Glory Chamber is a 10ft (3m) climb with fixed rope to squeeze into Darfar 2, discovered in 1983. Immediately right is tight descending passage which is very hard to get out of. Straight on is a hole in the floor to the top of Chamber Pot, 20ft (6m) deep. This is the main way to the bottom. Over the top of this the passage goes left and right. Left is awkward slide down to the Wind Tunnel, which can be reached easier from the top of Chamber Pot. The Wind Tunnel is a silty joint-controlled passage which draughts and ends in a dig within 30ft (9m) of Darfar Crag Swallet. The right hand way goes via a right hand bend and 7ft (2m) climb down to Canyon 2, a much larger hading rift. After a sloping descent of 20ft (6m) (use belay round chockstone), climb down through boulders to reach the river again (via a tight squeeze). To the right (upstream) is the link to Canyon 1. Left a short passage 3/4 full of water can be followed round a left hand bend to the top of the Toboggan Run. Note this has only about 1ft of air space. Do not attempt it if there is less than this. Chamber Pot is easily free-climbable to a small waterfall. Beyond this is the top of another pitch, Pedigree Pot, which is 55ft (17m) deep. Top 10ft (3m) is tight and sloping, but widens downwards. Fixed rope in place, but advise lifeline from below the narrow section. At the bottom is 20ft (6m) long, 10ft (3m) high passage with the river (from Canyon 2) entering on the right. A climb down at the downstream end of this passage enters the Toboggan Run, a steeply descending clean washed tube about 5ft (1.5m) wide and 3ft (1m) high carrying the river into the terminal sump after 70ft (23m) (in low water). Was dived in 1989 and found to be too tight to continue after 130ft (40m) at a depth of 50ft (15m). Toboggan Run has a fixed rope due to the large volume of water which flows down it in anything but very dry conditions.

Tackle:

Prospect Chamber: 20ft (6m) handline

Canyon 1:	25ft (8m) ladder; 30ft (9m) lifeline
Canyon 2:	20ft (6m) ladder; 30ft (9m) lifeline. (belay to chockstone).
Pedigree Pot:	55ft (17m) ladder; 70ft (21m) lifeline.
Toboggan Run:	100ft (30m) handline.

References: Brookes, S. 1989. O.C.C. N/L Vol.26. No.9/10. p.36. Johnson, S. 1983. Caves & Caving No.22. pp.10-11. Sketch survey. Milner, M. 1981. D.C.A. N/L No.48. pp.1-2. Milner, M. 1983. The Manifold Caver. pp.11-16. Survey. Milner, M. 1984. D.C.A. N/L No.56. p.13. Milner, M. 1984. The Manifold Caver. pp.9-11. Survey. Milner, M. 1987. D.C.A. N/L No.64, pp.14-15.

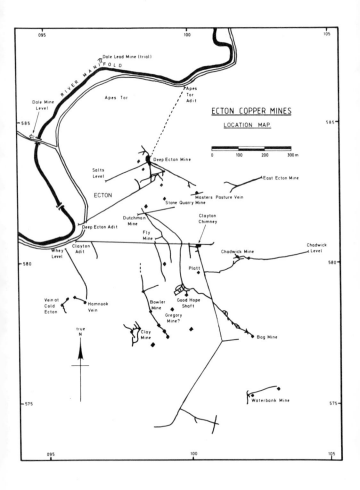

ECTON COPPER MINES

LOCATION MAP

DARFAR RIDGE CAVE   NGR 0980 5588   Grade I (Arch)
(Bone Cave)
Alt. 750ft (228m)   Length: 350ft (107m)
Gated. Key from Trent Valley Caving Group.

In crest of spur above Darfar Crag.

10ft (3m) entrance climb drops into large passage. Left into Old Series, a large muddy bedding plane. Right leads for 16ft (5m) to left hand bend and into New Series via muddy crawl to enter Aussie Chamber. Slide down on right into Link Passage to the Graveyard, because of skulls of small birds found here. At end on right is crawl to Root Chamber, near the surface. 7ft (2m) drop leads via short squeeze and crawl to Final Chamber. New Series was well decorated when found in 1981 by T.V.C.G.

Pleistocene and Neolithic remains.

References: Milner, M. 1981. D.C.A. N/L No. 48. pp.3-4. Milner, M. 1981. T.V.C.G. Review. pp.9-14. Milner, M. 1983. The Manifold Caver. pp.25-28. Survey. Nicholson, S. 1966. Peakland Archaeological Society N/L No.21. pp.20-25. Thomas, F.H. & Moore, R. 1962. Peakland Archaeological Society N/L No.18. pp.7-9.

DEEPDALE SHACKS   NGR 084 534   Digs
Alt. 1000ft (305m)
Beside Deepdale Farm.

Two active sinks, both silted up. The more northerly takes a fair amount of water off the shales. One has been opened up as a dig by Orpheus Caving Club and Birmingham Carabiner Club. The resurgence is not known.

DONKEY HOLE   NGR 0978 5498   Grade I
(One of "Radcliffe's Stables")
Alt. 570ft (171m)   Length: 50ft (15m)
The smaller and more northerly of two caves known as Radcliffe's Stables directly below Thor's Cave, about 30ft (9m) above the river bed.

The entrance is of the rock-shelter type. There is a choked passage to the right, and a crawl ahead to a chamber with water.

ECTON COPPER MINES   NGR 097 584   Grade II to IV
Alt. 600-1000ft (183-305m)   Length: c.¾ mile (1.2km)
These old copper mines are well known to cavers for their cave pearls and other formations in adits extending as much as ¾ mile (1.2km) into the hill. Beware of flooded shafts in the floor, which once led into workings 900ft (274m) below river level.

Most of former entrances sealed. Lid on Chadwick Shaft is locked and key kept by mineral rights owner, Mr.G.Cox, of Lees Farm, Back of Ecton, Wetton. Permission unlikely. Mr Cox also owns The Hillocks, Ecton, near Ashbourne (Tel. 129884 482) from where invited parties are conducted into Salts Level.

APES TOR LEVEL   NGR 0999 5862

Now blocked but formerly connecting Deep Ecton with the north end of the hill at river level.

BAG MINE   NGR 1021 5774

Shaft entrance high on the east side of the hill requires 30ft (9m) ladder. Ginging partly collapsed and unstable. Steeply sloping stopes lead to long adit going north west. Further 25ft (8m) ladder pitch into Goodhope/Dutchman Level, with climb up into Goodhope stopes on the left, at foot of Goodhope Shaft (110ft/34m) to surface.

CLAYTON ADIT   NGR 0959 5808

Adit on road side, up to knee deep in water. Now gated. Leads to underground winding and pumping chamber and long adit to Waterbank Mine. Beware flooded shafts. Turn right at Clayton Engine Chamber, then left into Chadwick Mine workings. Cross flooded shaft by plank to reach Chadwick Cascades, which can be climbed to old workings at the foot of Chadwick Shaft 100ft (30m) from the surface.

DALE MINE ADIT   NGR 0945 5845

Most of the Dale Mine is now inaccessible, but the adit is open for 1150ft (351m), at which point falls prevent further progress. The pipe workings appear to have been very extensive.

DEEP ECTON   NGR 0962 5813

Adit entrance gated. Up to 3ft (0.9m) of water. Leads into Engine Chamber and extensive series of level and stopes. Beware flooded shafts. Also accessible via 150ft (46m) of fixed ladders from Salts Level.

DUTCHMAN LEVEL   NGR 0981 5818

Close to largest hillock high on hillside. Half flooded and with good cave formations, links through to Goodhope and Bag Mines. Gated. No access – private water supply.

FLY MINE   NGR 0988 5809

Above and to the south of Dutchman Level. A sloping series of pipe workings.

SALTS LEVEL   NGR 0971 5829

Behind Ecton House. Leads into deep Ecton workings via a fixed ladderway. Gated.

WATERBANK MINE   NGR 1031 5755

A climbing shaft leads into the sough. Long hands and knees crawl leads to stopes on two levels.

WHEY LEVEL	NGR 0956 5805	Grade I
(Birch's Level)		
Alt. 700ft (213m)	**Length: 700ft (213m)**	

Obvious entrance at side of road. The level is easy walking with an occasional wet floor, ending at a forefield. The remains of valve gear can still be seen, from the storing of whey. It was used as a store for the Ecton Creamery in the 1920's – 1930's.

References: Kirkham, N. 1967. P.D.M.H.S. Special Publication. Survey. Robey, J.A. & Porter, L. 1972. Bull. P.D.M.H.S. Vol.5. No.2. pp. 93-106. Robey, J.A. & Porter, L. 1972. The Copper and Lead Mines of Ecton Hill. 92pp. Moorland Publ. Co., Hartington. Survey.

ECTON HILL CAVES   NGR 102 570   Grade I
Alt. 1025ft (312m)   Length: 17ft (5m) & 20ft (6m)

On a crag at summit of south east end of Ecton Hill.

Two entrances. One 3ft (0.9m) high becoming very tight before short descent to small chamber. The other is to the south in the same crag, longer, with one chamber.

ELDERBUSH CAVE   NGR 0978 5488   Grade I (Arch)
Alt. 900ft (274m)   Length: 150ft (46m)

In south west end of Thor's Crag.

Entrance chamber completely excavated. Fissure leads to lower series with good formations. Animals and human remains from Pleistocene to Romano-British.

References: Bramwell, D. 1947-1950. P.A.S. N/L Nos. 1-6 & 8. Bramwell, D. 1950. Trans. C.R.G. Vol.1. No.4. pp.47-52.

ELLISHILL CAVE   NGR 1303 4739   Grade I
Alt. 770ft (240m)   Length: 10ft (3m)

Overlooking Ellishill Brook on the west side of the gorge.

A short walk-in cave. In low flow conditions the brook is dry for nearly a mile from a sink point nearby.

ELLISHILL WOOD SINKS NGR 131 473 to 134 472 Digs
Alt. 700ft (213m)

Private grazing land adjoining steeply wooded flank of Ellishill area. Crossed by two North – South footpaths linking Swinscoe & Stanton villages.

Sinks occur between points where paths (mentioned above) cross Ellishill Brook.

Tributary from direction of Bullgap Lane (west) sinks on reaching dry bed of Ellishill Brook. Downstream course of brook becomes divided and less clearly defined for a distance of some hundred metres. Under conditions where Lee Wood Sink (1295 4763) overflows, brook may peter out along this section. In flood flow continues down brook's full length.

GUTTERHOLES   NGR 0729 4839   Grade IV
Alt. 970ft (295m)   Length: 200ft (61m)   Depth: 40ft (12m)

On west side of road past Cauldonlow Quarries. Entrance lies under concrete slabs which should be replaced.

A series of tight squeezes down between boulders leads to a steep slide to lip of The Funnel, a blind 25ft (8m) descent in the floor overhung by collapsed boulders. Way on is to the right via an awkward squeeze, then a brief climb into the roof, and through another squeeze before sliding down into a tall narrow rift. 10ft (3m) hole in floor drops into stooping sized phreatic passage, soon ending at Amatt's Rift, a 15ft (4.5m) easy descent. Extension from west end of rift leads back under valley floor into extensive collapse area. Digging has made a through route possible from here to the top of The Funnel, but care is needed in route finding, and with unstable rock.

Parts of the cave are active, depending on where the stream is sinking.

Dye testing has shown that the water resurges at Ilam.

References: Mellors, P.T. 1975. D.C.A N/L Nos.26. p.1-2 and 29. pp.1-3 Survey. Mellors, P.T. 1989. D.C.A. N/L No. 71. pp.2-9.

HAMPS VALLEY CAVE   NGR 1003 5350   Dig
Alt. 550ft (168m)

On north bank (left bank) of the River Hamps half a mile upstream of the confluence with the River Manifold. Just above the 3rd bridge.

A small cave entrance to a tight crawl that could be dug out.

HAYHOLE   NGR 1064 5407   Grade I
(The Hayloft)
Alt. 700ft (213m)

High in the face of Beeston Tor.

An obvious crescent shaped opening on a prominent joint in the reef limestone. Not to be confused with Jackdaw's Cave.

HELL HOLES CAVE   NGR 0943 5243   Grade I
Alt. 630ft (192m)

On right bank of River Hamps, downstream from Hell Holes Corner (marked on old two and a half inch maps) and 100ft (30m) above river level. Between bridges 5 & 6 from the confluence with the River Manifold.

A small cave in the cliff on the opposite side of the river from the Waterhouses to Beeston footpath.

HELL HOLES SINKS   NGR 0952 5211   Digs
Alt. 600ft (183m)

On National Trust land, and in river bed, with limited access.

In river bed and right hand bank of the River Hamps between the 6th and 7th bridges upstream from the confluence of the Hamps and Manifold.

A few small sinks in the river bed with obvious signs that once the sinks were much larger as there are large limestone blocks with eye bolts and holes for bolts in the bed of the river. Also upstream the river bed is lower than that downstream.

HEMMINGSLOW SWALLET NGR 0730 4882 Grade III
(Hemminslow Swallet)
Alt. 940ft (286m)   **Length: 100ft (30m)**   **Depth: 35ft (11m)**

In prominent blind valley on west side of road past Caldon Quarry, barely half a mile (0.8km) north of Gutterholes. Area is fenced and entrance fitted with hinged grille.

Stream is culverted to base of 10ft (3m) lidded concrete shaft through road widening rubble. Shaft is presumed to stand on site of original main sink, but digging here has been unproductive, with no sign of bedrock. In flood streamwater backs up in shaft and overflows to sink in northern corner of valley at foot of solitary limestone outcrop. Digging here in 1988 revealed a squeeze to the top of a tight pitch which can be free-climbed into a narrow phreatic rift, with several ways on including a 20ft (6m) high aven. All routes, however, soon become tight or are choked with clay or boulders.

The stream rises rapidly with the onset of rain and can make the entrance pitch impassable. The stream was positively dye tested to Ilam in June 1990.

The next hollow north also takes a small stream.

References: Mellors, P.T. 1973. D.C.A. N/L No.18. p.2. Mellors, P.T. 1989. D.C.A. N/L No.71. pp.2-9. Milner, M. 1988. D.C.A. N/L No.68. p.15.

HOFTEN'S CROSS SWALLET   NGR 071 479   Grade I
(Red Scar Swallet)
Alt. 1040ft (317m)   Length: 30ft (9m)

In stream bed, with lid.

A short length of low passage in solid rock from the foot of a brief pitch. Opened up in 1975 by Derbyshire Speleological Group. Floor of shingle and inwashed domestic refuse from disused tip. Water is believed to resurge at Ilam, 4 miles (6km) away and over 500ft (152m) lower.

References: Beasley, F. 1975. D.S.G. Bulletin Vol.1. Part 1. p.6. Beasley, F. 1975. D.C.A. N/L No.24 pp.2-4. Beasley, F. 1976. D.C.A. N/L No.27. p.4. Farey, J. 1811. A General View of the Agriculture and Minerals of Derbyshire. Vol.1. p.295.

HOO VALLEY MINE (north)   NGR 0912 5605   Grade I
                                                 (Mine)
Alt. 653ft (199m)   Length: 417ft (127m)

Just to the right of the footpath following the brook up the valley.

Stooping entrance leads to a 6ft (2m) climb down on the left. At bottom left is choked within a few feet, but right is stooping sized level with water. Soon enlarges to walking size. Cross 8ft (2.5m) deep flooded shaft on right with care, and continue for 80ft (25m) to foot of run in shaft from which a stream issues. Pass on right hand side at roof level to regain walking passage to junction. Right for 80ft (25m) through water to dead end. Ahead for 100ft (30m) to another dead end.

Another mine directly opposite on the south side of the valley consists of a walking size trial roughly 200ft (61m) long.

Reference: Milner, M. 1984. The Manifold Caver. pp.30-31. Survey.

HUDFORD BROOK RISING   NGR 092 461   Spring
Alt. 750ft (229m)

A small spring below the Weaver Hills, source of the Hudford Brook.

ILAM RISINGS   NGR 1314 5057   Dives
Alt. 450ft (135m)

MAIN RISING   NGR 1314 5057

The main rising of the River Manifold from its sink at Wetton Mill, 4 miles (6.4km) away. Water comes from beneath the path on the east bank close to Ilam Hall. Diving by C.D.G. members has passed a low area around 150ft (46m) in to reach a point 328ft (100m) from base.

RASPBERRY RISING   NGR 1313 5057

Upstream of and adjacent to Main Rising. Underwater digging revealed a large chamber where loose boulders prevented access.

ILAM WEIR RISING   NGR 1315 5056

A small culverted rising on the east bank just below the weir. Source unknown but alleged connections to the cellars of Ilam Hall and to Main Rising were not confirmed by dye testing. Too small for divers.

ILAM UPPER RISING   NGR 1309 5055

A few feet upstream of the main rising, and dye tests have proved a source in the River Hamps. Underwater digging enabled divers to reach a small chamber with no way on.

HINKLEY WOOD RESURGENCE   NGR 1283 5046

On the west bank between Ilam Main Risings and the Hamps Spring. Dye tests have proved a connection with Waterways Swallet 1 mile (1.6km) away and 470ft (143m) higher, and Gutterholes. Also connected to Ilam Main Rising. A possible dig?

HAMPS SPRING   NGR 1270 5078

Upstream from the Main Resurgence on the opposite (west) bank. The water rises through the muddy floor of a hollow with no obvious place to dig. Dye tests have proved a source at Waterhouses Sink (0916 5012). Dye takes 3 to 6 days and comes out at both the Hamps Spring and Ilam Upper Rising on opposite sides of the Manifold. Air bubbles appear in high water conditions and may indicate the proximity of air-filled passages.

MANIFOLD RIVER RISING   NGR 1273 5078

The river seeps up out of its bed a few yards up from the Hamps Spring. Probably an overflow from the Main Rising but dye tests have not confirmed this.

ST. BERTRAM'S WELL   NGR 1325 5060

A well leads to two short passages which have been dived in vain.

FLOW GAUGE RISING   NGR 1396 5074

0.6 mile (1km) downstream of St. Bertram's Well.

ILAM VILLAGE RISING   NGR 135 512

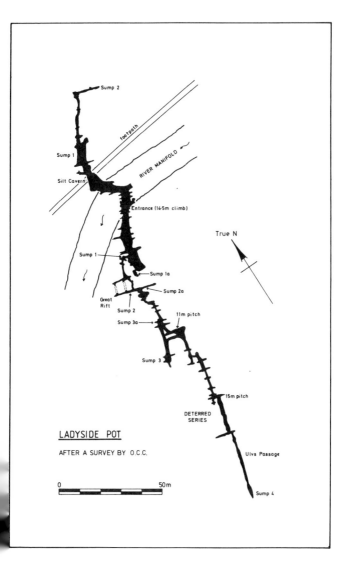

Sump 2

footpath

Sump 1

RIVER MANIFOLD

Silt Cavern

Entrance (14·5m climb)

True N

Sump 1

Sump 1a

Sump 2a

Great
Rift

Sump 2

11m pitch

Sump 3a

Sump 3

15m pitch

DETERRED
SERIES

LADYSIDE POT

Ulvs Passage

AFTER A SURVEY BY O.C.C.

Sump 4

0   50m

OKEOVER RISINGS   NGR 1440 4890
Small petrifying springs.

COWCLOSE WOOD SPRINGS   NGR 1465 4850

References: Ammatt, S., Drakeley, K., & Potts, J. 1981. Lyre No.5. pp.26-41. Brookes, S. 1987. C.D.G. N/L No. p. Survey. Brookes, S. 1986. D.C.A. N/L No.62. pp.2-6. Survey. Cave Diving Group. Various newsletters. Gill, D.W. 1973. British Caver No.60.p.62-64. Mellors, P.T. 1989. D.C.A. N/L No.71. pp.2-9.

J-POT   NGR 097 545   Sink/rising
Alt. 500ft (152m)

A small sink in the bed of the River Manifold, which becomes a rising under certain flow conditions.

JACKDAWS CAVE   NGR 1065 5408   Grade I
(Jackadaws Cave, Beeston Tor Cave, St Bertrams Chimney)
Alt. 700ft (213m)

High above St Bertram's Cave in the face of Beeston Tor.
An enlarged joint, similar to Hayhole, but less conspicuous. Connected to St. Betram's Cave by a very tight squeeze.

LADYSIDE CAVE   NGR 0960 5534   Grade I
Alt. 650ft (198m)   Length: 40ft (12m)

100ft (30m) above the valley floor. In thick undergrowth and difficult to find.
A rift entrance. A high passage some 30ft (9m) long diminishes in size and becomes mud choked.

LADYSIDE POT   NGR 0960 5498   Grade V
Alt. 550ft (168m)   Length: 1500ft (457m)   Depth: 70ft (21m)

Entered June 1975 by O.C.C. Extended 1976/7 by O.C.C. & C.D.G.
In the bed of the River Manifold, 750ft (228m) upstream of Ladyside Brook.
Warning: The entrance is in the bed of the river, and therefore the whole cave fills to the roof. No descent should be contemplated except in very dry settled weather.
The entrance is covered by a metal grid. The descent is tight, and the return is very difficult for large cavers. The rift widens out, and reaches the silt-covered floor of the stream passage after a total descent of 50ft (15m).
Upstream (north) leads to a fine phreatic passage with large silt banks, which ends in a sump. This has been passed by C.D.G. and after 30ft (9m) (not free-diveable) emerges into a further 250ft (76m) of phreatic passage heading in the direction of Redhurst Swallet, and ending at a second sump. A parallel rift containing another sump (Sump 2b) was entered in 1989.
Downstream (south) from the entrance, a hands and knees crawl passes an aven to two sumps. The first can be passed in drought (not free-diveable) to a sharp narrow climb, The Rasp, then a crawl to the Great Rift at the foot of which are two fluctuating sumps.

Traversing over the Great Rift leads to Deterred Series. A pitch of 35ft (11m) rejoins the streamway which sumps in both directions. A high level by-pass here leads to a number of rifts in the floor. The widest can be laddered for 60ft (18m) to a further 100ft (30m) of narrow stream passage to another sump. The muddy and arduous nature of the cave, despite its short length, make this an unpleasant spot.

Tackle:

Entrance: 50ft (15m) rope (prusiker & sling useful).

Deterred Series:
1st Pitch: 50ft (15m) ladder; 60ft (18m) lifeline.
2nd Pitch: 75ft (23m) ladder; 90ft (27m) lifeline; Long belay.

References: Allwright, P. 1977. O.C.C. N/L Vol.13. No.9. pp.46-47. Survey. Amatt, S. & Drakeley, K. 1975. O.C.C. N/L Vol.11. No.6. pp.33-35. Surveys. Drakeley, K. 1975. O.C.C. N/L Vol.11. No.5. pp.27-29. Survey. Drakeley, K. 1981. The Lyre No.5. pp.41-47. Survey.

LEE HOUSE QUARRY CAVE   NGR 086 503   Arch
(Waterhouses Fissure?)
Alt. 730ft (219m)

High in disused Lee House Quarry on the north east of the village.

Cave entrance difficult of access and has unstable roof. Easily visible. Has cave-earth fill just inside awaiting excavation. May be the same as Waterhouses Fissure recorded by Heath, 1882. It is also possible that Waterhouses Fissure may have been Bank End Quarry Fissure.

References: Aitken, J. 1873. Trans. Manch. Geol. Soc. Vol.12. Brown. 1864-5. Trans. Midland Scientific Assoc. p.34. Heath. 1882. Derbys. Arch. Jour. pp.164-5.

LEE WOOD SINK   NGR 1295 4763   Dig
Alt. 800ft (244m)

In bed of Ellishill Brook, where water passes from Bullgap Shales to Ellishill reef limestones. Site difficult to approach due to undergrowth.

Under low flow conditions brook sinks completely into mud, stones, and crevices, not always at exactly the same spot. In wet weather brook flows on to Ellishill Wood Sinks or beyond. Bed can be dry from Lee Wood Sink to downstream end of Catholes Wood where there is a gradual reappearance of water, with volume not fully restored till limestone beds are crossed again below Limestone Hill (east of Stanton village).

LOWER CHESHIRE WOOD CAVE AND SINK
NGR 112 534   **Grade I**
Alt. 550ft (165m)   Length: 15ft (4.5m)

A small sink close to a collapsed footbridge in the bed of the River Manifold, and a small cave 30ft above the sink in a grassy cliff.

The cave consists of a low crawl for 15ft (4.5m) to a small chamber whence a tube runs upwards to a choke. The roof is a single bed of limestone anticlinally folded.

LYNX CAVES   NGR 1067 5409   Grade I (Arch)
Alt. 700ft (213m)   Length: 150ft (46m)

20 yards (18m) downstream of St. Bertram's Cave, a climb up a steep gully leads to the Lynx Caves at the same altitude as Hayhole.

Upper Lynx Cave is a short old phreatic passage with remains of formations, eventually becoming too narrow.

Lower Lynx Cave a short distance to the east is a collapsed continuation of the upper cave, and contains only a short crawl.

Archaeological excavations revealed lynx, polecat, and reindeer remains. Finds in Natural History Museum, London.

References: Wilson, G.H. 1926. Some Caves and Crags of Peakland. pp.54-55.

MANIFOLD BADGER HOLES   NGR 0958 5486   Digs
Alt. 650ft (198m)

Opposite Ladyside Wood and Brook, 100 yards down valley from Ladyside Pot. 50-100ft (15-30m) above river level.

Several ancient sinks, now used (or have been used) as badger holes. Possible digs.

MILL CAVE AND POT   NGR 0965 5609   Grade I (Arch)
Alt.680ft (207m)   Length: 40ft (12m)   Depth: 25ft (8m)

On east bank of river 150 yards (137m) south of Wetton Mill, about 100ft (30m) above river level.

Two small entrances close together. First is to cave with large fallen roof block. Beyond is pot with 21ft (6m) ladder pitch into passage apparently leading behind cave but choked. Some stalactite formations. Various domestic animal remains as well as human remains and Middle – Late Bronze Age pottery.

Reference: Ryder, Longworth, & Gunstone. 1971. N. Staffs. Jour. Field Studies, Vol.11.

MOONMILK POT   NGR 0971 5603   Grade I
Alt. 635ft (194m)   Length: 40ft (12m)   Depth: 20ft (6m)

In gully above Darfar Pot.

A 10ft (3m) oil drum shaft leads via awkward squeeze to chamber with choked sump in floor at river level.

References: Johnson, S. 1980. T.V.C.G. Review. p.18-20. Survey. Milner M. 1981. D.C.A. N/L No. 48. p.1. Survey.

NAN TOR CAVE   NGR 0953 5615   Grade I (Arch)
(Wetton Mill Rock Shelter)
Alt. 640ft (192m)   Length: 115ft (35m)

Permit required from National Trust.

Just north of Wetton Mill Farm.

A limestone hummock riddled with holes from which one can emerge in the most unexpected places. A fossil swallow hole, probably once connected to small cave above Wetton Mill Sink.

Rock shelter on north side was excavated to reveal a late glacial to Iron Age sequence.

References: Kelly, J.H. 1976. Stoke Museum Publication. Warwick, G.T. 1953. Proc. 1st Int. Spel. Congr., Paris. Tome 2. pp.1-10.

OLD HANNAH'S HOLE   NGR 1002 5575   Grade I (Arch)
Alt. 800ft (244m)   Length: 45ft (14m)

On the west side of Redhurst Gorge, south of Wetton Mill.

A fissure entrance 10ft (3m) high and narrowing. Supposed natural explosions took place here and at Darfar Ridge Cave. Human remains excavated in 1896 are in the Hanley Museum, Staffs.

References: Bramwell, D. 1950. Trans. C.R.G. Vol.1. No.4. pp.47-52. Wardle, T. 1899. Trans. N. Staffs. Field Club. No.33. pp.97 & 105.

OSSUM'S CRAG CAVE   NGR 0958 5576   Grade I (Arch)
(Yellersley Tor Cave. Ossom Crag Cave)
Alt. 700ft (213m)   Length: 60ft (18m)

100ft (30m) up on the west side of the Manifold above Darfar Road bridge at the foot of a crag.

A fine phreatic passage soon becomes low and leads to a pool. Through this leads via a muddy rising passage to a hading rift. A small passage on the right is the continuation of the entrance passage, and has been dug for 7ft (2m). Fill blocks the way on, and spoil removal is a problem.

Late Palaeolithic remains found.

References: Bramwell, D. 1954. P.A.S. N/L No.11. pp.5-7. Bramwell, D. 1955. P.A.S. N/L No.12. pp.13-16. Bramwell, D. 1956. P.A.S. N/L No.13. pp.7-9. Bramwell, D. 1957. Lyre No.2. pp.20-22. Survey. Warwick, G.T. 1953. Proc. 1st. Int. Congr. Spel. Paris. Tome II. pp.1-10.

OSSUM'S CRAG FISSURE   NGR 0960 5575   Dig
Alt. 700ft (214m)   Length: 10ft (3m)   Depth: 10ft (3m)

In Ossom's Crag.

Narrow waterworn passage has been dug to a corner which needs enlarging.

Reference: Trent Valley Cave Exploration Group N/L.

OSSUM'S EYRIE CAVE ARCH   NGR 0960 5573   Arch
(Ossoms Eyrie. Ossums Eyrie Cave)
Alt. 780ft (234m)

In the face of Ossoms Crag.

A small archaeological bone cave discovered by P.A.S. in 1956. Noted for bird remains.

References: Bramwell, D. 1956. P.A.S. N/L No.13. pp.10-11. Bramwell, D. 1957. P.A.S. N/L No.14. pp.8-15. Bramwell, D. 1958. P.A.S. N/L No.15. p.8. Gee, S. 1956. P.A.S. N/L No.13. p.11.

PIKE LOW SWALLETS   NGR 0850 5150   Digs
Alt. 775ft (236m)

In field just west of Pike Low overlooking Bredon Brook.

Two small choked swallets taking drainage from shales. An attempt to trace the more southerly of these to Ilam Risings in 1988 proved inconclusive.

Reference: Mellors, P.T. 1989. D.C.A. N/L No.71. pp.3-9.

PLUGHOLE   NGR 0973 5525   Dig
Alt. 500ft (152m)

A mud filled joint in the bed of the River Manifold.

Digging caused the river to be engulfed in a large whirlpool during high flow.

PRITCHARD'S CAVE   NGR 1058 5407   Grade I
Alt. 630ft (192m)   Length: 60ft (18m)

A low entrance amongst brambles.

Entrance leads to two parallel joint passages which soon end after 60ft (18m) although digging may be possible.

References: O.C.C. N/L Vol.13. No.6. Phipps, M. 1981. The Lyre No.5. p.48. Survey. Wilson, H. 1926. Some Caves and Crags of Peakland. pp.35 & 55-58.

PROJECT POT   NGR 0969 5531   Grade I (Dig)
Alt. 500ft (152m)   Length: 70ft (21m)   Depth: 12ft (4m)

In middle of bed of River Manifold. Draughts strongly.

Entrance (with grille over – please replace) is a 10ft (3m) climb down. At bottom 2 ways on. Left leads to a very narrow rift. Right leads to an enlarged section ending in a bedding plane which is currently too tight for further progress. This is approx 45ft (14m) from West Passage in T-Pot.

Lowest sections sump in flood. Water originates from Redhurst Swallet via Wednesday Pot and T-Pot.

References: Milner, M. 1984. The Manifold Caver. p.16. Milner, M. 1985. D.C.A. N/L No.60. pp.8-9.

RABBITS HOLE   NGR 0906 5686   Grade II (Dig)
Alt. 670ft (204m)   Length: 150ft (46m)

Low entrance 10ft (3m) above the left side of the road.

Discovered 1979 by T.V.C.E.G. The entrance chamber leads up dip for 30ft (9m) to a tight squeeze through boulders into a small chamber. A low passage straight on leads after 10ft (3m) to a tight sloping squeeze down on the left. At the bottom a short passage leads to another, tighter squeeze, the Supermangle, which needs helmet and battery off to pass. Beyond a larger muddy chamber 10ft (3m) round is gained with low passages off which draught. Currently occupied by badgers.

References: Milner, M. 1980. D.C.A. N/L No.43. p.1. Milner, M. 1983. The Manifold Caver. pp.33-34.

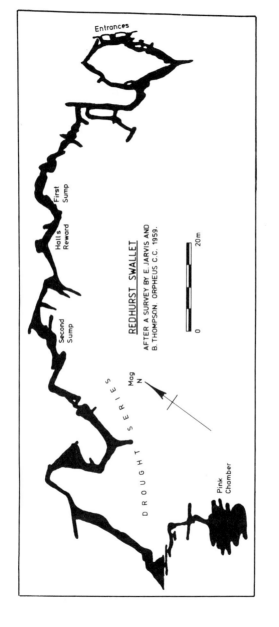

Entrances

First
Sump

Hall's
Reward

Second
Sump

D R O U G H T   S E R I E S

Mag
N

Pink
Chamber

REDHURST SWALLET

AFTER A SURVEY BY E. JARVIS AND
B. THOMPSON. ORPHEUS C.C. 1959.

20m

0

RADCLIFFE STABLES   NGR 0977 5498   Grade I
Alt. 570ft (174m)   Length: 50ft (15m)

Two small caves directly below Thor's Cave, some 30ft (9m) above the river.
  Name is applied either to the more southerly or both of the caves.
  Once used by a refugee from the Jacobite rebellion.

REDHURST SWALLET   NGR 0967 5570   Grade IV
Alt. 610ft (186m)   Length: 900ft (274m)

Warning: The first major swallet downstream of Wetton Mill, and therefore extremely liable to flooding. One hour's respite only. The cave between the Knifedge and Sump 4 floods very easily, with Sumps 2 & 3 rising BEFORE the others. Do not get cut off! Only go beyond Sump 1 in dry settled weather.

A number of small entrances on the south side of the river ¼ mile (400m) upstream of Redhurst Bridge. Only one entrance is open, and is covered by a metal grid (please replace).

Just inside the entrance, right leads back towards the crag, with a narrow climb down to Puke Sump (which dries up in summer) on the left. Back at the entrance, left soon enlarges to walking size, and after a sharp right hand bend a climb down (The Knifedge) leads to Sump 1. A passage to the right of this can be followed back to the other side of Puke Sump.

Sump 1 drains in summer and leads to a high narrow rift with the passage continuing at the far end, and soon reaching Sump 2. Halfway along the rift on the left is Shredder Passage. which is tight and nasty for 80ft (24m) to a 13ft (4m) pitch with a sump at the bottom.

Sump 2, passed by siphoning in 1959, drains in summer, and Sump 3 followed within a few feet. Sump 3 never drains, but an airspace may be present in a dry summer, when it is a short duck. Beyond, the passage rises to a large section with stal deposits in the roof. A tight rift on the left leads to Sump 4a, which is 7ft (2m) deep but too tight. Straight on is a slope down to Sump 4 (Bullyhead Sump), which has been dived for 7ft (2m) to a tight bedding.

A 20ft (6m) climb up to the right leads to Drought Series. A wide bedding passage leads via a Z-bend to a slope down for 40ft (12m). A sandy floored passage is then followed to a steeply rising sandy slope. At the top left soon gets too low, but a crawl under flakes reveals a short larger section. From here turn right and through a low archway to a rift. Left and then right leads to a larger section with many rifts leading off.

Pink Chamber can be reached by going up the slope to the right of the deep muddy rift in the floor, and after crossing over it a crawl leads to a muddy slope on the right into Pink Chamber, 20ft (6m) wide and up to 50ft (15m) high, approaching the surface.

References: Jarvis, E. 1965. The Lyre No.4. pp.28-35 & 38. Survey. Milner, M. 1984. The Manifold Caver. pp.21-23. Milner, M. 1985. D.C.A. N/L No.60. pp.9-10 & 1987 No.64. p.14. Potts, J. 1981. The Lyre No.5. pp.36-36.

REDHURST UPPER CAVE NGR 0967 5569 Grade I (Dig)
Alt. 670ft (193m)   Length: 20ft (6m)

On the crag top directly above the entrance to Redhurst Swallet.

Discovered by T.V.C.E.G. in 1986. A large mud-filled phreatic tube 20ft (6m) long. Could be dug further.

RIBDEN SWALLETS   NGR 075 471
Alt. 1000ft (305m)

SWALLET NO.1   **Dig**
In a depression near the road in a private garden. The main swallet. There is no obvious entrance but water sinks among boulders.

SWALLET NO.2   **Depth: 243ft (74m)**   **Grade IV (Mine)**
Across the road from (1) to the east. A large open mine shaft with a wall round it. Permission required from Ribden Farm.

Fine free hanging descent for 169ft (51.5m) to land on rubbish. A mined level leads off 5ft (1.5m) from the bottom, immediately breaking into natural passage, and forks.

Right via a short crawl to the high Fourways Aven. Ahead from here leads to a choke through which the stream enters. Climb on left via tight squeeze to a junction. Right leads to the same choke: left is too tight. Right from Fourways Aven leads to Manimal Passage, which splits into several silted tubes.

Back at the fork, left opens into walking sized passage scattered with refuse. A steep muddy ramp descends past deep holes in the floor to a rock bridge, the head of the second pitch, 21ft (6.5m) deep, landing in the large Chernobyl Chamber. A steeply descending tube leads shortly to a sump.

Water backs up into the entrance shaft in wet weather. The shaft is still being filled with rubbish.

Tackle:

Entrance Pitch:	170ft (52m) ladder; 180ft (55m) lifeline.
SRT:	180ft (55m) rope for free hanging descent.
Slope above	
Chernobyl Chamber:	33ft (10m) handline.
Chernobyl Chamber:	25ft (8m) ladder; 30ft (9m) lifeline.

SWALLET NO.3   **Dig**
In the fields adjacent to the farm about 100 yards (91m) to the south of (1). A group of shakeholes. No obvious entrances, although five of them have been seen to take water in wet weather.

The water from the swallets reappears at the foot of the Weaver Hills at 092 461, some 250ft (76m) lower in altitude.

References: Gill, D.I. 1966. E.P.C. Jour. Vol.7. No.1. pp.68-72. Survey. Robey. J.A. & Porter, L. 1971. Bull. P.D.M.H.S. Vol.4. No.6. pp.417-428. Survey. Robey, J.A. & Porter, L. 1972. Bull. P.D.M.H.S. Vol.5. No.1. pp.14-30. Survey. Tucker, S.J. 1987. D.C.A. N/L No.65. pp.6-9. Survey.

RIVERSIDE SINK   NGR 0970 5600   Grade II
(Riverside Swallet)
Alt. 610ft (186m)   Length: 150ft (46m)   Depth: 50ft (15m)
Warning: The lower areas near the end are very unstable.
50ft (15m) downstream of Wetton Mill Sink.

Oil drum entrance shaft (Grille over – please replace) 10ft (3m) deep leads to a steep clamber down a phreatic passage with water entering from the roof in many places. At bottom, right leads up slope for several metres before becoming too tight. On the left a squeeze down leads to an enlargement with a mud sump in one corner. Left of the squeeze over a mud bank enters a continuation. Straight on part of the river enters down a slope on the left and runs away through the boulders towards Darfar Pot. Right is a tight squeeze into another small muddy continuation where the water is last seen. The water reappears in Prospect Chamber in Darfar Pot.

References: Milner, M. 1984. D.C.A. N/L No.56, p.13. Milner, M. 1984. The Manifold Caver. pp.25-26. Survey. Potts, J. 1975. O.C.C. N/L Vol.11. No.9. p.43.

ST. BERTRAM'S CAVE NGR 1066 5407 Grade II (Arch)
Alt. 600ft (183m)   Length: 700ft (213m)

On the north bank of the River Manifold, opposite Beeston Tor Farm.

Two obvious entrances. The left hand one involves a short climb into a short blind joint passage. The right hand and larger entrance, formerly furnished with a door, leads to a small network of old phreatic passages, including a climb into the lofty Skull Rift (rope useful) and crawls into the "Cellars". An exit from the cave can be made by climbing a 30ft (9m) high rift, to emerge via a squeeze through the window higher in the cliff face, known as Jackdaw's Cave, or St.Bertram's Chimney. Archaeological excavations revealed evidence of occupation, including a hoard of Saxon coins. Remains in Buxton Museum, and British Museum London.

References: Amatt, S. 1975. D.C.A. N/L No.24. pp.7-8. Survey (grade 1). Amatt, S.N. 1981. The Lyre No.5. p.49. Survey. Holmes, F.A. 1909. Climbers Club Journal No.44. (Reprinted in P.A.S. N/L No.8. pp.10-12). Wilson, G.H. 1926. Some Caves and Crags of Peakland. pp.38-47. Wilson, G.H. 1934. Cave Hunting Holidays in Peakland. pp.47-56.

SALLYMOOR SWALLETS   NGR 08 46   Digs
Alt. 850-950ft (259-290m)

To the west and northwest of Kevin Quarry, below the main limestone escarpment of Wredon.

Several small intermittent swallets, all choked. Resurgences not known.

References: Beasley, F. 1975. D.C.A. N/L No.24. pp.2-4. Mellors, P.T. 1973. D.C.A. N/L No.18. p.2.

SEVEN WAYS CAVE   NGR 0982 5490   Grade I (Arch)
Alt. 900ft (274m)

On back of hill containing Thor's Cave, close to Elderbush Cave.

A short series of passages with seven branches or entrances. Dug archaeologically.

References: Anon. 1952. P.A.S. N/L No.8. pp.4-5. Bramwell, D. 1952. P.A.S. N/L No.8. pp.6-8, & No.10. pp.6-7.

SNOW HOLE

NGR 0965 5536

Dig

(Station Sinks)

Alt. 550ft (168m) | **Length: 15ft (4.5m)** | **Depth: 15ft (4.5m)**

On right hand bend in River Manifold below Ossom's Crag.

A series of sinks in fissures. One was dug to a depth of 15ft (4.5m) in a narrow joint where water could be heard ahead. Also dug horizontally for 10ft (3m) to narrower part under concrete in river bed.

References: Amatt, S. 1981. The Lyre No.5. p.48. Milner, M. 1983. The Manifold Caver. p.29. Warwick, G.T. 1953. lst Congr. Int. Speleo. Paris, Vol.2. Sect.1. pp.59-68.

T POT

NGR 0966 5538

Grade V

Alt. 585ft (178m) | **Length: 660ft (201m)** | **Depth: 25ft (8m)**

Warning: The entrance passage is awkward and tiring. The whole cave can flood to the roof. Do not descend in unsettled weather, or when the river is sinking downstream of the stone bridge near Redhust Swallet.

Entrance lies in bed of River Manifold on the right of the main stream channel, approximately 30ft (9m) downstream of Kyles Folly. Filter gate over. Please replace.

Tight, inclined bedding entrance. At bottom, right (downstream) is an awkward squeeze (head first) into continuing passage. Follow via upward sloping bedding to a squeeze down to a pool. Over this leads quickly to main passage. Left, East Passage, is walking size for 22ft (7m) to boulders. Straight on through the boulders is small phreatic tube which has been pushed for 60ft (18m). Left at the boulders leads after 12ft (4m) to narrowing rift with way on through flakes to the right. Beyond this slide over the mud slope to the left to regain larger passage. Beyond the mud slope is a confusing series of draughting joint-controlled passage which have so far been pushed for 150ft (46m) and are heading under the hill towards Wetton.

Back at the junction with the entrance passage, turning right is West Passage. Stooping for 20ft (6m) leads to larger section 10ft (3m) high and up to 15ft (5m) wide. On the left here is a short passage to a muddy pool, but straight on is a step down to 30ft (10m) of clean walking-sized passage. After a squeeze onto a ledge a wide muddy bedding passage continues for another 100ft (30m) towards Project Pot, gradually getting too low. Route finding is made difficult by silt banks and large flakes of chert.

References: Milner, M. 1983. T Pot. The Manifold Caver. pp.19-22. Survey. Milner, M. 1984. The Manifold Caver pp.16-17. Survey. Milner, M. 1981. D.C.A. N/L No.48. pp.2-3.

THOR'S CAVE

NGR 0986 5496

Grade I (Arch)

(Thyrsis's Cavern)

Alt. 870ft (265m) | **Length: 150ft (46m)**

Very obvious entrance in prominent crag south west of Wetton.

A large chamber, archaeologically excavated. Daylight penetrates most of it from the "West Window".

References: Bramwell, D. 1950. Trans. C.R.G. Vol.1. No.4. pp.47-52. Brown, E. 1865. Trans Midland Scientific Assoc. pp.1,19, & 70. Survey.

Carrington. 1866. The Reliquary Vol.6. pp.201-212. Dawkins, W.B. 1874. Cave Hunting. pp.127-129. Heath, T. 1882. Derbys. Arch. Jour. Vol.4. p.165. Warwick, G.T. 1947. P.A.S. N/L No.1. pp.4-5.

THOR'S FISSURE CAVERN
NGR 0985 5496   Grade I (Arch)
(Fissure Cave)
Alt. 850ft (259m)   Length: 60ft (18m)

Below and to the south of Thor's Cave West Window.

A fissure cave which has been archaeologically excavated. Late Palaeolithic to Roman sequence found.

References: Bramwell, D. 1974. Archaeology in the Peak District. Bramwell, D. 1950. Trans C.R.G. Vol.1. No.4. pp.47-52. Wilson, G.H. 1934. Cave Hunting Holidays in Peakland. pp.13-46. Wilson, G.H. 1937. B.S.A. Caves & Caving No.2. pp.61-69. Survey.

THOR'S FOX HOLE   NGR 1012 5372   Grade I
Alt. 870ft (265m)   Length: 60ft (18m)

Small cave entrance in base of 6ft (2m) cliff on south side of Wetton Valley in hill that contains Thor's Cave. Entrance faces road from Wetton Mill as it turns to face Thor's Cave.

A small phreatic cave entered by O.C.C. in 1976. Became impossible to push due to the smell (occupied by foxes).

THOR'S SINKS   NGR 0974 5500   Digs
Alt. 710ft (216m)

Several sinks in joints in the side and centre of the bed of the River Manifold below Thor's Cave between Donkey Hole and Radcliffe's Stables. Mostly filled with concrete and iron pipes. Some of the concrete has been removed, and water continues to sink.

WATERWAYS SWALLET   NGR 1260 4917   Grade III
(Waterings Swallet)
Alt. 935ft (285m)   Length: 500ft (152m)   Depth: 130ft (40m)

Warning: After prolonged heavy rain or rapid snowmelt, the stream overflows into the cave. Entrance Series and parts of Top Passage become impassable. Take care.

Entrance under iron lid inside fenced area at end of blind valley 200ft (60m) beyond present stream sink. Park in gated area just up the road on the opposite side to Waterings Farm. Use stile opposite the farm drive to reach the cave.

Entrance is short drop among boulders. Steeply sloping gap through boulder pile soon leads to sharp dogleg bend, and route then follows one solid wall down-dip to brink of climb down into first small chamber. A succession of short climbs and scrambles followed by a crawl across a steeply inclined bedding plane leads to a hole in the roof. This soon gives access to a descent into the large Main Chamber, 20ft (6m) square and boulder-strewn.

From Main Chamber a number of passages lead off. Ahead, hidden behind a fallen block, is 30ft (9m) pitch to large impressive sloping passage (The Gallery). To the right is Rift Passage, which can be followed by climbing down ledges. This is usual route to reach far end of The Gallery. Small slot on right next to Rift Passage rejoins main route via a choice of two dry waterfalls (Swirl Passage). Obvious opening above Rift Passage leads to tight and arduous uphill inlet route between boulders (Top Passage) which crosses over entrance series and ends at Omega Aven close to surface.

The Gallery is scene of a number of digs attempting to bypass massive terminal boulder collapse which underlies large shakehole seen on the surface near the cave entrance. Longest dig is via obvious inclined stooping passage which soon becomes flat out crawl past and under boulders jammed against solid left wall and into tight bedding plane.

The stream has been traced to Hinkley Wood Risings at Ilam.

References: Anon. 1974. O.C.C. N/L Vol.10. No.4. p.32. Drakeley, K. 1981. The Lyre No.5. pp.54-56. Mayer, D. 1962. British Caver No.36. p.48. Milner, M. 1987. D.C.A. N/L No.65. p.17. Potts, J. 1981. The Lyre No.5. pp.36-37. Potts, J. 1981. The Lyre No.5. pp.50-53. Survey. Potts, J. 1981. O.C.C. N/L Vol.10. No.6. p.49.

WEAG'S BRIDGE CAVE   NGR 100 540   Grade I
Alt. 540ft (165m)

100 yards (91m) downstream from the bridge, by the track.
    A small rift cave.

WEAGS BRIDGE RESURGENCE NGR 0995 5446 Grade I
Alt. 540ft (165m)   Length: 60ft (18m)

In the north bank of the River Manifold.
    A tight crawl for 60ft (18m). Acts as either a sink or a resurgence depending on river flow conditions.
    References: Allwright, P. 1976. O.C.C. N/L Vol. 12. No.5. pp.18-19. Survey.

WEAVER HILLS SPRING   NGR 093 461   Dig

A very small rising. The source of the Hudford Brook, which drains southwards to the River Churnet.
    Reference: Beasley, F. 1975. D.C.A. N/L No.24.

WEDNESDAY POT   NGR 0967 5544   Grade III
Length: 150ft (46m)   Depth: 15ft (5m)

Warning: The cave can quickly flood to the roof. Do not descend if the river is sinking below the stone bridge near Redhurst Swallet.

In right hand side of river bed under trees. Filter gate over – please replace.
    10ft (3m) climb down entrance rift leads to 2 ways on. Down and left is the upstream passage, 20ft (6m) of crawling becoming tight. A drop can be seen, but entry is not yet possible.

Right at the bottom of the entrance shaft is a squeeze along a bedding into larger downstream passage averaging 4ft (1.3m) wide and 3ft (1m) high. Follow to a pool and crawl through to larger section with perched sump on right. Passage can be followed for some distance until it gets too low approaching T-Pot (qv). Sometimes a stream is active along the whole downstream passage, its source being the perched sump.

The river can be heard roaring below the known cave under certain conditions, and when flooded has been traced to Redhurst Swallet. It flows to Project Pot via T-Pot.

References: The Manifold Caver 1984. p.19. Survey. The Manifold Caver 1983. p.23. Survey.

WETSTONES SWALLET   NGR 0985 4710   Grade II
Alt. 1060ft (323m)   Length: 20ft (6m)

In the plantation between Walk and Weaver Farms.

A small stream, fed from meres, sinks at the foot of a low crag. Digging has uncovered a short length of cave from the back of which it is possible to climb up into a loose roof area or down into a choked pot. Water has been traced to Ilam.

The crag bears traces of old flowstone and embedded pebbles, and cavity behind overhang at one end contains remains of old stalactites.

Reference: Mellors, P.T. 1973. D.C.A. N/L No.18. p.2. Mellors, P.T. 1989. D.C.A. N/L No.71. pp.2-9.

WETTON MILL HILL CAVE   NGR 102 562   Grade I
Alt. 900ft (274m)

In crag at top of west side of Wetton Hill near two isolated thorn trees.

A short muddy fissure passage.

WETTON MILL SINK   NGR 0970 5603   Dig
Alt. 610ft (186m)

500ft (152m) downstream from Wetton Mill Bridge.

A large volume of water, the entire river in dry weather, is engulfed by the river bed. Digging over many years has confirmed that the site is a huge boulder choke. Water can be heard roaring below. The nearby Darfar Pot (qv) has by-passed this choke, and meets the river underground. In wet weather the river overflows to sink at Redhurst Swallet, and progressively further downstream.

WETTON ROAD SINKS   NGR 0991 5562   Digs
Alt. 595ft (181m)

Just below road from Wetton Mill to Wetton Village, in river bed, 100 yards (91m) downstream from Redhurst Bridge where the road starts to rise (on bend) to leave river level.

A large hollow in river bed that has been completely concreted up and contains iron pipes to relieve pressure arising during flooding of the cave beneath. Some fissures have been dug, and the roar of water can be heard under certain conditions. All are too narrow for further progress.

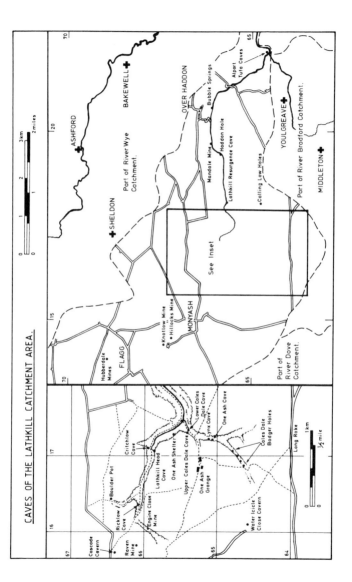

CAVES OF THE LATHKILL CATCHMENT AREA.

THE RIVER LATHKILL
CATCHMENT AREA

The Lathkill area has always been rather frustrating to cavers, for the most extensive caves are only accessible in drought. However, small fragments of abandoned high level cave such as Water Icicle give food for thought, and suggest the existence of an extensive high level network.

Lathkill Dale drains the structural basin centred on Monyash, and the risings from Lathkill Head Cave down to Cales Dale owe their position to a saddle-like structure on the eastern rim of the basin. Lavas outcrop in the valley floor further to the east, and this would keep the drainage on the surface were it not for the soughs which capture it in dry conditions.

There are no large allogenic sinks in the Monyash area, but a few small trickles which accumulate above the lavas do sink round the edge of the outcrop.

Lathkill Head Cave and Lower Cales Dale Cave are the most extensive systems. Both discharge a large volume of water in flood, and both are flooded after a short distance in all but very dry weather. Prospects for extension are good in both cases. At the limit of Lathkill Head Cave, long considered to be unpushable, a way was found through the choke in 1990 to enter a very large continuation which soon needed more digging. In the same year, the length of Lower Cales Dale Cave nearly doubled, and there is still a very powerful draught at the farthest limit.

Opposite Lathkill Head Cave lies Critchlow Cave, more frequently accessible, and pushed to a draughting choke after a gruelling crawl for some 2000ft (610m). Here again, determined pushing would undoubtedly reveal more cave, although we may end up with the longest flat out crawl in the world! Critchlow Cave can also discharge a large stream in very severe floods, suggesting a connection with the main drainage system somewhere far to the west.

The only other connection with the main drainage is in the Knotlow Mine, north west of Monyash. Here the miners have intersected natural tubes carrying a large stream which disappears into a very deep sump, and is thought to reappear at Lathkill Head Cave.

Careful investigation of other mines in the area, and some determined digging, may well reveal extensive (and large) vadose passages to the west of the known system. There is also the chance of superbly decorated high level cave associated with the Water Icicle tube network.

ALPORT TUFA CAVES   NGR 221 646   Grade I
Alt. 450ft (137m)   **Length: 20ft (6m)**
Alport by Youlgreave. Situated immediately north of the road.

A unique series of small rock shelter type caves in late Pleistocene tufa. Variously used as hen houses and cart park, but potentially of archaeological interest. One cave partly collapsed after 1963 frosts exposing moonmilk in cavities in tufa.

BOULDER POT NGR 164 665 Grade II
Alt. 875ft (267m)   **Length: 120ft (37m)**   **Depth: 110ft (34m)**

On left of track to Ricklow Quarry from Bakewell-Monyash road, among large boulders.

Narrow entrance leads to small bone chamber and a further descent to crawls. Very tight fissure allows slim cavers to reach bottom of pot. Entrance corked with boulders for safety – don't get shut in! Whole place is unstable.

BUBBLE SPRINGS NGR 206 661 Springs
Alt. 605ft (185m)

In the bed of the River Lathkill, close to the tail of Lathkill Dale Sough.

Water rises from beneath tufa in the bed of the Lathkill, above toadstone.

CALES DALE BADGER HOLES
NGR 167 646 – 172 648 Digs
Alt. 900-1000ft (270-300m)

On both sides of the south west branch of Cales Dale.

Five or six small badger holes, some large enough to enter. Require digging.

CALES DALE CAVE (Lower) NGR 174 654 Grade II-V
Alt. 675ft (206m)   **Length: 3460ft (1055m)**

Two low entrances below the footpath up Cales Dale, a short distance from the confluence with Lathkill Dale.

Warning: Almost the whole cave floods to the roof in wet weather, and beyond Figures of Eight chamber in all but drought. Trips to the end are extremely arduous.

Extended 1971 by P.T.Mellors and Eldon Pothole Club, and in 1976 and 1990 by the Technical Speleological Group.

Two entrances unite inside. Low phreatic passage for 125ft (38m) to the First Chamber. On the right the floor rises to Stalactite Chamber with closed avens above and 50ft (15m) of passage, blocked at the end. To the left of the First Chamber the passage can be followed for 40ft (12m) to the Second Chamber. A 40ft (12m) crawl on the right leads to the Rathole, dug through loose boulders in 1971 to a large chamber, the Dog House. A 32ft (10m) climb up the far wall leads to a junction after 25ft (8m). Passages to left and right are both blocked after 20ft (6m).

A crawl at floor level in the Dog House draughts strongly, and is being dug to by-pass the sump (September 1990).

From the Second Chamber 70ft (21m) of muddy passage can be followed to Figures of Eight Chamber, which is as far as can be explored in normal weather.

Beyond the Sump   **Grade III-V**

A tight descending squeeze to the left at the start of Figures of Eight Chamber leads to where the sump is normally met. Sump was first passed in 1959 drought, and a boulder choke is said to have been met after 60ft (18m). The sump was again passed in the 1976 drought. 100ft (30m) of glutinous muddy passage leads to a crawl on the right, but straight on the passage can be followed through a boulder choke for a further 180ft (55m) to where the way on is blocked, but draughts.

The arduous crawl on the right, "Armoured Mudball Crawl" leads to a small blind aven on the left after 130ft (40m). The crawl continues for a further 180ft (55m) to an aven 26ft (8m) long and about 40ft (12m) high. A crawl at the top may be the other end of the dig in the Dog House. Beyond the aven a further 100ft (30m) of muddy crawling arrives at a low wide bedding plane on the right, too low to enter, the outlet for the stream. Friday the Thirteenth Passage continues as a hands and knees crawl over a gravel floor to a T-junction after 525ft (160m). Right is blocked with clay immediately while left can be followed for 65ft (20m) to a boulder choke, which was passed in the 1990 drought.

A squeeze leads up into an aven. Two possible leads high in the aven are unpushed. A further squeeze down through boulders rejoins the main passage, Thursday the Thirteenth Passage, which continues for 330ft (100m) to a junction. The crawl on the right is thought to be the other end of Dawkes' Crawl in Lathkill Head Cave. It can be followed for 220ft (67m) to a junction. Left is silted while right ends after 20ft (6m) at a draughting choke.

Main passage continues for 155ft (47m) to a squeeze through boulders below a chamber. Another 155ft (47m) leads past more unpushed avens and inlets to a further choke. A very awkward upward squeeze leads into a chamber, and a climb down rejoins the main passage.

The passage soon becomes walking sized for the first time. 265ft (81m) beyond the chamber a further choke is met. Two parallel rifts immediately before the choke lead up through loose boulders into a low bedding plane which becomes too low for progress in all directions. A crawl on the right 120ft (37m) before the choke has been pushed to a junction. The left hand branch is unsurveyed, but the right branch, the Fallopian Tube, leads to a choke in a rift 560ft (171m) from the main passage.

References: Butcher, N.J.D. 1985. Jour. T.S.G. No.11. 1985. p.23 Coates, P. & Wicken, F. 1956. The Speleologist Vol.1. No.4. Survey. Gill, D.W. 1972. D.C.A. N/L No.12. p.3. Gill, D.W. 1977. Descent No. 35. p.8. Gill, D.W. 1976. D.C.A. N/L No.30. pp.10-12. Westlake, C.D. 1972. Eldon P.C. Journal Vol.8. No.1. pp.31-33. Survey.

CALES DALE CAVE (Upper)
NGR 1730 6544   Grade I (Arch)
(Churn Hole)
Alt. 775ft (232m)   Length: 200ft (60m)

Above and to the left of Lower Calesdale Cave on a shelf at the base of a small crag high on the west side of the dale.

There has been considerable confusion between this cave and One Ash

Cave, One Ash Shelter, and Lynx Cave, all at about the same altitude and given different names by cavers and archaeologists.

A stooping passage divides after 75ft (23m). Left is a blocked crawl, while right is a crawl terminating in a low clay-filled passage. The right hand passage may connect to a low clay-filled entrance on a shelf to the right of the main entrance.

Excavated material includes Iron Age and Roman pottery and animal remains, now in the Manchester Museum.

References: Coates, P. & Wicken, F. 1956. The Speleologist No.4. pp.174-175. Jackson, J.W. & Storrs Fox, W. 1913. Geol. Mag. Vol.60. pp.259-262. Pennington, R. 1875. Quart. Jour. Geol. Soc. Vol.31. pp.238-240.

CALES DALE NEW CAVE   NGR 1736 6538   Grade II
Alt. 670ft (204m)   Length: 65ft (20m)

A bedding crawl almost opposite Lower Cales Dale Cave entrance. Excavated in 1982 by O.C.C. but became too low for progress.

Reference: Morton, K. 1984. D.C.A. N/L No.56. p.2.

CALLING LOW HOLES   NGR 181 648   Digs
(Callenge Low Holes)
Alt. 1025ft (312m)

Situated east of the head of Cales Dale south of the farm.

A group of large shakeholes. One leads to a partially collapsed chamber, with small inlets and a rubble floor, said to have been dug out some years ago. Now partly filled in.

A small un-named cave lies nearby in the field overlooking the head of Cales Dale. A stooping entrance soon reduces to a tight crawl.

References: Farey, J. 1811. A general view of the Agriculture and Minerals of Derbyshire. Vol.1. (London). p.293. Mellors, P.T. 1971. D.C.A. N/L No.10. pp.2-3.

CASCADE CAVERN   NGR 158 664   Grade II
(Rumbling Hole)
Alt. 820ft (250m)   Length: 125ft (41m)   Depth: 60ft (18m)

Entrance shaft lies on south flank of Lathkill Dale, close to the Monyash-Bakewell road. It has been wrongly referred to as Eagle Mine, which lies at 158 661. It is likely to be Eagle Mine whose alternative name was Rumbling Hole.

Permission from Mr Mycock, Rowson House Farm, Monyash.

A wide mineshaft 40ft (12m) deep leads to a short passage. A further 15ft (5m) pitch (rotten wooden ladder to be avoided) drops into natural passage 100ft (30m) long with two waterfalls. Stream disappears into choked swallet. Natural phreatic clay filled passage has been dug by D.C.C. The cavern is said to have once connected to Knotlow Caverns.

Tackle:

Entrance Pitch:	40ft (12m) ladder; 50ft (15m) lifeline.
Second Pitch:	20ft (6m) handline.

Reference: Gee, S. 1957. The Lyre, Vol.1. No.2.

CRITCHLOW CAVE   NGR 1710 6593   Grade IV
Alt. 680ft (204m)   Length: 2000ft (610m) approx

Inside the Lathkill Dale Nature Reserve, which is managed by the Nature Conservancy Council. Evidence of membership of a club with NCA affiliation may be asked for by the wardens. Agreement with NCC forbids the use of carbide.

Directly opposite Lathkill Head Cave, but higher up the bank, by a lone bush.

Warning: The whole cave can fill to the roof in flood, and a stream can flow from the entrance. The cave often sumps in wet winter months at Eccles' Limit, cutting off the draught. A trip to the far end is an arduous undertaking even in dry conditions, and rescue would be extremely difficult.

Downward sloping entrance crawl (excavated by B.S.A. in 1947) for 20ft (6m) then sharp left turn through unpleasant muddy duck, and right turn with squeeze into Warren Chamber. Right hand crawl ahead leads through narrow channel with pools to a further chamber containing muddy flowstone. Continuing crawl develops into wide low bedding cave which veers to right (avoid obvious earlier right turn which is blind), through two small grottoes and over a gravelly floor to a fallen block. Squeeze down under the block (occasionally gravel-choked) into a wide low descending phreatic passage with gravel and stal floor and good formations. Branch to left at end after crawl through pool levels out but is muddy, and marks the limit of exploration by Eccles Caving Club in 1963.

From Eccles' limit the way on is a squeeze into a tight and awkward section with extensive breakdown. Wide low easier passage is regained beyond. A further 1500ft (457m) (Critchlow 2) was discovered in 1984. It is mostly crawling, but has some fine formations, and leads to the final chambers. One of these contains a mud slope from the roof. A low arch at the foot of this emerges into a boulder collapse area, with glimpses through boulders of a roof above. A strong draught blows through the boulders, and can be felt throughout the cave.

References: Beck, J., Gill, D., & Butcher, N. 1980 & 1984. Critchlow Cave survey. Eccles Caving Club. 1963. D.C.A. N/L No.8. Mellors, P.T. 1985. D.C.A. N/L No.57. pp.2-3.

EAGLE MINE   NGR 158 661   Dig (Mine)

A blocked mineshaft which has been confused with Cascade Cavern.

ENGINE CLOSE MINE   NGR 1605 6596   Grade II
Alt. 825ft (251m)   Length: 150ft (46m)   Depth: 30ft (9m)

In Ferndale, a south branch of Lathkill Dale.

A 10ft entrance shaft leads to a short level, with a blocked way out to the valley side. A 20ft pitch leads to a lower level 100ft long. Small natural solution cavities.

Tackle:

Entrance Pitch:	10ft (3m) ladder; 15ft (4.5m) lifeline.
2nd Pitch:	20ft (6m) ladder; 30ft (9m) lifeline.

Reference: George, T. 1989. Descent No.86. p.14.

FREEZELAND MINE   NGR 1608 6594   Grade II
Alt. 840ft (256m)   Depth: 20ft (6m)

In the field immediately south east of Fern Dale.

A 20ft shaft intersects a phreatic tube, backfilled with rubble. Shaft is presumed to have been deeper.

Reference: Milner, M. 1988. D.C.A. N/L No.68. p.15.

GREEN COWDEN CHERT QUARRY CAVE
NGR 200 678   Grade I
Alt. 870ft (260m)   Length: 20ft (6m)

In disued chert quarry, north of the Bakewell-Monyash road.

A small crawl passage with a boulder floor goes round two bends and is then choked with boulders. A possible dig.

HADDON HOLE   NGR 194 659   Lost
Alt. 550ft (167m)   Length: 30ft (9m)

In the bed of the Lathkill, east of the ruined Mandale Aqueduct.

A short crawl. Accessible only in drought, and often blocked by debris. Cannot now be located.

HILLOCKS MINE   NGR 145 672   Grade III
(Whalf Mine, Whalf Pipe)
Alt. 937ft (285m)   Length: 1963ft (598m)   Depth: 168ft (51m)

No prior permission necessary but please use stile.

North west of Monyash just south of the lane, 400ft (122m) east of junction with Green Lane.

Entrance is through oil drum in bottom of old open working. Easy walking for 310ft (94m) then flat crawl opening abruptly onto 9ft (3m) climb down. Squeeze through into 47ft (14m) straight coffin level to First Pitch of 23ft (7m). Several short scrambles lead to Second Pitch, where 50ft (15m) ladder is used for an involved series of short climbs and steep slopes. At the bottom a low arch leads to big levels.

Left becomes water filled after 90ft (27m). Right chokes after 60ft (18m) but half right is large 19th century level with the older coffin level in the roof. After 30ft (9m) rubble slope to right, beyond which very steep rubble slope descends to the left, ending in a coffin level and a flooded area, the lowest point in Hillocks Mine.

Large level continues through shallow pool to Main Chamber, 30ft (9m) in diameter and 130ft (40m) from arch at foot of Second Pitch. In roof is 190ft (58m) Engine Shaft capped at surface.

To right (SE) is roomy passage and up to left after 30ft (9m) is a series of climbing shafts ascending beside the Engine Shaft. Main route continues to end of workings 340ft (103m) from Main Chamber. Halfway along is a coffin level on the right, 55ft (16m) long to a choke.

To left (NW) in Main Chamber is comfortable undulating passage for 280ft (85m) passing Pool Chamber, but 130ft (40m) before the end is an obscure passage on the right which leads through several tight, loose, muddy crawls to Meccano Passage in Knotlow Cavern.

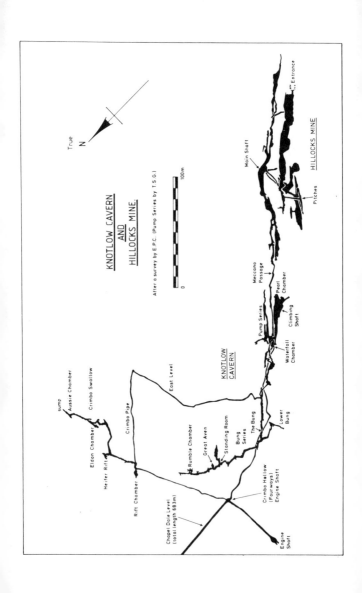

True N

KNOTLOW CAVERN
AND
HILLOCKS MINE.

After a survey by E.P.C. (Pump Series by T.S.G.)

0   100m

KNOTLOW
CAVERN

HILLOCKS MINE

Sump
Aussie Chamber
Crimbo Swallow
Eldon Chamber
Heifer Rift
Crimbo Pipe
East Level
Rift Chamber
Chapel Dale Level
(total length 683m)
Rumble Chamber
Great Aven
Standing Room
Bung Series
The Bung
Lower Bung
Crimbo Hollow
(Fourways) Engine Shaft
Engine Shaft
Pump Series
Waterfall Chamber
Meccano Passage
Climbing Shaft
Pearl Chamber
Main Shaft
Pitches
Entrance

Tackle:

	Ladder	Belay	Lifeline
First Pitch:	25ft (8m)	2ft (0.6m)	35ft (11m) (or SRT rope)
Second Pitch:	50ft (15m)	10ft (3m)	60ft (18m) (or SRT rope)
			(Bolt belays)

References: Gilbert, J.C. 1952. Cave Science Vol.3. No.21. pp.223-226. Survey. Mellor, D. 1983. Eldon P.C.Journal Vol.9. No.3. pp.1-6. Robey, J.A. 1961. Bull. P.D.M.H.S. Vol.1. No.5. pp.30-36. Robey, J.A. 1962. Bull. P.D.M.H.S. Vol.1. No.6. pp.29-35. Robey, J.A. 1963. Bull. P.D.M.H.S. Vol.2. No.1. pp.51-56.

HUBBERDALE PIPE CAVERNS   NGR 14 69   Lost

Sough tail in Deepdale at 161 695.

A pipe vein said to be 150 yards (137m) wide, running a little west of north, intersected by the level from Deepdale at 46 fathoms depth. No details known, and all shafts and level blocked (the latter about 1000ft (305m) in). Old accounts suggest that it would be very extensive and interesting if access could be gained.

References: Worley, N. et al. 1978. P.D.M.H.S. Bull. 7 (1) pp.31-39. survey. Kirkham, N. 1958. P.D.M.H.S. Bull. 2 (4) pp.206-209. Smith, P. 1957. Lyre No.2. pp.54-68.

KNOTLOW CAVERN
NGR 1438 6739 (climbing shaft)   Grade III-V (Mine)
Alt. 960ft (290m)   Length: 1.25 miles (2km)   Depth: 250ft (76m)

Warning: Crimbo Swallow and Crimbo Pipe inlet are dangerous except in dry weather.

The climbing shaft is fitted with a lid. Spanner required. At time of publishing this is available from "The Hobbit", Monyash. Contact D.C.A. for up to date details. Permission for Crimbo Hollow Engine Shaft from Knotlow Farm.

Various entrances between Dale House and Knotlow Farm, northwest of Monyash. Access via Cross Lane, turning off B5055 at double bend just west of Monyash. Park at junction of Cross and Blackwell Lanes. Crimbo Hollow Engine Shaft is amongst trees towards Knotlow Farm, where permission should be obtained.

Reopened by Eccles Caving Club in 1959. Extensions by E.P.C., S.U.S.S., and B.S.A. (T.P.U.) 1968-1972.

Entrance to Rift Chamber   **Grade III**

Very interesting system with both natural and mined passages, including some of the finest coffin levels in Derbyshire. First Pitch is climbing shaft 50ft (15m) deep, followed by a low arch to Second Pitch of 25ft (8m) into Pearl Chamber. Muddy passage leads to a climb down, and a hole on the right opens partway down the 210ft (64m) Chapel Dale Engine Shaft. Further scrambles lead to a wide low chamber with the route ahead to the Bung Series.

To the right, more scrambling leads to a 30ft (9m) pitch into Waterfall Chamber, wet on lower part. At the far end fixed ladders lead up into Meccano Passage, 350ft (107m) of difficult caving with squeezes, mud and loose boulders to the north east passage of Hillocks Mine. Waterfall Chamber can also be reached direct by 210ft (64m) Chapel Dale Engine Shaft.

The flooded shaft in the floor of Waterfall Chamber has been pumped out by TPU and EPC to find 500ft (152m) of levels normally completely submerged. A tub and rag-and-chain pump were recovered.

Water can be followed 502ft (153m) downstream from Waterfall Chamber through coffin level (with deep water towards the end) to the foot of Crimbo Hollow Engine Shaft ("Fourways Shaft"), 175ft (53m) deep, an alternative entrance. On the left is 180ft (55m) of large mine level to the foot of another big engine shaft. Ahead is Chapel Dale Level, very dull paddling for 2291ft (698m). To the right (downstream) is another coffin level 300ft (92m) long with deep water. On the left at the end is Rift Chamber, 25ft (8m) long and 10ft (3m) wide.

Crimbo Pipe Inlet and Crimbo Swallow   Grade V

Turning right at Rift Chamber, a big inlet is met with all the water disappearing under the left wall. The water can be followed downstream in dry weather through a long duck, then a part-mined passage. On the left is a low passage leading to Heifer Rift, probably another miners' route in, but now blocked. Stream flows into low crawl, Crimbo Swallow. 128ft (39m) of very wet crawling (water backs up on return) leads to Eldon Chamber, with a high aven and very wet pitch to a sump. Traverse across and partway down the pitch to another long crawl to Aussie Chamber. A 15ft (5m) climb rejoins the stream, which immediately sumps.

Upstream from the junction with Crimbo Pipe is Crimbo Pipe Inlet, a fierce passage with tight ducks in fast flowing water, leading to the foot of a waterfall. Beyond is a further squeeze and bouldery crawls to East Level, a coffin level 1253ft (381m) long, ending at a T-junction. To the right is the Bung Series, while left up an 8ft (2m) climb leads back to the chamber near the Waterfall Pitch.

Bung Series   Grade III

Beyond the junction with East Level the passage contracts to a squeeze, The Bung. A T-junction follows. Left leads to a very tight pitch into a sump, or into a small chamber in drought. Right is 196ft (59m) of flat out crawling to Standing Room 10ft (3m) high from the top of which a traverse back over the rift leads to a crawl to a high narrow aven. Other way is straight on with Great Aven on right. A 70ft (21m) flat crawl leads to Rumble Chamber. In the floor is the Lower Bung Series. A 13ft (4m) pitch and tight squeeze lead to bedding plane, usually with a stream, which probably goes to Crimbo Pipe Inlet. Beyond Rumble Chamber a crawl can be followed for 40ft (12m) until it is too low.

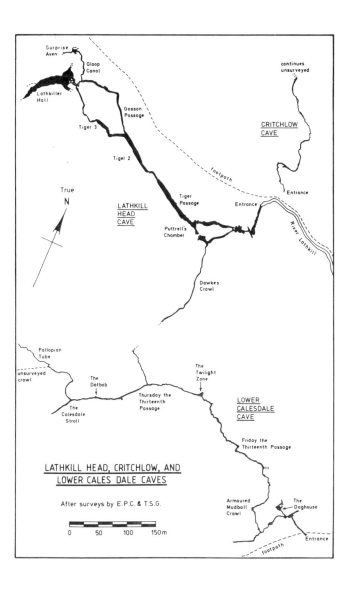

Surprise Aven

Gloop Canal

Lathkiller Hall

Tiger 3

Gasson Passage

Tiger 2

True N

LATHKILL HEAD CAVE

Tiger Passage

Puttrell's Chamber

Dawkes Crawl

continues unsurveyed

CRITCHLOW CAVE

footpath

Entrance

Entrance

River Lathkill

Fallopian Tube

unsurveyed crawl

The Datbob

The Calesdale Stroll

Thursday the Thirteenth Passage

The Twilight Zone

LOWER CALESDALE CAVE

Friday the Thirteenth Passage

Armoured Mudball Crawl

The Doghouse

Entrance

footpath

LATHKILL HEAD, CRITCHLOW, AND
LOWER CALES DALE CAVES

After surveys by E.P.C. & T.S.G.

0   50   100   150 m

Tackle:

| | Ladder | Belay | Lifeline |

Climbing Shaft Route:

First Pitch:	50ft (15m).	Short belay.	60ft (18m) (or SRT rope).
Second Pitch:	25ft (8m).	25ft (8m).	40ft (12m) (or SRT rope).
Waterfall Pitch:	30ft (9m).	10ft (3m).	40ft (12m) (or SRT rope).

Engine Shafts:

Chapel Dale:	210ft (64m). Short belay. 225ft (69m). (SRT: 230ft/70m rope).
Crimbo Hollow:	180ft (55m). Short belay. 200ft (61m). (SRT: 200ft/61m rope).
Eldon Chamber:	20ft (6m).	10ft (3m).	30ft (9m).
Lower Bung Pitch:	15ft (5m).		Crowbar & short belay.

References: Batey, J. 1969. S.U.S.S. Jour. Vol.1. No.5. pp.221-223. Cooper, G.W. & Westlake, C.D. 1970. E.P.C. Jour. Vol.7. No.3. pp.9-28. Mellor, D. 1983. E.P.C. Jour. Vol.9. No.3. pp.1-6. Survey. Robey, J.A. 1961. P.D.M.H.S. Bull. Vol.1. No.6. pp.29-35., 1962. Vol.1. No.6. pp.29-35., 1963. Vol.2. No.1. pp.51-56. Saville, B. 1960. The Lyre No.3. pp.37-41. Survey. Westlake, C.D. 1966. E.P.C. Jour. Vol.7. No.1. p.20. Westlake, C.D. 1970. E.P.C. Jour. Vol.7. No.3. pp.48-52. Westlake, C.D. 1970. S.U.S.S. Jour. Vol.1. No.6. pp.236-237.

LATHKILL HEAD CAVE   Grade II, III, IV
(Lathkill House Cave)

RIVER ENTRANCE   NGR 1707 6588
Alt. 680ft (207m)

TOP ENTRANCE   NGR 1671 6596
Alt. 815ft (248.5m)

Length: 5000ft (1525m)   Vertical Range: 135ft (41.5m)

The only large obvious entrance on the south side of Upper Lathkill Dale. Wet weather resurgence of the River Lathkill.

Warning: The whole system floods to the roof in wet weather, and the further limits are full in normal weather. The choke at Handshake Chamber is loose and very dangerous.

Extended 1965 by E.P.C., 1969 by S.U.S.S. and E.P.C., 1974 by O.C.C., 1976 by E.P.C., 1990 & 1991 by T.S.G.

Entrance Series   **Grade II**

The large entrance soon reduces to a 200ft (61m) long bedding plane crawl over large slabs to Rift Chamber. Crawl on right leads to The Spiral, a descent among boulders to a low wide bedding cave. Straight on and then to right is squeeze down into lower bedding plane. In normal weather the stream is soon met at a junction after a short crawl.

Puttrell's Chamber & Dawkes Crawl   **Grade III**

Left soon sumps, but in dry weather can be followed for 150ft (46m) to a junction. Right leads back to Puttrell's Chamber via a very tight crawl over and between boulders (Mullen's Mistake). Left is Dawkes Crawl, 500ft (152m) of flat out crawling explored in 1976 by E.P.C. to a choke, passed in 1977 to a further 30ft of very tight crawl. Strong outward draught in drought.

Right at the first junction leads upstream and again soon sumps, but in dry weather Oval Pot can be reached after 150ft (46m) of crawling. Climb Oval Pot and along low bedding with boulders to Puttrell's Chamber, limit of exploration up to 1965. Left leads through boulders to Mullen's Mistake.

Further Limits   **Grade IV**

Straight on from Puttrell's Chamber E.P.C. dig leads to 350ft (107m) of flat out crawling (Tiger Passage) leading to Bridge Chamber, followed by Fan Chamber. This is the only section where it is possible to walk. The rest of the cave is only accessible in drought. Low bedding plane crawl (Tiger 2) continues for 200ft (61m) to a junction, the limit of exploration up to 1969. Left leads to 480ft (146m) of flat out crawling (Tiger 3) leading to Handshake Chamber.

Right at the junction is Gasson Passage, a 500ft (152m) bedding plane crawl which also leads to Handshake Chamber. Just before Handshake Chamber a small hole on the right leads to Gloop Canal, which can be followed on hands and knees through water for 180ft (55m) to Surprise Aven. An exposed climb up of 35ft (11m) enters a small chamber with a silted inlet passage. Another passage to the south west is blocked after 60ft (18m). The side passages draught strongly.

From Handshake Chamber a very dangerous route up through a loose boulder choke (The Lathkiller) was pushed in 1990 to a large decorated chamber (Lathkiller Hall). A crawl, and climb through a further choke lead into a very large chamber, the Waiting Room. The Top Entrance pitch (65ft/20m) enters at the far end. Main route continues from Lathkiller Hall for approximately 1000ft (305m), and is presently still being explored.

Tackle:

Surprise Aven: 50ft (15m) handline.

Top Entrance: 65ft ladder. 80ft lifeline or SRT rope. Bolt or stal belay.

References: Bamber, H.A. 1948. B.S.A. Cave Science. Vol.1. No.5. pp.148-150. Bamber, H.A. 1951. B.S.A. Cave Science Vol.2. No.15. pp.293-301. Drakeley, K. 1974. D.C.A. N/L No.22. p.6. Drakeley, K. 1974. O.C.C. N/L Vol.10. No.8. pp.65-67. Ford, T.D. (ed) 1977. Limestones and Caves of the Peak District. Chapter 20. Geo Books. Norwich. Gasson, I.D.H. 1970. E.P.C. Jour. Vol.7. No.3. pp.62-3. Survey. Gill, D.W. 1976. D.C.A. N/L No.30. pp.10-12. Gill, D.W. 1974. D.C.A. N/L No.22. p.4. Lord, P.J. 1971. S.U.S.S. Jour. Vol.2. No.1. pp.26-27. Lord, P.J. 1969. S.U.S.S. Jour. Vol.1. No.5. p.224. Survey. Westlake, C.D. 1966. E.P.C. Jour. Vol.7. No.1. p.20.

LATHKILL RESURGENCE CAVE
NGR 1813 6568   **Grade II**
(Pudding Springs)
Alt. 600ft (183m)   Length: 200ft (61m)

About 1 mile downstream of Lathkill Head Cave, below a waterfall.

First entered during the 1959 drought. The entrance and the whole cave are normally under water. The cave consists of a long crawl with small chambers, eventually becoming too low. Developed entirely in tufa below the valley floor. Formations consist of tufa-encased roots.

References: Commander, B. 1983. T.S.G. N/L No.10. pp.11-14. Survey. Mort, J.B. 1956. The Lyre No.2. pp.11-12 & 14. Survey.

LYNX CAVE   **NGR 1723 6509**   **Grade I (Arch)**
Alt. 775ft (232m)   Length: 30ft (9m)

Two obvious entrances on a shelf some 15ft (4.5m) above the valley floor on the north side of the buttress containing One Ash Cave on its south side.

Higher entrance drops into roof of lower tube a few feet inside. A stooping passage leads to a partial blockage of rotten flowstone after 30ft (9m). Believed to be the cave excavated by Storrs Fox to reveal remains of Lynx.

Reference: Storrs Fox, W. 1906. Proc. Zool. Soc., Vol.1. pp.65-72 & 77.

MANDALE MINE **NGR Incline: 197 661 Grade III (Mine)**
Alt. 550ft (165m)   Length: ¼ mile (0.4km) approx

Incline entrance at cliff foot above the sough tail. Mandale Founder Shaft lies on the rake at 190 663.

One of the oldest lead mines in Derbyshire. The incline leads into the main level, usually knee deep in water. Various old stopes can be reached along it, and evidence of sand filled solution cavities seen in places. The sough tail by the footpath can be followed under the old engine house, but is blocked beyond. Workings extend 1 mile to the north west, beneath Mandale Founder Shaft, over 300ft (91m) deep.

References: Ford, T.D. & Worley, N.E. 1976. Bull. P.D.M.H.S. Vol.6. No.3. pp.141-143. Survey. Rieuwerts, J. 1963. Bull. P.D.M.H.S. Vol.2. No.1. pp.9-30. Survey. Thornton, D.R. 1960. Bull. P.D.M.H.S. Vol.1. No.3. pp.3-4. Sketch survey. Tune, R. 1969. Bull. P.D.M.H.S. Vol.4. No.1. pp.67-74. Survey.

ONE ASH CAVE   **NGR 172 651**   **Grade I**
Alt. 780ft (234m)   Length: 100ft (30m)

On the west side of the dale in the narrow gorge section, some 325 yards (297m) east south east of One Ash Grange, on the south side of a buttress.

The cave is on a shelf some 30ft (9m) above the dale floor. A stooping size tube lowers to a crawl which has been dug. Blocked with corroded flowstone. There is an unnamed cave on the same shelf a little way to the south, blocked with clay. Not to be confused with Lynx Cave on the north side of the buttress.

Reference: Mellors, P.T. 1969. Bull. B.S.A. No.83. pp.5-6.

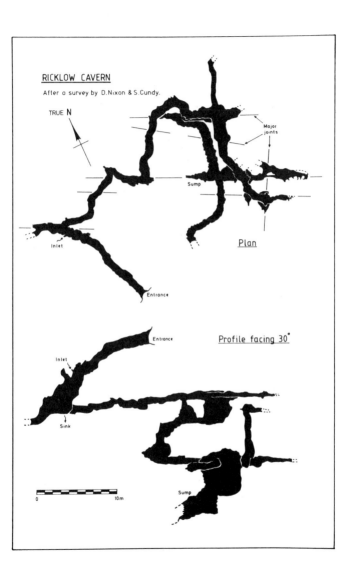

RICKLOW CAVERN

After a survey by D.Nixon & S.Cundy.

TRUE N

Major joints

Sump

Inlet

Plan

Entrance

Profile facing 30°

Entrance

Inlet

Sink

Sump

0   10m

ONE ASH SHELTER   NGR 1730 6556   Grade I (Arch)
Alt. 775ft (232m)

At base of crag high up and northwest of footbridge.

A rock shelter with a low blocked phreatic tube. Archaeologically excavated to reveal remains of late Upper Palaeolithic Man and animals.

RAVEN MINE   NGR 1609 6590   Grade II (Mine)
Alt. 880ft (268m)   **Depth: 100ft (30m)**

On the south east side of Fern Dale.

A partly natural shaft 35ft (11m) deep leads very soon to a second pitch of 50ft (15m), choked at the bottom. 15ft (5m) down the pitch a natural passage leads off. Up and then down a small hole to a passage with a false floor and bedding crawls off to the left. All passages soon choked.

First pitch was blocked, but was reopened by Darfar P.C. in 1989.

Tackle:	Ladder	Lifeline
First Pitch:	35ft (11m)	50ft (15m)
Second Pitch:	50ft (15m)	60ft (18m)

RICKLOW CAVE   NGR 1636 6607   Grade II
Alt. 750ft (225m)   **Length: 431ft (131m)**   **Depth: 51ft (16m)**

Small entrance at base of cliff on north side of valley floor immediately below Ricklow Marble Quarry tip.

Short passage leads to 15ft climb down. Water sinks at bottom in wet weather. Was excavated for 14ft (4m) by Fourways Club in 1962 and backfilled from dig in left hand crawl. Dig progressed for 60ft (18m) in mud and water.

Right hand crawl leads through pools to 12ft (3.5m) pitch into small pot. Three passages enter in roof but all close shortly. A tight rift at one end of the pot has been enlarged down to a small passage, which are also enlarged to give access to a flooded rift. Small passages continue, and are currently being dug (1991).

The quarry above has a partly collapsed choked cave entrance at the extreme east end which may be worth digging, as well as marble mines which are now in a dangerously unstable condition.

Tackle – 20ft (6m) handline.

References: Anon. 1962. D.C.A. N/L No.3. p.1. Milner, M. 1985. D.C.A. N/L No.57. p.20. Milner, M. 1985. D.C.A. N/L No.58. pp.2-3. Survey.

WATER ICICLE CLOSE CAVERN
NGR 1610 6460   **Grade II**
Alt. 1065ft (325m)   **Length: 700ft (213m)**   **Depth: 105ft (32m)**

No known access restrictions. Park at end of green lane.

A capped and lidded shaft in the field north of the end of the green Derby Lane, close to a plantation.

The shaft is 105ft (32m) deep in solid limestone, and descends through the roof of a chamber at the junction of three fairly large passages. The south passage leads into a mined out vein about 120ft (37m) long and 70ft (21m) high. The north passage is about 320ft (98m) long, gradually descending into a clay fill. The north west passage is about 350ft (107m) long with dcads stacked at the sides and remnants of stalagmites and some small avens. It ends at a boulder choke which has been dug into a high aven with much loose debris. The choked passage appears to continue beyond.

Tackle – 110ft (33m) ladder; Short belay; 130ft (40m) lifeline.

References: Lord, P.J. 1971. S.U.S.S. Jour. Vol.2. No.1. pp.27-28. Lord, P.J. & Batey, A. 1970. S.U.S.S. Jour. Vol.1. No.6. pp.247-248. Phipps, M. 1981. The Lyre. No.5. pp.12-13. Smith, M.E. 1968. Bull. P.D.M.H.S. Vol.3. No.5. pp.281-284. Survey. Westlake, C.D. 1970. E.P.C. Jour. Vol.7. No.3. pp.57-58. Survey.

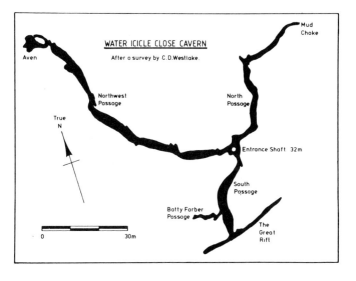

WATER ICICLE CLOSE CAVERN

After a survey by C.D.Westlake.

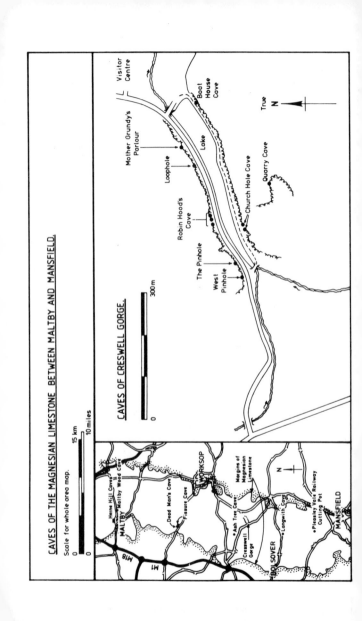

CAVES OF THE MAGNESIAN LIMESTONE BETWEEN MALTBY AND MANSFIELD.

Scale for whole area map.

0   15 km

0   10 miles

CAVES OF CRESWELL GORGE.

0   300 m

Visitor Centre

Mother Grundy's Parlour

Loophole

Robin Hood's Cave

The Pinhole

West Pinhole

Lake

Boat House Cave

Church Hole Cave

Quarry Cave

True N

MALTBY

Hesne Hill Caves

Maltby Wood Cave

Dead Man's Cave

Fissure Cave

WORKSOP

Ash Tree Cave

Margins of Magnesian Limestone

Creswell Gorge

BOLSOVER

Langwith Gorge

Pleasley Vale Railway Cutting Pot

MANSFIELD

N

CAVES OF
THE MAGNESIAN LIMESTONE

A number of caves, mostly of archaeological importance, occur in the Magnesian Limestone of East Derbyshire. Cresswell Gorge and its caves are now a National Nature Reserve, and the caves are gated and locked. Permission to visit must be sought from the Ranger, Creswell Caves Visitor Centre (at the east end of the gorge) which has displays of archaeological material from the caves. Access to the Herne Hill Caves at Maltby is now controlled by D.C.A., and for this reason they are included here.

ASH TREE CAVE   NGR 515 762   Grade I (Arch)
Alt. 395ft (120m)   **Length: 23ft (7m)**   **Depth: 10ft (3m)**

Obvious entrance in cliff on south side of shallow valley 650 ft (200m) west of road. Slope down into chamber. Continuation is choked by fill although further open passage can be glimpsed beyond. Neolithic burial found.

    References: Armstrong, A.L. 1950-1955. Derbys. Arch. Soc. Jour. Armstrong, A.L. 1956. Derbys. Arch. Soc. Jour. 76. pp.57-64.

BOAT HOUSE CAVE   NGR 537 742   Grade I (Arch)
Alt. 250ft (75m)   **Length: 180ft (55m)**

Obvious low arched entrance near the east end of the crags on the south side of Cresswell Gorge. At rear of entrance chamber gently winding passage 4ft (1.2m) high leads beneath a variety of small avens to a sandy choke. Important archaeological site. Do not disturb fill or deposits.

    Reference: Armstrong, A.L. Derbys. Arch. Jour. Vol.57. p.129.

CHURCH HOLE CAVE   NGR 534 741   Grade I (Arch)
Alt. 250ft (75m)   **Length: 250ft (75m)**

Obvious large entrance on south side of gorge. Gated. Smaller entrance a short distance to the west. Entrances unite in a roomy tunnel, gradually lowering, to easy climb up sloping tube into final small chamber and calcited choke. Important archaeological site. Do not disturb fill or deposits. Excavated material now in British Museum.

    References: Armstrong. Reports in Derbys. Arch. Jour. from Vol.55. onwards. Heath, Thomas. 1882. Derbys. Arch. Jour. Vol.4. pp.173-176. Mem. Geol. Surv. 1913. The northern part of the Derbyshire Coalfield. pp.107-108.

DEAD MAN'S CAVE   NGR 533 831   Grade I (Arch)
Alt. 280ft (85m)   **Length: 30ft (9m)**

Wide entrance in Anston Stones crags next to the A57 road.

    Passage constricts to a crawl leading to a low chamber. Archaeological remains found. Take care not to disturb sediments.

FISSURE CAVE   NGR 535 830   Grade II (Arch)
Alt. 170ft (52m)   Length: 33ft (10m)

Entrance in small depression in Anston Stones crags next to the A57 road.

A squeeze leads to a chamber 25ft (8m) long and 10ft (3m) high, with a tight crawl continuing. Archaeological remains found. Take care not to disturb sediments.

HERNE HILL CAVE 1   NGR 533 922   Grade II
Alt. 350ft (107m)   Length: 550ft (168m)   Depth: 35ft (11m)

Discovered M.S.G. 1973. Behind the supermarket on the north side of the main street in Maltby. Gated.

Crawl entrance drops steeply for 15ft (4.5m) to First Chamber, 20ft (6m) by 12ft (4m), and up to 10ft (3m) high. At upper end of chamber a shaft drops 15ft (4.5m) into Second Chamber, also reached down obvious boulder slope. Narrow rift on left of slope enters small blind chamber.

On right of Second Chamber two short passages unite in a low chamber. To the left a squeeze up into a rift leads to 70ft (21m) of passage below the quarry floor. Main route from Second Chamber is a crawl into the Third Chamber. Small passages to the right are blind, while those to the left lead to the Fourth Chamber, about 30ft (9m) by 15ft (4.5m).

Beyond Fourth Chamber route lowers, with holes to the left to a parallel passage. Route steps up into Fifth Chamber. On the right of the Fifth Chamber a squeeze leads to a further chamber 25ft (8m) long.

References: Ryder, P. 1974. M.S.G. Journal No.7. pp. 16-17. Survey. Ryder, P. 1979. M.S.G. Journal No.10. pp.23-24. Survey.

HERNE HILL CAVE 2   NGR 533 922
Length: 210ft (64m)

Discovered 1980. Entrance lies between the supermarket wall and the cliff face.

Entrance drops into a low chamber. A narrow rift descends into a second chamber with three routes leading on. Crawling and squeezing over concrete (poured down a borehole) leads to a further chamber with small speleothems. A tube on the left leads to a wide low bedding chamber, and via a squeeze into a larger passage leading back to the second chamber. The other way on from here led back under the entrance chamber to a choke.

Reference: Ryder, P. 1980. B.C.R.A. Caves & Caving No.11. p.6 & p.26. Survey.

LANGWITH CAVE   NGR 518 695   Grade I (Arch)
Alt. 295ft (90m)   Length: 100ft (30m)

Large entrance on north bank of River Poulter, a short distance west of a public footpath and almost due north of Upper Langwith Church. Entrance drops into a roomy chamber from which much material has been removed by archaeologists. Several sandy crawls lead off. The longest is to the left, ending in a small chamber with tree roots. A Neolithic burial was found.

References: Hinton, M.C.A. 1913. Derbys. Arch. Jour. No.35. pp.157-158. Keith, A. 1913. Derbys. Arch. Jour. No.35. pp.155-157. Kennard, A.S. & Woodward, B.B. 1913. Derbys. Arch. Jour. No.35. pp.153-155. Mullins, E.H. 1913. Derbys. Arch. Jour. No.35. pp.137-153.

LOOPHOLE   NGR 535 742   Grade I (Arch)
Alt. 250ft (76m)   Length: 50ft (15m)

Small entrance at cliff foot east of Robin Hood's Cave. Small spidery cave with upper entrance on ledge. Important archaeological site. Do not disturb fill or deposits.

MALTBY WOOD CAVE   NGR 549 917   Grade I
Alt. 230ft (70m)   Length: 131ft (40m)

Obvious entrance in the north wall of a mineral railway cutting. Entrance crawl forks almost immediately. Left is a crawl down a slope into a chamber 25ft (8m) x 13ft (4m). The right hand passage is a crawl into a bouldery chamber, then a further crawl 10ft (3m) wide and 3ft (1m) high. After 20ft (6m) a crawl up a rubble slope leads into a chamber 16ft (5m) in diameter. A draught blows from the rubble round the edge of the chamber.

Reference: Ryder, P. 1987. M.S.G. Jour. No.11. p.32. Survey.

MOTHER GRUNDY'S PARLOUR
NGR 5358 7426   Grade I (Arch)
Alt. 280ft (85m)   Length: 50ft (15m)

Large obvious rock shelter near east end of north side of Cresswell Gorge. Small passage at rear soon ends in a little chamber. Important archaeological site. Do not disturb fill or deposits.

Flints and bones excavated can be seen in British Museum, London.

References: Campbell, J.B. 1969. Derbys. Arch. Jour. Vol.89. pp.48-52. Survey. Campbell, J.B. 1970. Peakland Arch. Soc. Bull. No.25. pp.13-15. Survey. Geological Survey Memoir 1913. The Northern Part of the Derbyshire Coalfield. p.108. Heath, T. 1882. Derbys. Arch. Jour. Vol.4. p.176. Mello, Rev. J.M. 1880. Trans. Manch. Geol. Soc. Vol.XV. pp.290-314.

PINHOLE CAVE   NGR 533 741   Grade I (Arch)
Alt. 300ft (91m)   Length: 170ft (52m)

Obvious large entrance, gated. High but narrow passage opens into lofty chamber, with short low branch to right. Ahead, climb through wedged boulders into narrow passage with stalagmite flows, choking after a squeeze and a 6ft (2m) drop.

The cave furnished the most complete record of animal and human occupation of any British Caves. Finds can be seen in Derby Museum, Manchester University Museum, The British Museum London, and Middlesborough Museum.

Reference: Heath, T. 1882. Derbys. Arch. Jour. No.4. p.169.

PLEASLEY VALE RAILWAY CUTTING POT
NGR 520 649   Grade III (Arch?)
(Yew Tree Cave?)
Alt. 450ft (137m)   Length: 295ft (90m)   Depth: 75ft (23m)

Warning: Continuing rock movements mean that visits to the chamber below Rift Chamber Pitch are not recommended.

An unusual slip-rift system. Obvious entrance on south side of disused railway cutting. May be the same as the "Yew Tree Cave" mentioned in early archaeological literature.

Drop of 10ft (3m) into rift. Straight ahead is rift with hole in floor leading back into Main Rift. Back under cutting is T-junction with Main Rift. Right is climb down to feet-first squeeze into chamber, with various short rift passages beyond. Left is climb down through boulders onto 15ft (4.5m) Rift Chamber Pitch. Belay to any safe boulder above. Ahead is unsafe high level chamber, rift on left to choked chamber, and scramble up to lip of 20ft (6m) Second Pitch into final chamber.

Tackle:

	Ladder	Belay	Lifeline
Entrance:			20ft (6m)
Rift Chamber:	20ft (6m)	20ft (6m)	20ft (12m)
Second Pitch:	20ft (6m)	5ft (1.5m) + stemple	60ft (18m)

References: Dawkins, W.B. 1869. Quar. Jour. Geol. Soc. Ransom, 1866. Report of the British Association.

QUARRY CAVE   NGR 535 740   Grade I
Alt. 295ft (90m)   Length: 50ft (15m)

In north wall of large disused quarry 295ft (90m) south of Creswell Crags. Obvious entrance drops into large passage with much sandy fill, which meets roof after a short distance in each direction.

ROBIN HOOD'S CAVE   NGR 5341 7419   Grade I (Arch)
Alt. 300ft (91m)   Length: 950ft (290m)

Three obvious entrances in Creswell Gorge, all gated.

A series of roomy dry chambers and galleries, owing much of their size to removal of fill by archaeologists. At end of passage running straight in from east entrance is 20ft (6m) aven leading only to short choked passage. Two routes from rear of large chamber just inside central entrance connect in an interesting round trip, including an easy chimney and a squeeze. In floor of large chamber is climbable 11ft (3.5m) shaft to short lower passage. More complex low level series is reached via 8ft (2.5m) shaft at the side of the portal of the west entrance.

An important archaeological cave. Do not disturb fill or deposits. Finds in British Museum, London, and Manchester Museum.

References: Geological Survey Memoirs. 1913. The Northern part of the Derbyshire Coalfield. pp.106-107. Survey. Campbell, J.B. 1969. Derbys. Arch. Jour. No.89. pp.52-57. Arch. Survey. Campbell, J.B. 1970. P.A.S. Bull. No.25. pp.11-12. Arch. Survey. Heath, T. 1882. Derbys. Arch. Jour. No.4. pp.170-173.

WEST PINHOLE   NGR 533 741   Grade II (Arch)
Alt. 245ft (75m)   Length: 200ft (60m)

Several entrances near the west end on the north side of Creswell Gorge.

Entrance to the right into semi-daylight chamber, that to the left into high rift passage pinching out after 50ft (15m). On right of rift passage is a low chamber. On left two routes into a series of low crawls with a squeeze and small avens.

Betweeen West Pinhole and Pinhole, and between Pinhole and Robin Hood's Cave are a few short small caves up to 30ft (9m) in length. All the caves are important archaeological sites. Do not disturb fill or deposits.

WHALEY CAVE   NGR 511 721   Arch

Two archaeological caves excavated by A.L.Armstrong. Nearby are some rock shelters.

Reference: Radley, J. 1967. Derbys. Arch. Jour. No.87. pp.1-17. Survey.

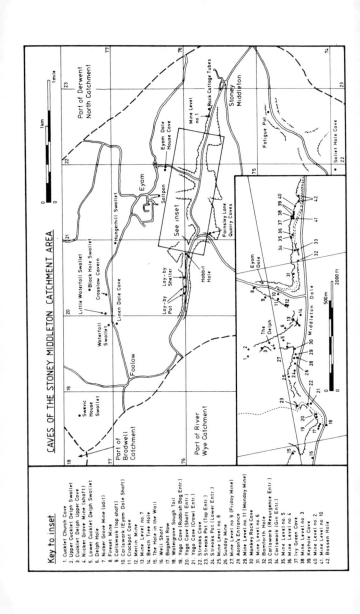

CAVES OF THE STONEY MIDDLETON CATCHMENT AREA

Key to inset

1. Cucklet Church Cave
2. Upper Cucklet Delph Swallet
3. Cucklet Delph Upper Cave
4. Nicker Grove Mine (shaft)
5. Lower Cucklet Delph Swallet
6. Delph Hole
7. Nicker Grove Mine (adit)
8. Firest Mine
9. Cariswork (top shaft)
10. Cariswork (Eyam Dale Shaft)
11. Crockpot Cave
12. Merlin Mine
13. Mine Level no. 7
14. Beech Tree Hole
15. The Hole in the Wall
16. Well Shaft
17. Bagshot Row
18. Watergrove Sough Tail
19. Yoga Cove (Rubbish Bag Entr.)
20. Yoga Cove (Short Entr.)
21. Yoga Cove (Crawl Entr.)
22. Streaks Cove
23. Streaks Pot (Top Entr.)
24. Streaks Pot (Lower Entr.)
25. Mine Level no. 8
26. Sunday Mine
27. Mine Level no 9 (Friday Mine)
28. Aaron's Entrance
29. Mine Level no. 11 (Monday Mine)
30. Monkey Rock Cave
31. Mine Level no. 6
32. Bamforth Hole
33. Cariswork (Resurgence Entr.)
34. Cariswork (Gin Entr.)
35. Mine Level no. 5
36. Mine Level no. 4
37. Ivy Green Cove
38. Mine Level no. 3
39. Keyhole Cove
40. Mine Level no. 2
41. Mine Level no. 10
42. Bassen Hole

Part of Derwent North Catchment

Part of Bradwell Catchment

Part of River Wye Catchment

Foolow

Swevic House Swallet

Waterfall Swallet

Little Waterfall Swallet

Black Hole Swallet

Crosslow Cavern

Linen Dale Cave

Hungerhill Swallet

Eyam

Saltpan

Eyam Dale House Cave

Mine Level no. 1

Rock Cottage Tubs

Stoney Middleton

Fornsley Lane Quarry Caves

Fatigue Pot

Sollet Hole Cave

Lay-by Shelter

Hobbit Hole

Lay-by Pot

See inset

The Delph

Eyam Dale

Middleton Dale

1 mile

1 km

THE STONEY MIDDLETON CATCHMENT AREA

The easily accessible caves of Stoney Middleton Dale have provided many cavers with their first introduction to the sport.

The geology is ideal for the formation of an extensive cave system. A series of swallets on the shale/limestone junction to the west of Eyam take streams which must follow the strike eastwards beneath Eyam. The drainage is uncomplicated by lavas in the area, for the highest of these, the Cressbrook Dale Lava, lies well below the floor of Stoney Middleton Dale.

Four periods of downcutting have occurred in the area, and this is reflected by the four cave levels in Stoney Middleton Dale. The older caves are generally silt filled, but even some of these are penetrable for several hundred feet (ie. Ivy Green Cave).

The original risings undoubtedly lay in the floor of Stoney Middleton Dale, but the water has been captured by soughs. The Resurgence Entrance to Carlswark Cavern can still discharge a large stream in flood. Only two swallets have been penetrated for any distance (Waterfall Swallet and Hungerhill Swallet) and neither gives access to the major cave which must lie beneath.

Carlswark is the largest system. Together with Streaks Pot and parts of Merlin Mine it represents the downstream end of a system whose most distant feeder swallets lie far to the west beyond Foolow. Only a small proportion of this system is known, although many new discoveries have been made in the last twenty years.

Caves are occasionally met in the quarries on the south side of Stoney Middleton Dale. They tend to be penetrable only for short distances, but are often well decorated (ie. Sarah's Cave), and are fragments of early abandoned drainage systems.

Prospects for a large breakthrough are still good, though the digs tend to be remote (ie. the West Choke of Streaks Pot and the Dynamite Series of Carlswark Cavern). There is still a potential drop of just over 200ft (61m) from the lowest point reached in Waterfall Swallet to the Bedpan Sump of Carlswark Cavern.

Although included in the Stoney Middleton area, the drainage of Coombs Dale, to the south, is really separate. The only significant cave is Fatigue Pot, which ends at a very small passage with a tantalising draught. It is still possible that a penetrable system exists beneath Coombs Dale.

BAGSHOT ROW   NGR 2109 7585   Grade I
Alt. 673ft (205.1m)   Length: 35ft (11m)

Three entrances in the lowest cliff on the north side of the A623 immediately west of the sharp bend. The right hand entrance is a crawl for 25ft (8m) to emerge at the middle entrance. The left hand entrance is a larger tube, completely silted after a few feet.

BAMFORTH HOLE   NGR 2205 7580   Grade I Dig
Alt. 600ft (183m)   Length: 30ft (9m)

Somewhat confused. There has been a great deal of argument over this cave first referred to by Short (1734) as a narrow passage at the end of which was a climb into a cave. The cave corresponds with the east end of Eyam Passage in Carlswark Cavern (Oyster Chamber). The most likely entrance is a small mine level approximately 100ft (30m) west and slightly above Carlswark's Lower (Resurgence) Entrance.

A short descending passage ends at roof falls after 30ft (9m). If dug for a considerable distance, it probably connects with the Gin Entrance to Carlswark Cavern.

References: Gill, D.W. 1976. Eldon P.C.Journal Vol.9. No.1. pp.11-12. Kirkham, N. 1948. British Caver Vol.18. pp.21-26. Pilkington, J.A. 1789. A View of the Present State of Derbyshire. 2 Vols. Short, T. 1734. A History of the Mineral Waters of Derbyshire, Lincolnshire, and Yorkshire. p.34 & 95. Smith, M.E. 1971. Bull.P.D.M.H.S. Vol.5. No.5. pp.370-374. S.

BEECH TREE HOLE   NGR 2180 7590   Grade I
Alt. 646ft (196.9m)   Length: 55ft (16.7m)

A silted cave passage at the base of the Lower Shell Bed, just west of trial workings on Old Oak Scrin. Excavated by Chesterfield Caving Club for 55ft (16.7m). Work continues (1990).

BLACK HOLE SWALLET   NGR 2035 7732   Lost
Alt. 1000ft (300m)

100 yards (90m) south west of Black Hole Mine. Now filled in.

The shakehole was a large one, but only occasionally took a stream.

BOSSEN HOLE   NGR 2233 7573   Grade I
(Badger Hole, Tacko Hole, Windy Ledge Cave)
Alt. 625 ft (190.5m)

On north side of Stoney Middleton Dale. A footpath leads to an exposed ledge midway up the Castle Buttress. The cave is at the east end of the ledge.

After walking a few feet and climbing up 8ft (3m), rest of cave is a crawl right through the buttress. A left hand branch becomes too tight. The through tube may be too draughty for naked lights at times. Care is needed on the ledge.

Reference: Smith, M.E., Jour. S.U.S.S. Vol.1. No.2. Survey.

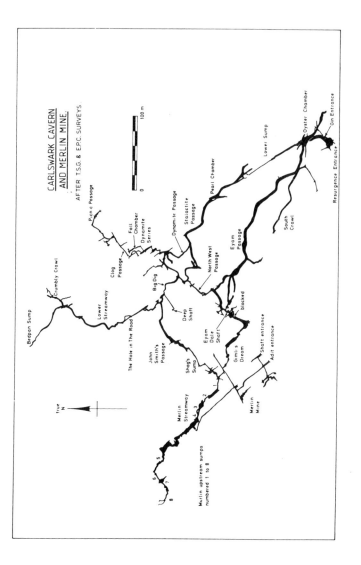

CARLSWARK CAVERN
AND MERLIN MINE.

AFTER T.S.G. & E.P.C. SURVEYS.

0   100 m

true N

Bedган Sump

Crumbly Crawl

Plane Passage

Fall Chamber

Dynamite Series

Clog Passage

Lower Streamway

The Hole in The Road

Big Dig

Dynamite Passage

Stalactite Passage

Pearl Chamber

Lower Sump

John Smith's Passage

Deep Shaft

North West Passage

Shog's Sump

Eyam Dale Shaft

blocked

Eyam Passage

Oyster Chamber

Gin Entrance

Gimli's Dream

Adit entrance

South Crawl

Resurgence Entrance

Shaft entrance

Merlin Streamway

Merlin Mine

Merlin upstream sumps
numbered 1 to 8

1 2 3 4 5 6 7 8

CARLSWARK CAVERN
(Charleswork, The Wonder Cavern)

Grade III-V

RESURGENCE ENTRANCE   NGR 2207 7580
Alt. 572ft (174.5m)

EYAM DALE SHAFT   NGR 2184 7596
Alt. 644ft (196.3m)

GIN ENTRANCE   NGR 2207 7581
Alt. 623ft (190m)

STUB SCRIN SHAFT   NGR 2184 7603
Alt. 757ft (230.6m)

Length (Merlin/Carlswark combined): 10641ft (3243m)
Vertical Range: 200ft (61m).

Lower (Resurgence) Entrance is at the foot of a cliff midway between Stoney Middleton and the Eyam road turning on the A623. The Gin Entrance is about 50ft (15m) vertically above, and slightly west of the Lower Entrance, reached by a rough track. Eyam Dale Shaft is opposite the electricity sub-station in Eyam Dale. A deep shaft entrance lies high above Eyam Dale Shaft, a little further to the north.

The Lower Entrance is a low crawl into a sizeable chamber which is frequently flooded in winter. The main route is to the right for 290ft (89m) to a sump which must not be free dived as it is over 90ft (27m) long. A difficult 30ft (9m) climb up a rift to the right leads to the Oyster Chamber in the Upper Series (Eyam Passage).

The entrance on the Gin is the most popular entrance, and is an open rift on a terrace at the base of the cliff. An easy 30ft (9m) scramble down leads to a junction with Eyam Passage. Right is soon blocked, but left leads quickly to Oyster Chamber and the connection with the Lower Series. The main route is ahead: all other passages off are blocked. Three inlet passages enter at roof level in Eyam Passage. The first, 150ft (45m) is very tight. The second, 290ft (89m) is South Crawl and ends at a fall. The third, 99ft (30m) is also tight.

Eyam Passage reduces to a crawl between South Crawl and the third inlet, but enlarges again to Noughts and Crosses Chamber, where another fall blocks the way. The way on is to the right of the fall into a low chamber with three ways off. The first is soon blocked by mud, the second is tight at first and leads up close to Eyam Dale Shaft. The main route is right, following a small stream, to a junction with North West Passage. At this junction, left leads to Eyam Dale Shaft, 36ft (11m) deep and 1165ft (355m) from the Gin Entrance. A crawl 10ft (3m) up the shaft leads to a chamber where the connection with Gimli's Dream in the Merlin Mine was made (now blocked for safety).

Back at the junction in North West Passage, turning right and following the small stream the size reduces to a crawl, which improves to hands and knees and eventually leads to an awkward left hand squeeze and a low junction. Left leads to Big Dig, and right leads via Cockle Passage and a duck to a junction with Stalactite Passage, now badly vandalised. Dynamite Passage soon enters on the left, and can be followed back to Big Dig. The main passage continues to Pearl Chamber, after which the main route ends at a climb down into a rift. In the rift, a mine level on the right leads to the upstream end of the sump in the Lower Entrance passage. The sump has been passed in drought, but is rarely open. The formerly well-decorated Aladdin Crawl is reached by a traverse over the rift.

The Dynamite Series, 1065ft (322m) long, is reached by taking the first obvious right turn off Dynamite Passage, a squeeze through boulders. The route consists of a series of joint-oriented chambers connected by mostly tight crawls. The largest is Prospect Chamber, which leads to the very tight Porth Crawl, continuing via a tight ascending rift into Clog Passage. Right ends at a boulder choke, and straight on to Old Man workings, in which the bottoms of run-in shafts can be seen. Natural passage is re-entered beyond, and soon leads to another high aven. A keyhole passage leads to two more avens via tight squeezes, and a passage at floor level (Picnic Passage) can be followed as a very tight crawl for about 250ft (76m). This could still be dug, and may provide a connection with nearby Eyam Dale House Cave.

The Big Dig Series is 1803ft (549m) long. Big Dig is a roomy crawl reached by turning left at the bottom of North West Passage, and again left at a T-junction. 150ft (46m) of crawling, often in water, leads past the blocked route to the deep shaft entrance (three pitches total 180ft (55m)), and through a boulder choke to a T-junction with the streamway, carrying a large stream which dries up in late summer. Left (upstream) is John Smith's Passage, 280ft (85m) of canals, crawls, and a short walking sized stretch to the downstream end of Shag's Sump in the Merlin Mine.

Right at the junction, a crawl leads to a rift passage where the stream flows into an impenetrable slot. Follow the rift for 60ft (18m) to a pit (The Hole in the Road). Part of the stream enters at the bottom. Either climb down to a watery crawl, or traverse over to rejoin the stream where the Cowlishaw Vein crosses the cave. 300ft (90m) of stooping passage follows, passing Ted's Inlet (too tight) where most of the stream re-enters. A right hand branch, Crumbly Crawl, is next, and leads to a cross rift after 75ft (23m) with a very tight continuation at roof level. The main streamway continues, soon sumping in wet weather, but penetrable in summer for another 300ft (90m), becoming more and more disagreeable until it is too low.

Tackle:
Eyam Dale Shaft: 40ft (12m) ladder; 60ft (18m) lifeline; (Ring bolt belay).
Gin Entrance: 60ft (18m) handline for novices; Belay to tree.

References: Beck, J.S. 1975. Trans. B.C.R.A. Vol.2. No.1. pp.1-12. Beck, J.S. 1979. T.S.G. N/L No.8. Survey. Beck, J.S. and Christopher, N.J. 1977. Trans. B.C.R.A. Vol.4. No. 3. pp.361-365. Survey. Beck, J.S. and Gill, D.W. 1974. D.C.A. N/L No.20 pp.1-2. Buckley, A.L. 1974. D.C.A. N/L No.21. Jefferson, D.P. 1961. Bull. P.D.M.H.S. Vol.1. No.4. pp.37-43. King, B. 1962. Cave Science Vol.4. No.32. pp.377-383. Survey. Mellor, D. 1972. Eldon P.C. Jour. Vol.8. No.1. pp.14-15. Smith, M.E. 1971. Bull. P.D.M.H.S. Vol.4. No.5. pp.370-374. Survey.

CRACKPOT CAVE   NGR 2182 7596   Grade I
(Hardwark)
Alt. 686ft (209m)   Length: 70ft (21m)
Above and to the left of Eyam Dale Shaft entrance to Carlswark.

Originally 10ft (3m) long. Dug out for 10ft (3m) through a hole in the calcite roof to 50ft (15m) of well decorated passage ending in a calcite choke. Formations now destroyed by vandals.

Reference: Noble, M. 1975. D.C.A. N/L No.24. p.6.

CREEP CAVE   NGR 215 758   Lost?
Alt. 800ft (244m)   Length: 110ft (34m)

In Eyam Quarry, below Farnsley Lane, halfway up quarry face. Now thought to be buried.

Phreatic tube 2ft 6in (0.8m) diameter for 70ft (21m) to a small aven. Further 40ft (12m) of passage to a calcite blockage.

References: Gill, D.W. 1972. British Caver Vol.57. p.102. Lord, P.J. 1971. Jour. S.U.S.S. Vol.2. No.1. p.26

CROSSLOW CAVERN   NGR 2030 7706   Lost
Alt. 1000ft (305m)   Length: 300ft (90m)   Depth: 80ft (24m)

Shaft in enclosure in south west corner of field no.281, 200 yards (182m) south west of Black Hole Mine.

A lost cavern listed by Farey, and rediscovered by Peak District Mines Historical Society. On Crosslow Rake. A 60ft (18m) ladder pitch and 20ft (6m) scramble into mine workings. A short passage goes west into natural cavern once used as a washing floor and largely filled with "deads". Drainage towards Waterfall Swallet. The site has been "restored" and the entrance obliterated.

Reference: Robey, J. 1964. Bull. P.D.M.H.S. Vol.2. No.3. 151-152. Survey.

CUCKLET CHURCH CAVE   NGR 2154 7619   Grade I
Alt. 800ft (240m)

High on the west side of Cucklet Delph at the north end.

A series of through arches in a prominent buttress. Used each year for the plague commemoration service.

Reference: Pearce, A. 1974. Bull. P.D.M.H.S. Vol.5. No.5.

CUCKLET DELPH UPPER CAVE
NGR 2156 7610   Grade I
(Smokey Hole)
Alt. 656ft (200m)   Length: 50ft (15m)

Small cave about 6ft (2m) above the stream on the west side of the path.

A short bedding crawl was dug out to 50ft (15m), completely blocked at the end by clay.

DELPH HOLE   NGR 2165 7595   Grade II
Alt. 697ft (212.5m)   Length: 187ft (57m)

High on the east side of Cucklet Delph below Auton Crofts plateau.

Entrance is 6ft (2m) high mine level. After 60ft (18m) from entrance step across a shaft in the floor (with care) to a passage on right. After 25ft (8m) is a natural chamber 30ft (9m) long with a silted passage descending to the left, dug for some distance during 1977. Down the shaft (easy climb 8ft/2.5m) is a mine level which ends at a forefield.

References: Pearce, A. 1974. Bull.P.D.M.H.S. Vol.5. No.5. pp.243-257. Survey. Pill, A.L. 1950. Cave Science No.15. p.223.

DELPH SWALLETS   Digs

DELPH TOP SINK   NGR 2157 7618
Alt. 661ft (201m)   **Depth: 60ft (18m)**

Close to the brook directly below Cucklet Church. Concrete cover on oil-drum shaft.

A 12ft (4m) oil-drum shaft opens into a large rift dug out to a depth of 60ft (18m). Water backs up to the 50ft (15m) mark and sinks in narrow cracks.

Water dye tested to Moorwood Sough without passing through the known Carlswark Cavern system.

DELPH BOTTOM SINK   NGR 2158 7597
Alt. 626ft (191m)

By the side of the path up Cucklet Delph 140 yards (128m) north of the main road.

Water sinks in the bed of the stream. The sink is soon overpowered and water flows on to join the Dale Brook. Dug in the early 1970's, but no bedrock was found. Water dye tested to the Merlin Streamway.

Reference: Beck, J.S. 1975. Trans B.C.R.A. Vol.2. No.1. pp.1-11.

EYAM DALE HOUSE CAVE   NGR 2196 7626   Grade III
Alt. 760ft (232m)   **Length: 1050ft (320m)**   **Depth: 183ft (56m)**

Permission required IN ADVANCE from Mr C. Baker, Eyam Dale House Residential Home for the Elderly. The shaft entrance lies in the grounds of the house close to the line of the sewer. The manhole cover just off the line of inspection pits is a mineshaft.

60ft (18m) hading entrance shaft discovered by tracing the old sewer (now diverted!) in 1985. Shaft enters natural chamber, with second pitch 35ft (11m) leading only to a further climb down into tight rifts. From base of entrance shaft pass the second pitch and follow crawls into a parallel rift to the head of a 20ft (6m) pitch which can be free climbed with care. Passage enlarges until the roomy North West Chamber is reached, with various digging possibilities.

Back at the base of the 20ft pitch follow a flat-out crawl to the Pearly Gate, a squeeze between stalagmite pillars. Crawl continues well-decorated (care needed to avoid stals) to an 8ft (2.5m) climb down to a bouldery chamber. A fine grotto (The Room with a View) is up the flowstone slope to the left. This looks out along a large rift (The Other Side), 200ft (61m) long and with a vertical range of over 100ft (30m). Climb down boulders and follow rift until the floor drops away and traverse continues. Rift ends at all levels in either boulders or flowstone. Has been climbed to the base of a mineshaft to surface.

A series of sharp muddy rifts and crawls leads in the other direction from the climb down boulders to The Other Side. Appears to draught from Dynamite Series in Carlswark Cavern.

Tackle:

Entrance Shaft:	60ft (18m) ladder; 80ft (24m) lifeline.
	(Belay to tree or take a short bar).
2nd Pitch:	40ft (12m) ladder; 50ft (15m) lifeline.
	(Bolt belays).
20ft climb:	20ft (6m) ladder; 30ft (9m) lifeline.

Reference: Beck, J.S. 1985. T.S.G. Jour. No.12. pp.10-14. Survey.

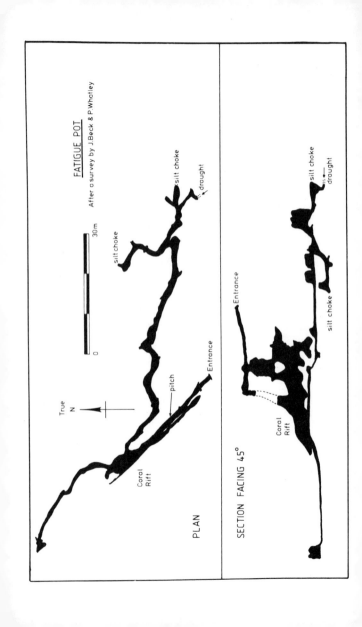

FATIGUE POT

After a survey by J.Beck & P.Whatley

30m

True N

PLAN

silt choke

silt choke

draught

pitch

Entrance

Coral Rift

SECTION FACING 45°

Entrance

Coral Rift

silt choke

silt choke

draught

FARNSLEY LANE QUARRY CAVES
NGR 211 757   Grade I
Alt. 700ft (210m)   Lengths: 10-50ft (3-15m)

Permission from Wimpey's Quarry at the bottom of Eyam Dale. Not usually granted.

Various caves in the lower bench of what used to be Eyam Quarry, by the sharp bend on the main road.

One tube 15ft (5m) up the face is about 30ft (9m) long. Directly below Farnsley Lane is a large blind mine level, and to the right of this is a large phreatic tube about 50ft long ending at a clay choke.

At present (1991) these entrances are buried by "landscaping".

FATIGUE POT   NGR 2268 7485   Grade III
(Colliers Peril Cave)
Alt. 600ft (183m)   Length: 620ft (189m)   Depth: 82ft (25m)

No known access restrictions, but please replace cover.

20ft (6m) above the valley floor on the north side of Coombes Dale. Small entrance blocked by removable steel door. Very difficult to find.

Small, muddy, smelly entrance crawl for 30ft (9m) to head of 25ft (8m) pitch. Replacing the cover carefully will help to stop foxes making the crawl worse.

Follow the rift down several short climbs and drop through tight hole in boulders for 15ft (4.5m) into wide rift passage (handline useful for return). Traverse along the rift above tight holes in the floor for 50ft (15m) approximately. Two crawls on the right. The first leads to 300ft (91m) of low passage with avens at the end, and a strongly draughting continuation which is too tight. The second crawl is very tight for 100ft (30m) with very restricted turning space.

References: Beck, J.S. 1979. Jour. Eldon P.C. Vol.9. No.1. pp.1-3. Survey. Tottle, P. 1954. The Speleologist No.1. pp. 85-91.

FIRESET SHAFT   NGR 2189 7607   Grade II
Alt. 700ft (213.3m)   Length: 154ft (47m)   Depth: 84ft (25.5m)

Shaft excavated in 1982 for 50ft (15m) to a short sidestep into a stope which ends at forefields in both directions. Small hole in the floor gives access to a very narrow level with soot-coated walls, which has been driven by the old method of firesetting, ie without the use of explosives. The level ends at a narrow shaft with further short backfilled fireset workings leading westwards. Draught is thought to come from the Dynamite Series of Carlswark.

Reference: Whitehouse, R.H. 1986. T.S.G. Jour. No.12. pp.6-9. Survey.

HAWKEN EDGE CAVE   NGR 218 757   Lost
Alt. 650ft (198m)   Length: 52ft (16m)

At the west end of Dalton's (now Wimpey's) Quarry on the south side of the Dale, by the footpath to Lane Head. 50ft above the road.

A large entrance 15ft (5m) high, which soon closed. Quarrying has now either buried or removed the cave.

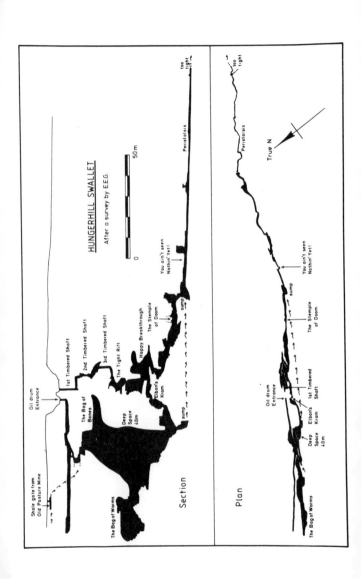

HUNGERHILL SWALLET

After a survey by E.E.G.

0   50m

Section

Shale gate from Old Pasture Mine

Oil drum Entrance

1st Timbered Shaft

2nd Timbered Shaft

3rd Timbered Shaft

The Tight Rift

The Bog of Bones

Deep Space 40m

Elbon's Kram

The Bog of Worms

Happy Breakthrough

The Stemple of Doom

sump

You ain't seen Nothin' Yet!

Peristalsis

too tight

sump

Plan

True N

Oil drum Entrance

1st Timbered Shaft

Elbon's Kram

Deep Space 40m

The Bog of Worms

The Stemple of Doom

sump

You ain't seen Nothin' Yet!

Peristalsis

too tight

HAWKENEDGE WELL   NGR 2156 7583   Dig
(Oakenedge Sough)
Alt. 600ft (183m)

Small resurgence on the south side of A623 in Middleton Dale, opposite
Cucklet Delph.

Discharges a fairly constant flow. Possibly the tail of a sough, though shafts
immediately upstream will be under quarry debris.

References: Kirkham, N. 1967. Bull. P.D.M.H.S. Vol.3. No.4. pp.197-218.

HOBBIT HOLE   NGR 2083 7597   Grade I
Alt. 715ft (218m)   Length: 35ft (11m)

At road level in the lowest section of Furness (Ben Bennett's) Quarry.

A short unpleasant flat-out crawl to a complete flowstone choke.

HOLE IN THE WALL   NGR 2096 7604   Grade I
Alt. 786ft (240m)   Length: 230ft (70m)

25ft up the north face in the main part of Furness (Ben Bennett's) Quarry,
directly opposite the entry point of the track.

An ancient cave passage intersected by the quarry. Entrance about 10ft
(3m) high. Dig is about 230ft long. Ends 30ft into a boulder choke.

HUNGER HILL SWALLET   NGR 2096 7695   Grade V
(Pippin Swallow? Duss Pit?)
Alt. 920ft (280m)   Length: 1200ft (305m) approx.   Depth: 250ft (76m)

**Warning: The timbered shafts will deteriorate and become slippery and
unstable. Some of the squeezes in the cave are very tight and awkward, or
through poised boulders. The big pitch (Deep Space) and the streamway
(Peristalsis) may quickly become impassable in wet weather.**

Permission from Mr. H. Eyre, Hungerhill House.

A tree lined shakehole in field west of Hungerhill House, the whitewashed
cottage to the north of the road. Excavated 1985-1987. Swallet stream
captured by shale gate from Little Pasture Mine, seen in a tiny shaft west of
the main shakehole, where the stream flows into an impenetrable bedding.

The Timbered Shaft Entrance lies in the ruined shelter against the south wall
of the shakehole. The first shaft is 28ft (8.5m) deep, and leads via a timbered
tunnel to a further timbered shaft of 15ft (4.5m). Beware of loose boulders at
the bottom. The third timbered shaft is 25ft (8m) deep. All the shafts are free-
climbable with care, but the timbers are becoming slippery (Aug. 1990).

Crawl under loose boulders with care into a rift passage. A tight descent
down a slot in the floor leads to the head of a 25ft (8m) pitch (belay to boulder
jammed in the head of the rift). The pitch lands in a chamber, "Happy
Breakthrough".

The Mine Level Entrance consists of an oil drum shaft in the shakehole
floor at the west end. Cover may be buried under silt from road drains. Short
(10ft/3m) ladder is needed for exit! Follow wet and muddy mine level into a
chamber. Level continues to a forefield, but an obvious crawl in the floor
leads to a tight and awkward squeeze down into the Top Streamway.

Follow stream in small passage over short cascades to the head of the spectacular 130ft (40m) pitch, "Deep Space". This may become impassable in flood. The pitch begins as a long narrow rift and becomes progressively bigger. The landing is on a boulder slope, down which the stream cascades into a small passage and a choked sump.

At the top of the boulder slope a climb and short crawl lead into a breakdown chamber. A further climb and crawl at the far end lead to the head of a flowstoned boulder slope in the "Bag of Worms". The far end of this second chamber consists of a large choke, which has been dug upwards into a short continuation through very loose boulders 70ft (21m) above the floor.

A climb above the sump (beware of dangerous boulders) leads via a narrow rift to the bottom of "Elbon's Kram", a strenuous climb up a tight rift to a very awkward squeeze. Two further squeezes lead through to the bottom of the 25ft (8m) pitch below the timbered shafts.

From the bottom of the 25ft (8m) pitch, climb down slabs and double back to scramble into a parallel rift. A short crawl leads to a further breakdown chamber. Small stream sinks at the far end, but follow a crawl just above (beware of the dangerously balanced "Stemple of Doom" just beyond). The route continues under more loose boulders to a climb down into a sump pool where the stream from Deep Space emerges.

A narrow stream passage continues along the joint, and turns right into a very tight section, "You Ain't Seen Nothin' Yet!" 150ft (46m) of crawling leads to a small chamber where miners' deads are seen. The miner's way down is blocked with large boulders in the roof. A tight squeeze through boulders leads to 40ft (12m) of frustrating crawling in the stream to Bang Corner.

Bang Corner looks passable at roof level, but it is only passable in dry weather by lying in the stream. The next 120ft (37m), "Peristalsis", necessitates wriggling in the stream in a passage about a foot wide, round some very sharp bends. It is sumped in all but dry weather. A tiny cross rift is reached. A short distance beyond, progress in the stream becomes impossible. Wet weather overflow water leaves to the right via the cross rift, which is an unpromising, remote, horrible dig.

Tackle:

Timbered Shaft Entrance:	30ft (9m) ladder; 50ft (15m) lifeline.
Tight Rift Pitch:	25ft (8m) ladder; 60ft (18m) lifeline. (Long belay to wedged boulder)
Oil Drum Entrance:	10ft ladder or handline.
Deep Space:	130ft (40m) ladder; 150ft (46m) lifeline.
SRT:	160ft rope + bolts for deviations.

Reference: Beck, J.S. 1988. Jour. T.S.G. No.13. pp.26-33. Survey.

IVY GREEN CAVE   NGR 2225 7580   Grade II
Alt. 655ft (199m)   Length: 740ft (225m)

High in the cliff, just east of the terrace, and west of Cliff Stile Vein. An awkward climb up to the entrance.

Rift-like entrance soon becomes a phreatic tube. Right branch after 90ft (27m) was dug for over 100ft (30m) to a choke in Cliff Stile Vein. Main

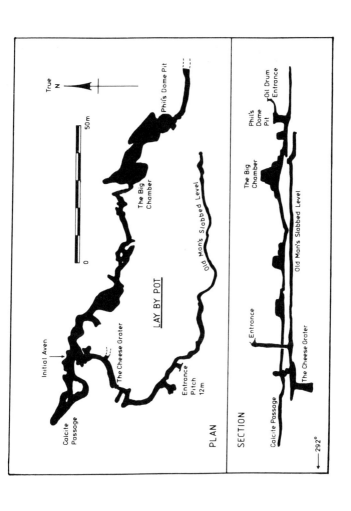

LAY BY POT

PLAN

SECTION

Initial Aven

Calcite Passage

The Cheese Grater

The Big Chamber

Phil's Dome Pit

Old Man's Slabbed Level

Entrance Pitch 12m

Entrance

Old Drum Entrance

292°

True N

0   50m

passage continues through some tight squeezes to a final calcite choke. There is no draught at the end but small silted passages on the left appear to draught from a mine level at 2214 7582 (Middleton Dale Mine Level No.5).

References: Beck, J.S. 1975. Trans.B.C.R.A. Vol.2. No.1. pp.1-11. Noble, M. 1975. D.C.A. N/L No.24. p.7. Smith, M.E. 1969. S.U.S.S. Jour. Vol.1. No.5. pp.208-210. Survey.

KEYHOLE CAVE   NGR 2226 7580   Grade I
Alt. 655ft (199m)   Length: 50ft (15m)

Immediately east of Cliff Stile vein and east of the terrace.

The obvious downstream continuation of Ivy Green Cave before quarrying intersected the passage. A large passage filled with sandstone pebbles has been partly dug out, and leads right through the buttress with a window in the cliff face halfway through.

LAY-BY POT   NGR 2035 7599   Grade II
Alt. 810ft (247m)   Length: 1215ft (370m)   Depth: 76ft (23m)

On north side of dale, opposite the second lay-by coming from Wardlow. Behind an earth bank and vegetation.

A short mined passage slopes down to the head of a 46ft (14m) pitch, dug out by South West London Caving Club in 1973. Belay ladder to tree. At base of pitch a crawl to the east leads to the 200ft (61m) long "Old Man's Slabbed Level", a dry-stone level which runs beneath the road and ends at a collapse.

The other direction at the base of the pitch leads after 100ft (30m) natural passage to the Cheese Grater, a 23ft (7m) pitch to a static pool. Passage continues to a collapse and an upward slope to a T-junction. Left is the 80ft (24m) long Calcite Passage, passing Initial Aven, where the date "1818" is scratched in the flowstone. Right at the junction leads after 60ft (18m) to Silhouette Grotto. A crawl at the far end of the chamber leads after 30ft (9m) to another low chamber with avens. A further crawl, wet at first, leads after 100ft (31m) to a large chamber about 50ft (15m) long, 20ft (6m) wide, and 25ft (8m) high. A further 60ft (18m) of passage leads to Phil's Dome Pit. The crawl continues beyond this aven, but is soon blocked by clay and breakdown.

Second Entrance: A short drop through an oil drum leads through two tight squeezes to a choice of ways down into Phil's Dome Pit. Either crawl ahead to a 15ft (4.5m) pitch, or follow very tight squeeze between boulders into a lower passage which emerges over a hole in the floor of the main aven.

Tackle:

Entrance Pitch:	50ft (15m) ladder; 60ft (18m) lifeline.
	Long belay to tree.
Phil's Dome Pit Pitch:	15ft (4.5m) ladder; 20ft (6m) lifeline.

References: Beck, J.S. & Gill, D.W. 1973. D.C.A. N/L No.18. Beck, J.S. 1976. E.P.C. Jour. Vol.9. No.1. pp.6-7. Gill, D.W. 1976. E.P.C. Jour. Vol.9. No.1. pp.4-5.

LAY-BY SHAFT 2   NGR 2030 7599   Grade II
Alt. 805ft (245m)   **Depth: 27ft (8m)**

Just west of the Lay-by Pot shaft.

A natural shaft excavated to 27ft (8m) depth by Chesterfield Caving Club in 1987. Becomes too narrow for progress.

LAY-BY SHELTER   NGR 205 760   Grade I
Alt. 770ft (235m)   **Length: 20ft (6m)**

Immediately west of Hanging Flat Mine, opposite the third lay-by down from Wardlow.

A large entrance easily visible to westbound traffic. Soon closes to flat out crawls choked with flowstone.

LINEN DALE CAVE   NGR 1989 7696   Grade I
Alt. 950ft (290m)   **Length: 45ft (14m)**   **Depth: 25ft (8m)**

At the north end of the valley, south of the Foolow Road, in small walling stone quarry.

A tight dug out crawl to the head of a pot full of mud and boulders. Dug to its present depth by Stockport Caving Group.

Reference: Beck, J.S. 1975. Trans. B.C.R.A. Vol.2. No.1. p.7.

LITTLE WATERFALL SWALLET   NGR 2003 7710   Dig
Alt. 870ft (265m)

A large tree-lined shakehole 150 yards (137m) north east of Waterfall Swallet, with a stream sinking against the south wall.

Reference: Beck, J.S. 1975. Trans B.C.R.A. Vol.2. No.1. p.2.

MERLIN'S MINE   NGR 2177 7591   Grade III (Mine)
(Merlin Mine. Merlin's Cavern. Merlin's Cave)
Alt. 686ft (209m)   **Length: 3200ft (975m)**   **Depth: 90ft (27m)**

Two entrances, of which the lower (adit) entrance is most used. High above Carlwark's Eyam Dale Shaft, but closer to the road junction.

The lower adit entrance is small, but soon opens out to an enlarged natural rift which leads to a crossroads. Right leads to the bottom of the 23ft (7m) upper entrance shaft. Left leads to a natural chamber, with a crawl on the right to a muddy dig, and left to a small passage which ends at the boulder-lined Laxative Pot, 50ft (15m) deep. Other small passages soon end.

Straight on at the crossroads soon leads to a short climb up into a natural chamber, and the level continues in Merlin's Pipe to a T-junction. Left leads to some natural rifts, and right over a collapse to a further junction. To the left is a mine level leading after 276ft (84m) to a blind shaft 33ft (10m) deep on Cowlishaw Vein. Ahead are three shafts in the floor. S1 is 18ft (5.5m) deep, with climbs into loose workings. S3 is also blind, 20ft (6m) deep.

The second shaft, S2, is 26ft (8m) deep to the top of a boulder slope in a stope. A squeeze down in the floor at the bottom of the slope leads to a junction. Left leads to Gimli's Dream, and straight on leads to the Merlin Streamway.

Gimli's Dream: A series of short crawls lead to a series of chambers which were extremely well decorated when first discovered. Further crawls and climbs lead eventually to the original connection with Carlswark, now blocked.

The Merlin Streamway: Turning right after a few yards of mine level leads to Sump Pool Chamber, usually occupied by a fast flowing stream, but dry in dry summers. To the right is a low arch or short sump leading to a bedding cave, and a climb down into a rift leading to the tight Shag's Sump. The stream reappears in John Smith's Passage in Carlswark Cavern, and has been pumped out and surveyed in drought.

To the left at Sump Pool Chamber is Sump 1, 60ft (18m) long, constricted at its inner end, and not free-diveable. 66ft (20m) of large passage follows to Sump 2, 30ft (9m) long and emerging in large passage again. Sump 3 lies to the right and is by-passed. Sump 4 is a flat out crawl in water. Merlin 5 is 265ft (80m) of fine large passage up to Sump 5. The first 4 sumps often drop far enough to be passable without diving in late summer.

Sump 5, 115ft (35m), was passed in the 1976 drought to an airbell. In the 1990 drought Sump 6, 40ft (12m) was passed to a roomy chamber. Sump 7, 20ft (6m) follows, and a short passage leads to Sump 8. 40ft (12m) into Sump 8 the route forks. Left was baled over dams and continued for 30ft (9m) to become too tight. Right was baled out to give access to a tiny cross rift. A squeeze led into a higher bedding plane continuation which became too low.

Tackle:

Cowlishaw Shaft:	35ft (11m) ladder; 50ft (15m) lifeline.
Laxative Pot:	50ft (15m) ladder; 70ft (21m) lifeline.
S1 Shaft:	20ft (6m) ladder; 30ft (9m) lifeline.
S2 Shaft:	30ft (9m) ladder; 40ft (12m) lifeline.
S3 Shaft:	20ft (6m) ladder; 30ft (9m) lifeline.

References: Beck, J.S. 1975. Trans. B.C.R.A. Vol.2. No.1. pp.1-11. Area plan. Beck, J.S. 1976. E.P.C. Jour. Vol.9. No.1. pp.9-11. Christopher, N.S.J. & Beck, J.S. 1977. Trans. B.C.R.A. Vol.4. No.3. pp.361-365. Survey. Rieuwerts, J. 1960. Bull. P.D.M.H.S. Vol.1. No.3. pp.3-6. Survey.

MIDDLETON DALE MINE LEVELS   Grade I-II (Mines)

LEVEL 1   NGR 2262 7565
Alt. 590ft (180m)   Length: 150ft (46m) approx.

In garden of first house below the filling station.

A short working in Paul Pipe intersects a level on a north east – south west vein. Two awkward scrambles for 10ft (3m) to a lower level. A tight phreatic tube at the south west end leads to a small solution chamber.

LEVEL 2   NGR 2231 7577
Alt. 645ft (196m)   Length: 50ft (18m) approx.

Three trial levels one above the other at the west end of Windy Ledge.

A hard climb is necessary to reach the top level, which is about 40ft (12m) long. The lower two close almost immediately.

LEVEL 3   NGR 2223 7579
Alt. 650ft (198m)   Length: 20ft (6m) approx.
On Cliffstile Vein between Ivy Green and Keyhole Caves.
   A large open rift. Until about 1968 a level led out at the back, and ended at a small chamber with a boss of flowstone in the centre after roughly 100ft (30m). The roof was dangerous, and has now collapsed.

LEVEL 4   NGR 2215 7582
(Triple Hole. MKP. The Tuesdig. Lower Bamforth Hole).
Alt. 610ft (186m)   Length: 300ft (91m)
At the base of the upper cliff, on the terrace, 180ft (55m) east of Carlswark's rift entrance.
   A vertical drop of four feet into a partly natural level. This runs north west for 60ft (18m) then turns along a north east vein. After 40ft (12m) a natural passage on the left leads via a muddy chute and short sump to two natural chambers (dug into by TSG 1976/7). Beyond junction main level becomes a dangerous crawl under stacked deads to a blind and unstable shaft after 200ft (61m).

LEVEL 5   NGR 2214 7582
(Fingal's Cave. Incorrectly referred to as Bamforth Hole).
Alt. 620ft (189m)   Length: 205ft (62m)
Large rift like entrance above the terrace, 150ft (46m) east of Carlswark's rift entrance.
   Soon closes down to a small mine level. A short climb up a shaft and along a higher level leads to a natural chamber with phreatic tubes to right and left. Right is soon blocked by flowstone, but there is a strong draught, thought to come from Ivy Green Cave. Passage to left now blocked by collapse of shaft in roof, but was entered by digging and found to be hopelessly blocked by silt and flowstone.

LEVEL 6   NGR 2195 7589
Alt. 690ft (210m)   Length: 300ft (91m)
At base of top cliff, 150ft (56m) east of Shining Cliff.
   Small mine level. Intersects Shining Cliff Scrin after roughly 60ft (18m) and runs northeast. Becomes very loose and ends at a collapsed floor shaft.

LEVEL 7   NGR 2166 7588
Alt. 600ft (183m)   Length: 350ft (106m) approx.   Depth: 130ft (40m)
At valley floor level at south east corner of The Delph.
   Small entrance leads to level with small solution cavities. Another level directly above leads to a shaft to the lower level. Hope Shaft entrance (alt.730ft/222m) at 2177 7585 has been dug into and drops into top level.
Tackle for through trip:
Hope Shaft: 100ft (30m) ladder; 110ft (34m) lifeline; Bolt belays.
Internal Shaft: 30ft (9m) ladder; 40ft (12m) lifeline; Bolt belays.
   Reference: Whitehouse, D. 1980. D.C.A. N/L No.46. pp.1-2.

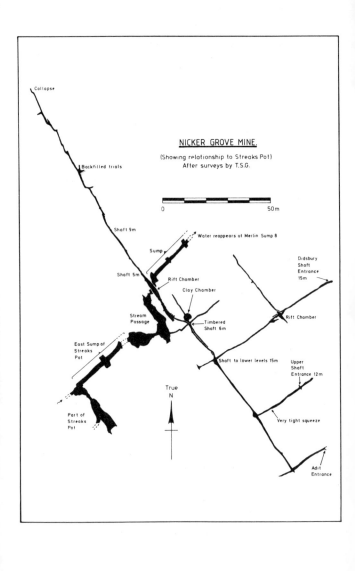

Collapse

Backfilled trials

Shaft 9m

Sump

Water reappears at Merlin Sump 8

NICKER GROVE MINE.

(Showing relationship to Streaks Pot)
After surveys by T.S.G.

0   50m

Shaft 5m

Rift Chamber

Clay Chamber

Didsbury
Shaft
Entrance
15m

Stream
Passage

Timbered
Shaft 6m

Rift Chamber

East Sump of
Streaks
Pot

Shaft to lower levels 15m

Upper
Shaft
Entrance
12m

True
N

Part of
Streaks
Pot

Very tight squeeze

Adit
Entrance

LEVEL 8   NGR 2145 7596
Alt. 710ft (216m)   Length: 100ft (30m)   Depth: 23ft (7m)

In gully between two buttresses of the top cliff, west of The Delph.
    A tiny shaft 23ft (7m) deep leads to a level. Can be followed north to a solution chamber.

LEVEL 9   NGR 2140 7594
(Friday Mine. Good Friday Mine)
Alt. 660ft (201m)   Length: 250ft (76m)   Depth: 80ft (24m)

On hillside west of The Delph, about 40ft (12m) above the road.
    A blocked adit entrance and 17ft (5m) shaft above. The shaft leads to a level which runs back into the hillside. A 70ft (21m) shaft in the floor leads to a short level which is blind. Nothing natural.

LEVEL 10   NGR 2224 7579
Alt. 609ft (185.7m)   Length: 50ft (15m)

A short roomy pipe working directly below Ivy Green Cave entrance.

LEVEL 11   NGR 2150 7592
(Monday Mine)
Alt. 664ft (202.4m)   Length: 170ft (52m)   Depth: 70ft (21m)

Narrow descending entrance passage leads to a hole in the floor which can be climbed down to a stope with no way on, and a shaft to surface slabbed over at the top. Straight ahead leads to a second shaft in the floor which can be climbed to a static blind sump.
    Reference: Noble, M. 1985. T.S.G. Jour. No.11. pp.7-8. Survey.

MONKEY ROCK CAVE   NGR 2153 7592   Grade I
Alt. 725ft (221m)   Length: 32ft (9.7m)

A short solution cave on a major joint in the topmost cliff.

NICKERGROVE MINE   Grade II (Mine)
(Wrongly referred to as Great Cucklet Mine)
Adit   NGR 2155 7596   Didsbury Shaft   NGR 2155 7603
Alt. Adit: 675ft (206m)   Didsbury Shaft: 662ft (202m)
Length: 1900ft (579m)   Depth: 80ft (24m)

On the west side of Cucklet Delph. Adit almost directly above end of wall in valley floor. Shaft entrance further north, a short distance up the hillside.
    The obvious adit turns sharp right after 60ft (18m) at a hole in the floor which leads nowhere. A level on the right after a further 100ft (30m) leads via a very tight squeeze to the bottom of a shaft to surface. The main internal shaft is reached after a further 110ft (34m). Cross carefully. The level becomes much smaller, and breaks out into a large rift chamber, the floor of which descends in a series of steps to the continuation of the level. Two more shafts have to be traversed over (both are blind) before a complete run-in of sludge and rock is reached 790ft (241m) from the entrance.

The main shaft was excavated to a total depth of 80ft (24m) but the bottom 30ft was backfilled from the Clay Chamber dig. A level to the north east at 25ft (8m) leads via a series of short free climbs to a rift chamber. A further climb down on the far side of the chamber leads to a junction. A level to the north is blind after 130ft (40m), while that to the north east leads into the "Didsbury Shaft" 15ft (5m) from surface. The shaft continues down to 50ft (15m) to short blind levels and a blind sump.

At the 50ft (15m) level in the main internal shaft, a short level leads south west to a forefield, and a level with rails in the floor (from the 1984 dig) leads north to the Clay Chamber. A short level continues beyond, and a timbered shaft in the floor leads to a short stretch of large stream passage between two sumps. The large upstream sump is the downstream end of Streaks East Sump, and downstream the water is next seen in the Merlin Streamway. The downstream sump was penetrated in the 1990 drought through a very tight squeeze to a roomy chamber. The passage continued for a further 60ft (18m) to a large cross rift beyond which the route sumped.

Tackle:

	Ladder	Belay	Lifeline
Main Shaft:	50ft (15m)	3ft (0.6m) to log	60ft (18m)
Didsbury Shaft:	50ft (15m)	10ft (3m) to tree	60ft (18m)

References: Beck, J.S. & Worley, N.E. 1977. Bull. P.D.M.H.S. Vol.6. No.5. pp.175-179. Survey. Gunn, J. 1975. D.C.A. N/L No.24. p.5. Pearce, A.J. 1974. Bull. P.D.M.H.S. Vol.5. No.5. pp.243-257.

PIPPIN SWALLOW   Lost

The Pippin Swallow is likely to have been Hungerhill Swallet, or a swallet now unknown somewhere near Eyam Square. A field north of the square is known as Pippin Close.
Reference: Woods, W. 1842. The History and Antiquities of Eyam.

ROCK COTTAGE TUBES   NGR 2273 7570   Grade I
Alt. 580ft (177m)

In cliff directly above cottage and adjacent garage.
Three small phreatic tubes, all silted.

SALLET HOLE CAVE   NGR 2192 7395   Grade II
Alt. 900ft (274m)   Length: 75ft (23m)   Depth: 200ft (61m)

High on the west side of a shallow gully above Sallet Hole Mine.
Entrance chamber leads to left passage with 15ft (4.5m) deep pot in the floor, and right passage (partly mined) with 200ft (61m) shaft in the floor. This shaft used to connect with Sallet Hole Mine (now being actively worked) but the lower level is now run-in.

THE SALTPAN   NGR 2158 7636   Gorge
Alt. 730ft (223m)

At the north end of Cucklet Delph.
A narrow gorge with all the features of a vadose streamway with no roof.

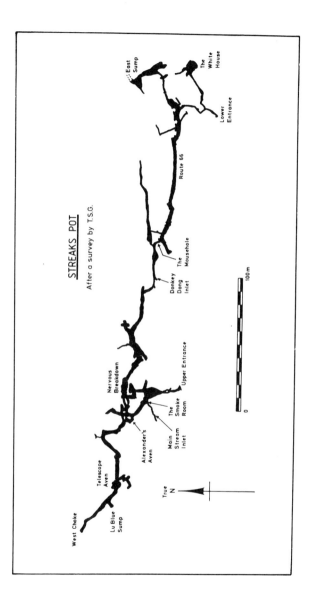

STREAKS POT

After a survey by T.S.G.

West Choke

Telescope Aven

Lu Blue Sump

Nervous Breakdown

Alexander's Aven

Main Stream Inlet

The Smoke Room

Upper Entrance

Donkey Dong Inlet

The Mousehole

Route 66

Lower Entrance

East Sump

The White House

True N

0   100 m

SARAH'S CAVE   NGR 2151 7572   Lost
Alt. c.700ft (213m)

In Hawkenedge Quarry (now Wimpey's Quarry) in a position almost opposite The Delph.

A large well decorated cave discovered during quarrying operations. Part of the cave was certainly destroyed, but some may remain. Fragments of phreatic cave keep appearing in this part of the quarry, but the actual horizon of Sarah's Cave is below the floor of the main bench.

References: Anon. 1970. D.C.A. N/L No.7. p.8. Gill, D.W. 1976. E.P.C. Jour. Vol.9. No.1. p.2. Lord, P.J. & Wright, A. 1971. S.U.S.S. Jour. Vol.2. No.1. pp.24-25. Survey.

STREAKS CAVE   NGR 2121 7590   Grade I
Alt. 665ft (202.7m)   Length: 90ft (27m)

Above and to the right of Yoga Cave, below Streaks Footpath.

A lower mined entrance leads after 40ft (12m) to a short climb up into a rift chamber which continues for a further 40ft (12m). From the top of the climb, a natural hands and knees crawl leads to an entrance directly above the lower one.

STREAKS POT   NGR 2121 7596   Grade IV
(Saturday Pot)

(Top Entr.) NGR 2121 7596	**(Lower Entr.) NGR 2140 7593**
Alt. 748ft (228m) (Top Entr.)	**636ft (194m) (Lower Entr.)**
Length: 2549ft (777m)	**Depth: 135ft (41m)**

Upper Entrance Series

A small mined entrance at the base of a low cliff, close to the highest cliff line, east of Streaks Footpath.

A low mined crawl leads after 15ft (5m) to the head of a 40ft (12m) pitch. Belay to tree outside. Possible to traverse over the pitch and free climb down beyond. A passage 10ft (3m) above the floor of the pitch leads to a breakdown chamber with a bouldery rift passage in the right hand corner. Scrambling along this through breakdown leads to an aven where an easy climb down a narrow rift (care not to dislodge stacked rocks) leads to a short horizontal section. Enter feet first with care as roof is supported by rotten timbers. An easy 30ft (9m) climb follows (but beware of loose rocks). At the bottom a short muddy tube leads to the stream.

Lower Entrance Series

Approx.12ft (4m) above the road roughly 200 yards (183m) west of Hawkenedge Well. Entrance via two oil drums, not to be confused with Sunday Mine to the east which is four oil drums deep. Short ladder useful for exit from drums.

Crawl at the bottom leads to a fork. To the right is a tight crawl to a chamber. Left is main way on, and leads to a T-junction. Right leads to a series of muddy chambers and crawl, and the stream is seen briefly between two sumps.

Left at the T-junction leads through a mined area into Route 66, a spacious sandy crawl which may carry a large stream in wet weather. The crawl reduces to flat-out beyond an area of breakdown, and a crawl on the right soon leads to the stream, with an unpleasant crawl in water for 200ft (61m) to a sump. Beyond the crawl is a small chamber. Low passage on the left leads to a boulder choke, while ahead is a tiny crawl, the Mousehole. After a wet flat out crawl, a tight squeeze into a small breakdown chamber, and a duck, the passage continues past Donkey Dong Inlet on the left, and through a dry stretch to a T-junction with the Main Stream.

Downstream to the right becomes too tight, but upstream becomes more roomy until a crawl round a breakdown pile leads to a short stretch of walking-sized passage. A window leads to a parallel tube which carries most of the stream. Nervous Breakdown follows–a chaos of boulders in the streamway with crawls in and out of the water. The final descent to the stream is a few feet before the rift where the Upper Entrance Series joins the route.

The Upstream Series

Beyond the bottom of the Upper Entrance Series the stream comes from two tubes. Either route is a very sporting crawl in the stream. The tubes join, and a T-junction is reached.

The stream comes from the left, where a larger passage leads to a small chamber. The stream comes from the Main Stream Inlet, a crawl which becomes too tight. A silted crawl also leads to a rift directly below the floor of the Upper Entrance Series.

To the right at the T-junction leads to a rift chamber and crawl that becomes too low. An obscure way ahead at the T-junction leads through boulders into Alexander's Aven, and continues into a roomy crawl. A breakdown chamber is soon reached, and the passage continues, becoming steadily larger to the base of the impressive Telescope Aven. This was climbed for 100ft (30m), but the tubes at the top still await a very thin determined explorer. Beyond Telescope Aven a left hand branch leads to Lu-Blue Sump, dived and pronounced too tight in 1980 but more recently a way on down was found. The main passage attains a consistent walking size for the first time in the cave, with a vadose trench starting to appear. It ends abruptly at a boulder choke, which draughts strongly.

Tackle:

Upper Entrance: 40ft (12m) ladder; 50ft (15m) lifeline.
         Long belay to tree outside.

References: Beck, J.S. 1981. T.S.G. N/L No.9. pp. 1-10. Survey. Davenport, J. 1988. C.D.G. N/L No.87. p.19.

SUNDAY MINE   NGR 2145 7593   Grade II
Alt. 641ft (195.2m)   Length: 200ft (61m) approx.

An oil drum shaft 14ft (4m) deep, now in a poor state of repair, leads via a low crawl to a large natural rift with a small branch mine level. The rift ends at a choke of large boulders. A shaft was sunk from surface (now collapsed) to intersect the continuation, a large natural passage with a silt fill which ended at a scree run. A new entrance (Aaron's Entrance) was constructed here, and lies 115ft (35m) east of Sunday Mine. There is no connection now to the rift.

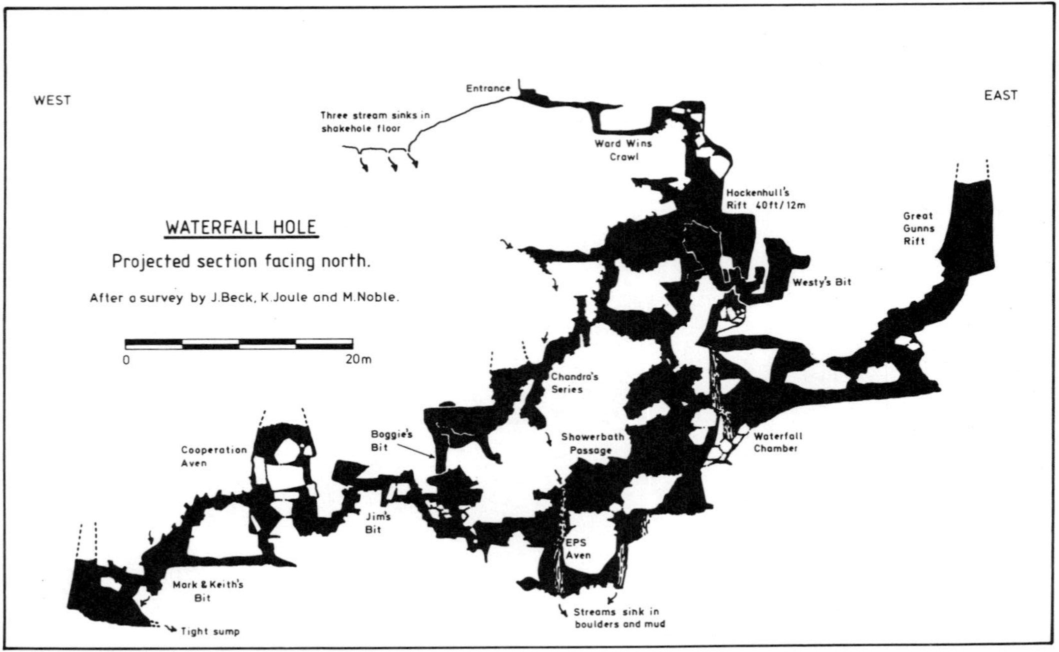

WATERFALL HOLE

Projected section facing north.

After a survey by J.Beck, K.Joule and M.Noble.

WEST

EAST

Three stream sinks in shakehole floor

Entrance

Ward Wins Crawl

Hockenhull's Rift 40ft/12m

Westy's Bit

Great Gunns Rift

Chandra's Series

Showerbath Passage

Waterfall Chamber

EPS Aven

Streams sink in boulders and mud

Bogie's Bit

Jim's Bit

Cooperation Aven

Mark & Keith's Bit

Tight sump

0   20m

SWEVIC HOUSE SWALLET   NGR 1869 7746
Alt. 975ft (297m)   Length: 20ft (6m)

Digging not allowed.

In the more northerly of two shakeholes in the south east corner of field, 230 yards (210m) west of Swevic House Farm.

At present a 20ft (6m) long crawl in the stream which becomes too low. Has been reported as having been dug for 200ft (61m) to the west in a 3ft (1m) high stream passage.

WATERFALL HOLE   NGR 1988 7705   Grade IV
Alt. 896ft (273m)   Length: 1150ft (350m)   Depth: 140ft (43m)

Warning: In extreme flood the entrance passage sumps. Do not descend if water is backing up significantly in the shakehole. A very loose cave in places, and rescue would be almost impossibe through the tight entrance passages.

A large open pothole on the north side of the Eyam-Foolow road, with a stream falling into it and trees all round. No access restrictions. Landowner asks cavers to park sensibly, not in entrances or on the sharp road bend.

Discovered in 1959 by Eldon Pothole Club after clearing debris.

An easy walk down into the shakehole on the east side. Stream sinks at three places in the floor, overflowing into a bedding cave on the north east side in flood. A low bedding crawl for 30ft (9m) to a drop of 6ft (2m). Small passage at the bottom, Ward Wins Crawl, leads to a small chamber. Ward Wins Crawl sumps in flood. Scramble through boulders, taking care not to fall down Hockenhull's Rift, 35ft (11m) deep. Belay to boulders above the pitch head.

Main Route: Many ways down at bottom of rift. Easiest is a small hole, down which the stream can be heard, close to the bottom of the ladder. Follow the noise of water, and scramble down to the stream. The stream falls over a 20ft (6m) pitch, but step across and down into small chamber. In far corner is another 20ft (6m) drop, and care is needed to enter a bedding 3ft (1m) down, feet first. Turn round and climb down on far side of tiny bedding chamber. Scramble down into Waterfall Chamber.

At base of waterfall scramble through boulders to a right turn. Traverse over a 20ft (6m) drop with the stream in the bottom, and enter Showerbath Passage. At extreme end of Showerbath Passage, on the right, a small hole drops into EPS Aven (30ft/9m). Long belay needed. Stream reappears in the bottom and sinks in a hopeless boulder choke. This is the lowest point.

Jim's Bit: Halfway down the EPS Aven pitch step across onto a ledge. A series of muddy passages can be followed through tortuous squeezes and scrambles to a short drop into a narrow rift which opens into Co-operation Aven. The roof is a choke of huge boulders. A further climb down leads into a muddy rift, and a tight crawl was pushed in 1987 to a further series of rifts in which the stream from a new sink directly below the waterfall in the surface shakehole was met. **Do not have an accident here: rescue would be virtually impossible.**

Westy's Bit: Follow obvious passage down boulder slope from bottom of Hockenhull's Rift ladder. Climb into flowstoned rift right at the end, and by squeezing to its extreme end, the right wall is found to consist of a flake. A

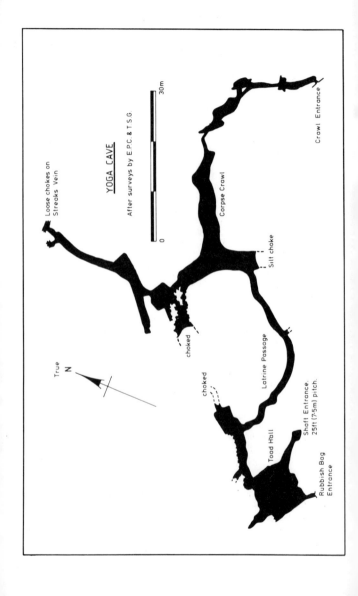

YOGA CAVE

After surveys by E.P.C. & T.S.G.

30m

0

True N

Loose chokes on Streaks Vein

choked

choked

Toad Hall

Shaft Entrance. 25ft (7.5m) pitch.

Rubbish Bag Entrance

Latrine Passage

Silt choke

Corpse Crawl

Crawl Entrance

very difficult sideways manoeuvre lies above a drop. Climb down, and a further series of rift passages leads south eastwards under the east end of the shakehole.

Chandra's Series: Climb down into boulders before the entrance to Westy's Bit. A tiny chamber and a short climb open above a drop which goes right through to the roof of Showerbath Passage. At the top, a right hand passage leads back to the Main Route below Hockenhull's Rift. The left hand passage is a tight rift leading to a small chamber. Climb boulder slope to squeeze on left. Through squeeze is a climb down into a rift, and a boulder slope leads down to an inlet from the boulder roof. A passage on the right before this leads to an inclined chamber, and further rift passages. Parts of Chandra's Series are very loose.

Tackle:
Hockenhull's Rift: 40ft (12m) ladder; 60ft (18m) lifeline.
                     10ft (3m) belay to boulders above pitch.
EPS Aven Pitch: 30ft (9m) ladder; 50ft (15m) lifeline.
                     10ft (3m) belay to boulder on floor.

References: Beck, J.S. 1975. Trans. B.C.R.A. Vol.2. No.1. pp.1-11. Beck, J.S. 1985. T.S.G. Jour. No.11. pp.1-4. Full survey. Gill, D.W. & Lord, P.J. 1970. D.C.A. N/L No.8. pp.5-6. Gunn, J. 1974. Trans. B.C.R.A. Vol.1. No.3. pp.159-164. Hatherley, P. S.U.S.S. Jour. Vol.2. No.6. pp.40 & 42. Survey. Hurt, L. 1968. D.C.A. N/L No.48. p.21. King, B. 1962. B.S.A. Cave Science No.32. pp.381-382. Lord, P.J. 1971. S.U.S.S. Jour. Vol.2. No.1. p.26. Lord, P.J. & Batey, A. 1970. S.U.S.S. Jour. Vol.1. No.6. p.248. Yonge, C.J. Undated. S.U.S.S. Jour. Vol.2. No.2. p.31. Survey.

WATERGROVE SOUGH   Grade III
NGR Tail at 2110 7579   Shaft at 2091 7592
Alt. Tail at 640ft (195m). Shaft at 670ft (204m)   Length: 800ft (244m)

The sough tail lies between the sharp bend and the bottom of Farnsley Lane in Stoney Middleton Dale, where the water is piped under the main road.

A shaft under a small corrugated iron shed (Well Shaft) lies north of the road a little further west. The 30ft (9m) shaft drops directly into the sough, which is accessible downstream for approx. 100ft (30m), and upstream for approx. 700ft (213m). The trip upstream involves several ducks in wet weather, and may become impassable. Some small stopes are passed near the end, and a southward branch leads immediately to the base of a run-in shaft. Progress is halted by large scale collapse.

Tackle – 30ft (9m) ladder; Short belay. 40ft (12m) lifeline.

YOGA CAVE   Grade II
NGR 2122 7589 (Crawl Entr.)   NGR 212 759 (Rubbish Bag & Shaft Entr.)
Alt. 650ft (198m)   Length: 600ft (183m)

On the north side of the road, 15ft (5m) above the road just east of the sharp bend by Eyam Quarry. Rubbish Bag entrance is in the corner of the quarry north of Streaks Footpath, with the shaft entrance on a ledge 20ft (6m) above.

Low crawl excavated in places leads after 150ft (46m) to a 'T' junction. Left to a clay blockage, but a crawl on the right before the blockage leads to a chamber. To the right is a dig, but to the left is a scramble up through very loose boulders into a large natural chamber entered by the miners, "Toad Hall". Various ways off the cavern soon end, except for a passage up a slope to the left, which closes down to a crawl leading to the bottom of the 20ft (6m) deep unstable Shaft Entrance, excavated in 1980. A narrow slot high in one wall of the cavern is Rubbish Bag Entrance, dug by Masson Caving Group in 1989.

Turning right at the first 'T' junction leads into chamber which has been entered by miners. A dig on the left terminates at a blockage after 30ft (10m), but is known to connect with the chamber at the end of the crawl.

Straight on leads to a second larger chamber with a short passage on the left. A short climb up boulders at the far end leads to a continuation, which soon ends in Streaks Vein, in a dangerous state of run-in. The cave has been used by foxes and contains many bones.

Tackle:

Rubbish Bag Entrance:	12ft (4m) handline and krab.
Shaft Entrance:	20ft (6m) ladder; 30ft (9m) lifeline.

References: Beck, J.S. & Gill, D.W. 1974. D.C.A. N/L No.21. p.2. Chandler, P. 1990. D.C.A. N/L No.73. pp.8-9. Survey. Gill, D.W. 1973. D.C.A. N/L No.18. p.1. Gill, D.W. 1976. E.P.C. Jour. Vol.9. No.1. p.7. Survey.

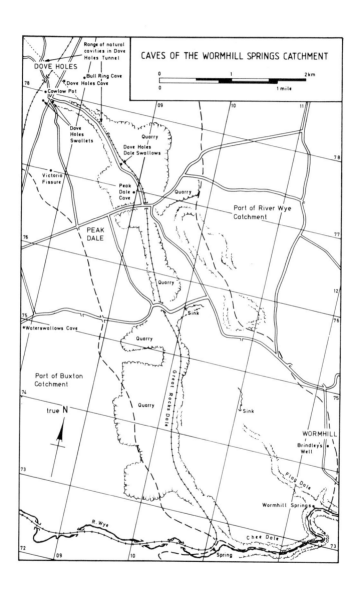

CAVES OF THE WORMHILL SPRINGS CATCHMENT

THE WORMHILL
CATCHMENT AREA

Wormhill Springs is one of the largest risings in the limestone area, with an estimated discharge of at least 10 mgd., and the catchment is probably the most promising area in the White Peak for an undiscovered large cave system.

The springs lie to the south of the axis of the Wormhill–Priestcliffe Syncline close to a fault parallel to the axis. To the north west the Upper and Lower Millers Dale Lavas have concentric outcrops, while between Great Rocks Dale and the shale margin extensive faulting gives rise to complex dolerite and lava outcrops. There is little evidence of high level cave development, suggesting that the Great Rocks Dale and Wormhill Springs have been the main outlets for a considerable period. Numerous small dolines exist on the margins of the lava outcrops, but none have been dug.

Apart from Cow Low Pot, the major swallets at Dove Holes have not been extensively dug, but have been dye tested to the impenetrable fissures in the Dove Holes railway tunnel. It has also been claimed (along with some very unlikely claims!) that they were tested many years ago to the Great Rocks Dale risings.

The driving of the railway tunnel effectively captured the drainage, sending it to the Irish Sea via the Mersey instead of to the North Sea via the Trent. The artificial lowering of water levels may have rendered more cave penetrable than would otherwise have been the case. Further digging should bring interesting results.

Wormhill Springs responds fast in flood conditions, and becomes milky in colour, suggesting that the catchment area includes the floors of the quarries in Great Rocks Dale. Rumours of a hole with a large stream flowing in it appearing in the quarry floor have not been substantiated but should not be entirely discounted. The drainage from Dove Holes must pass through faults in the Lower Millers Dale Lava to reach either the springs at Great Rocks Dale or the Wormhill risings. Eastwest faults may carry water eastwards to Great Rocks Dale, while faults further to the north carry water eastwards to join the Wormhill system.

Perched groundwater rises above the Upper Millers Dale Lava around Bole Hill and Withered Low, flows over both lavas, and sinks again. Digging at these small sinks may well prove worthwhile.

The existence of the floodprone Wormhill springs, the swallets nearly four miles away at Dove Holes, the many dolines, and the favourable geological structure suggest the existence of a large cave system. The rising itself may be a deep one, but large vadose canyon passages could exist further upstream. Perhaps a JCB at Wormhill Springs could be the answer!

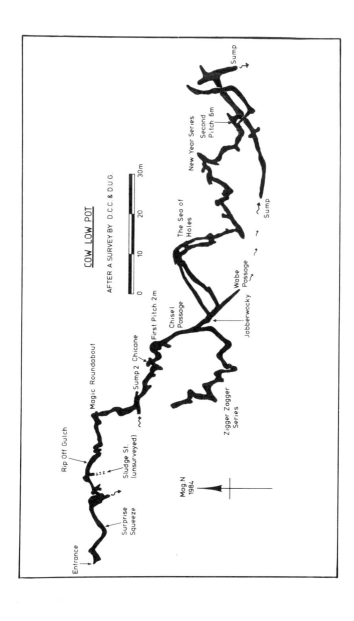

COW LOW POT

AFTER A SURVEY BY D.C.C. & D.U.G.

0 10 20 30m

Mag N
1984

Entrance
Surprise Squeeze
Rip Off Gulch
Sludge St. (unsurveyed)
Magic Roundabout
Sump 2 Chicane
First Pitch 2m
Chisel Passage
Zigger Zagger Series
Jabberwocky Passage
Wobe Passage
The Sea of Holes
New Year Series
Second Pitch 6m
Sump
Sump

BRINDLEY'S WELL   NGR 123 743   Spring
Alt. 1050ft (320m)

A small spring which feeds the well in Wormhill village.

BULL RING CAVE   NGR 079 783   Grade I
Alt. 1075ft (327m)   Length: 28ft (8m)

On the west side of the old tramroad cutting.

A 4ft (1.2m) by 3ft (.9m) phreatic tube 28ft (8m) long ends at a clay fill.

COWLOW POT   NGR 075 780   Grade IV
Alt. 1075ft (327m)   Length: Approx. 600ft (183m)   Depth: Approx. 50ft (15m)

Discovered by members of Disley Underground Group in 1981.

Situated to the south of Station Road, Dove Holes, through ginnel between houses. Entrance is lidded oil drum shaft by wall, above stream sink. Permission and the key to the lid must be obtained from Mr Burton, Old House Farm, Back Lane, Dove Holes.

Warning: Some sections are tight and awkward, and rescue from beyond would be extremely difficult. The cave floods to the roof in places in wet weather. Danger of infection from broken glass and rubbish in initial stages, also known discharge of sewage into the cave.

Drop down shaft to streamway. In a few feet stream passes under slot. Way on is squeeze through vertical crack above, Surprise Squeeze. The Surprise is an occasional dousing with bathwater from cracked drain above! Forward into small chamber. Stream sinks through choked slot ahead.

Way on is left. Drop down and back under into crawl, bearing left then right after several feet. Ahead is wet and muddy tube. Left is upward draughting crawl, Rip-off Gulch.

Crawl through muddy tube, Sludge Street, drop and crawl left, then right through confusion of miniature cross rifts to meet small pool with sharp flake of rock. Cross pool and flake, crawl through water, then follow water to short flowing duck. Follow water beyond duck to meet Sump 1.

Just before muddy tube, way on is up Rip-off Gulch. Follow this crawl through pool and awkward bends (Magic Roundabout) and drop down to cross rift with small stream and Sump 2. Continue along crawl ahead on opposite side of stream, through tight left and right squeeze (The Chicane) to top of muddy bank (the 1st Pitch). Drop down this (handline useful). Crawl left is Chisel Passage above small stream which sumps below and is seen through slots in floor. Climb up out of Chisel Passage. Right leads to Zigger Zagger Series. Tube on right comes to short upward climb. Awkward bend follows with water and small stream.

Straight on from Chisel Passage leads to Jabberwocky. Short climb down boulder and partially dug crawl (Wabe Passage) is seen ahead. Way on is left through short upward crawl with pool to emerge into boulder strewn rift, The Sea of Holes. Left leads through muddy crawl to hole in floor through which Jabberwocky can be seen and entered once more.

Two routes to the right in the Sea of Holes eventually unite in a narrow rift. The area is confusing. The narrow rift becomes a crawl to a right hand bend followed by an awkward squeeze up by a large boulder (take care). This is the start of the New Year Series. Meandering passage eventually leads to a low too-tight bedding crawl, with too-tight branches. Two thirds of the way along New Year Series is a slot. This is the head of the 2nd Pitch, 20ft (6m) deep to a longish passage with a stream. Short upstream section leads nowhere. Downstream leads to too-tight streamway and gravel filled muddy tube.

Dye tested to inlets on the left hand wall of the Dove Holes railway tunnel.

Tackle:
1st Pitch:	Short handline.
2nd Pitch:	25ft (8m) ladder; 30ft (9m) lifeline.

DOVE HOLES CAVE   NGR 077 782   Grade I
Alt. 1075ft (327m)   Length: 10ft (3m)

Near the recreation ground, behind Marchington's lorry park.

Discovered in 1962 by Eldon Pothole Club after clearing rubbish from the entrance, which is 3ft (0.9m) wide and 1ft (0.3m) high. Leads into 10ft (3m) square chamber. Possible dig.

DOVE HOLES DALE SWALLOWS
NGR 176 778, 087 773, 089 772   Digs
Alt. c.1000ft (305m)

In the floor of Dove Holes Dale.

Three abortive digs in small swallows.

Reference: Frost, R.V 1954. The Speleologist, Vol.1. No.3. p.95.

DOVE HOLES TUNNEL CAVES
NGR 083 778 to 074 784   Grade I
Alt. c.940ft (287m)

A number of inlets were encountered during the construction of the Dove Holes railway tunnel. All are close to the limestone/shale boundary, and still give a large quantity of water which is culverted under the lines to the north end of the tunnel, thus diverting the water from the North Sea to the Irish Sea! All the inlets soon become impenetrable. No access is allowed.

1) Two small inlets on the west wall. Impenetrable.

2) Walled off inlet. Discharges a small stream.

3) Three inlets close together. The first two are too tight, but the third is a large inlet 13ft (4m) long to a climb up of 13ft (4m). Water emerges from impenetrable bedding plane.

4) At mark 46 on the east wall is an inlet rift blocked with boulders.

5) Just beyond No.4 is a 23ft (7m) climb against the tunnel lining, tight at the top, emerging in a chamber approx 20ft x 20ft (6m x 6m), approx 10ft (3m) high, with an inlet in the roof which is too tight.

Dye tested from Cowlow Pot and Dove Holes Swallet 1.

DOVE HOLES SWALLET 1   NGR 075 779   Dig
Alt. c.1065ft (325m)

In garden of house on west side of A6.

The main sink, which takes a very large volume of water in wet weather.

DOVE HOLES SWALLET 2   NGR 076 779   Dig
Alt. c.1060ft (323m)   **Length: 30ft (10m)**

Access not normally granted.

Opposite the Queens Hotel on the south east corner of the crossroads. A small stream sinks, but the swallet takes a large volume of flood water.

Three possible digs in the same artificially deepened shakehole. The first is too tight. The second is a tight crawl for roughly 30ft (10m) blocked with mud. Could be a good dig. The third consists of tight possibilities in large boulders.

Reference: Eldon Pothole Club Newsletter Vol.2. No.12.

GREAT ROCKS DALE SPRING   NGR 1114 7266   Spring
Alt. 740ft (225m)

A large spring on the west side of the junction of Great Rocks Dale and the Wye Valley. A possible destination of water from the Water Swallows area.

PEAK DALE CAVE   NGR 090 770   Lost
Alt. 1000ft (305m)   **Length: 90ft (27m)**

South of road, opposite signal box, in quarry entrance which has been bridged over.

A low entrance into a passage 5ft (1.5m) high and 2.5ft (76cm) wide, with 2ft (61cm) of water. Ended in a fine grotto which has been largely destroyed in attempts to push further. Water has been pumped out and a crack leads to a narrow pitch. The cave is below a waste lime tip and the water is mildly caustic. A calcite film soon forms on the water if left undisturbed. Now completely buried by "landscaping".

Reference: Gill, D.W. 1973. The Burial of Peak Dale Cave. D.C.A. N/L No.17. p.3.

VICTORY QUARRY FISSURE   NGR 07 77   Lost

A unique fissure containing Pliocene (pre-Ice Age) mammal remains. Now quarried away. Others may be awaiting discovery. Animal remains include "sabre toothed tiger". Remains now in Buxton and Manchester Museums, and in the Natural History Museum, London.

References: Dawkins, W.B. 1903. Quart. Jour. Geol. Soc. Vol.59. pp.105-129. Spencer, H.E. & Melville, R.V 1974. Bull. Geological Survey of Great Britain. No.48. pp.43-53.

WORMHILL SPRINGS   NGR 123 735   Dig
Alt. 700ft (213m)

On the north bank of the River Wye where Flag Dale meets Cheedale.

A series of large springs, the most westerly of which yields an impressive amount of water, and is presumed to have its furthest source at Dove Holes. The springs turn milky in wet weather as a result of runoff from the Great Rocks Dale quarries.

The large pit immediately upstream from the main rising was dug by the Derbyshire Pennine Club around 1936. The ring bolt embedded in a tree is their work.

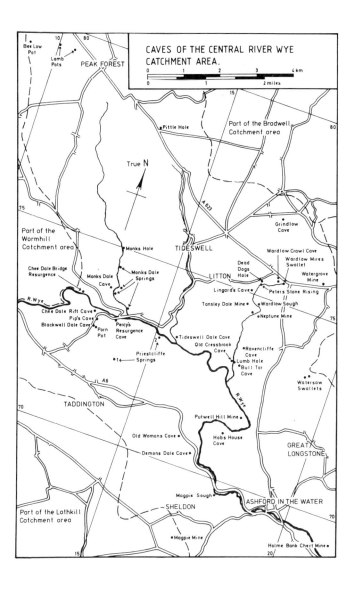

CAVES OF THE CENTRAL RIVER WYE
CATCHMENT AREA.

0 1 2 3 4 km
0 1 2 miles

Bee Low Pot

Lamb Pots

PEAK FOREST

Pittle Hole

Part of the Bradwell Catchment area

True N

Part of the Wormhill Catchment area

Monks Hole

TIDESWELL

Grindlow Cave

Chee Dale Bridge Resurgence

Monks Dale Cave

Monks Dale Springs

Wardlow Crawl Cave

Wardlow Mires Swallet

Watergrove Mine

LITTON

Dead Dogs Hole

R.Wye

Chee Dale Rift Cave

Pip's Cave

Blackwell Dale Cave

Porn Pot

Percy's Resurgence Cave

Lingard's Cave

Peters Stone Rising

Tansley Dale Mine

Wardlow Sough

Neptune Mine

Tideswell Dale Cave

Old Cressbrook Cave

Priestcliffe Springs

Ravencliffe Cave

Lumb Hole

Bull Tor Cave

Watersaw Swallets

R.Wye

TADDINGTON

A6

Putwell Hill Mine

Old Womans Cave

Hobs House Cave

GREAT LONGSTONE

Demons Dale Cave

Part of the Lathkill Catchment area

Magpie Sough

SHELDON

ASHFORD IN THE WATER

Magpie Mine

Holme Bank Chert Mine

THE RIVER WYE
CATCHMENT AREA

The catchment of the central River Wye, covering an area of almost 100 square kilometres, represents the largest area of limestone in the Peak District, but contains few caves of any significance.

The River Wye is the largest of the two permanent rivers on the limestone. The river crosses several lavas in its course across the central limestone area, and these are a major factor in the river's surface course throughout. The flow is increased by numerous springs on both banks, but to date all have proved to be impenetrable. The increase in volume between Buxton and Bakewell is more than can be accounted for by the known springs, and it is likely that a lot of water rises from undetected risings in the river bed.

The tributary valleys are normally dry, but Monks Dale, Tideswell Dale, Cressbrook Dale and Deep Dale carry surface streams except in very dry conditions. These are generally fed by risings close to the valley floors which carry local perched groundwater.

The area contains many dolines, although many have been filled in by farmers or modified by surface and underground mineral workings along the rakes. Few have been dug. There are no major allogenic sinks, but the lack of surface streams and the high rainfall suggest that extensive underground systems may exist.

The catchment area boundary reflects the surface topography, and underground drainage does not necessarily coincide with this. Thus the only major sink at Wardlow Mires, which is a resurgence in flood, probably drains eastwards via the Watergrove Sough to Stoney Middleton in normal conditions.

The major rising at Lumb Hole, in Cressbrook Dale, represents the best possibility for a breakthrough in the area. It is thought to drain the western end of Longstone Edge, and it is a dramatic rising during floods. There is even a short stretch of accessible cave to give the digger a little encouragement.

A further possibility exists in the large risings at the foot of Taddington Dale, although here it is less clear where a worthwhile dig could be started.

The complex geology and mineralisation of the area gives rise to a complex and little understood hydrology. The reader is referred to the cited references for detailed information.

ARBOR SEATS SOUGH NGR 1746 7461 Grade I (Mine)
Alt. 750ft (228m)   Length: 300ft (91m)

Adit on west side of Cressbrook Dale, in line with shafts on hillside above and with Neptune Mine opposite.

Adit, with roof sections of stacked deads. Some run-ins have been dug through and a draught blows through the present limit of exploration.

Furthest shaft at 850ft (259m) and 173746 is into impressive hading stope over 60ft (18m) high.
Reference: Beck, J.S. 1978. Bull P.D.M.H.S. Vol.7. No.2. pp.107-115.

ASHFORD BLACK MARBLE MINE
NGR 191 697   Grade I (Mine)
(Rookery Mine)
Alt. 550ft (168m)   Length: ½ mile (800m) approx.

Entrance in small quarry at top of Rookery Wood beside Ashford Road off A6.
An intriguing network of roomy walking passages and mined out flat-roofed cavities, popular with novice cavers, and an impressive example of former pillar and stall mining of black marble.
Reference: Ford, T.D. 1964. Bull. P.D.M.H.S. Vol.2. No.4. pp.179-188. Survey.

BEE LOW POT   NGR 092 793   Dig
Alt. 1325ft (403m)

Near a group of boulders behind Bee Low Quarry.
A heavily fluted shaft ends in a tight fissure. Entrance is now blocked.
Tackle – 25ft (8m) ladder; 40ft (12m) lifeline.

BLACKWELL DALE CAVE   NGR 133 728   Grade I
Alt. 825ft (251m)   Length: 355ft (108m)

Access to the final chamber is controlled by the Orpheus Caving Club.
Opens from the east side of the main Millers Dale – Taddington road in Blackwell Dale.
Stooping for the first 25ft (8m), then opens into a chamber 15ft (5m) high. Continues through pools and crawls for 160ft (49m) to an excavated crawl through a choke (fitted with a gate) to a decorated chamber with the choked passage continuing beyond. A crawl on the left (facing into the cave) is wet and muddy, and after 110ft (34m) emerges in the valley side on a ledge.
Reference: Turner, D. 1951. S.T.P.C.Jour. Vol.1. No.1. p.13.

BULL TOR CAVE   NGR 1742 7313   Grade I
(Good Friday Cave)
Alt. 1000ft (305m)

High on the side of Cressbrook Dale, to the south of Ravencliffe Cave.
Entrance about 6ft (1.8m) wide into a long crawl with a badger lair.

CHEE DALE BRIDGE RESURGENCE NGR 127 735 Dig
Alt. 655ft (200m)

A short distance upstream from the footbridge on the north bank of the River Wye.
A large volume of water rises from scree. Possibly controlled by the intersection of the outcrop of the Lower Millers Dale Lava with the valley floor.

Reference: Christopher, N.S.J. Unpublished PhD Thesis. University of Leicester.

CHEE DALE RIFT CAVE   NGR 132 732   Grade I
Alt. 660ft (201m)   Length: 160ft (48m)   Depth: 40ft (12m)

On the south bank of the River Wye, 120ft (36m) above river level.

Discovered Eldon P.C. 1968. Entrance drops steeply to a 10ft (3m) pitch. A high rift 5ft (1.5m) wide can be followed for 40ft (12m) narrowing down to a crack. A 20ft (6m) climb up in the roof leads to a short high level continuation. At the base of the 10ft climb the north west continuation of the rift can be followed for 50ft (15m) before it becomes too narrow. 12ft (4m) down the entrance slope a small passage on the right can be followed to a junction. Right soon ends at an earth fill while left arrives at a further junction. Right is blocked, while left rises up a climb to the top of the 10ft pitch.

300 yards (274m) down dale on same side (1325 7319) is a small unnamed cave near river level, blocked with mud after 12ft (4m).

Reference: Bridger, R. 1975. D.C.A. N/L No.25.

CHELMORTON CAVERN

Listed in Caves of Derbyshire 1984. Probably does not exist, as the cave referred to by Farey was first described by Pilkington, and is almost certainly Thirst House Cave.

DEAD DOGS' HOLE   NGR 1725 7538   Grade I
Alt. 900ft (270m)   Length: 50ft (15m) approx.

High in the crags opposite Peter's Stone. On Nature Conservancy land.

A winding tube dug out by TSG.

Reference: Beck, J.S. 1978. Bull. P.D.M.H.S. Vol.7. No. 2. p.110.

DEMONS DALE CAVE   NGR 1689 7045   Grade I (Arch)
(Taddington Dale Resurgence Cave)
Alt. 650ft (198m)   Length: 15ft (5m)

Close to the path from the car park into Deep Dale.

A large rock shelter archaeologically excavated for 15ft (5m) being 5ft (1.5m) high ending in large scale breakdown. Large volume of water resurges in flood. Neolithic and Roman remains found.

References: Armstrong, A.L. 1948. Archaeological Newsletter p.5. Orpheus Caving Club Newsletter 1974. Vol.10. No.3.

GRINDLOW CAVERN   NGR 1725 7713   Grade II
Alt. 975ft (292m)   Length: about 100ft (30m)   Depth: 40ft (12m)

Owner is Mr P. Furness, Cartledge Farm, Great Hucklow.

30 yards south of a small walled quarry in field, 50 yards east of the Grindlow-Tideswell road.

The 25ft (8m) entrance shaft has a large rock wedged in the top. Capped with smaller blocks. Tight squeeze past big block. Shaft drops into a bedding

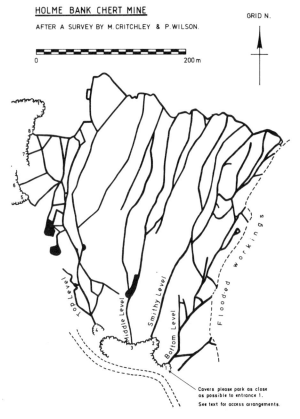

HOLME BANK CHERT MINE

AFTER A SURVEY BY M. CRITCHLEY & P. WILSON.

0   200 m

GRID N.

Top Level

Middle Level

Smithy Level

Bottom Level

Flooded workings

Cavers please park as close
as possible to entrance 1.
See text for access arrangements.

Note: only entrances 1 and 8 are readily accessible.
Entrance 4 is buried and bad air may be met in Top Level area.

cave which extends for 50ft (15m) to the west. Squeezes and climbs down between boulders lead to a short lower level, with crawls in a decorated extension to the north which becomes too tight. A short crawl to the east of the shaft quickly closes.

Tackle:
25 ft (8m) ladder; 40ft (12m) lifeline. Bar or scaffold pole and short belay.

Reference: Lord P.J. & Smith, M.E. 1969. Jour. S.U.S.S. Vol.1. No.6. pp.234-5. Survey.

## HOB'S HOUSE CAVE	NGR 176 712	Grade I (Arch)
(Hob Thirst Hole, Hob Hurst House, Hob's Hurst Cave, Monsal Dale Cave)
**Alt. 800ft (240m)	Length: 80ft (24m)**

At the back of the landslips on the north side of Fin Cop.

A narrow descending fissure. A human skeleton of early British date was found among the debris at the bottom. No attempt at further excavation is recorded.

Has been confused with Thirst House in Deepdale.

Reference: Fox, W. Storrs. 1913. A human skeleton in Monsal Dale. Derbys. Arch. Jour. No.35. pp.99-102.

HOLME BANK CHERT MINE
## NGR 213 694	Grade II (Mine)
**Alt. 590ft (180m)	Length: 2.2 miles (3500m) approx.**

Key can be obtained during the week from the block works (Smith's Runners Ltd) in the middle quarry. (Phone Bakewell 812636).

At weekends park near the mine entrance and walk down to the cottages to collect key from Mr. L. Moseley, 1 New Lumford.

Entrance 1 lies on right of track, below crane. 2 & 3 in old quarry above the crane. 4 to right of track just before gate. 5,6,7 and 8 are in the quarry on the hill top. 1 & 8 were the main entrances.

Very complex, with over 70 junctions. From entrance 8, facing an old hut, the mine starts as an unstable passage about 8ft (2.5m) square. A passage immediately on the left eventually leads to entrances 1,2, & 3. Main passage continues to the right and links eventually to entrance 4. Branch passages on the right leads to entrances 5,6, & 7 in the quarry. Another passage on the right leads to New Year Chamber, with New Year Pot, natural pot 10ft (3m) deep to a silted bedding plane. Several passages on the left link with the main passages to entrances 1,2,& 3.

Passage on left inside entrance 8 heads north east with several branches on the right, then a sharp bend and a drop into another passage. Turn right and then left to a chamber. Right here leads to a passage with more branches to the right. Second, third, fourth and fifth branches lead to entrance 3. Sixth, seventh and eighth branches lead to entrances 1 & 2. Main passage continues ahead to the flooded sections.

The amount of accessible passage varies according to water levels.

Reference: Critchley, M.F. & Wilson, P.J. 1975. Bull. P.D.M.H.S. Vol.6. No.1. pp.1-5. Survey.

LAMB POTS NGR 100 795 to 104 795 Grade I (Digs)
Alt. 1150-1200ft (285-300m) **Depth: 30-60ft (9-18m)**

On hillside ¼ mile (0.4km) west of Chambers Farm, west of Peak Forest.

A series of 7 open natural shafts, choked at depths of 30-60ft (9-18m) with boulders. Other pots on the same hillside choked to surface.

LINGARD'S CAVE NGR 1706 7506 Grade I
Alt. 900ft (274m) **Length: 60ft (18m)**

On west side of Cressbrook Dale 150ft (46m) above the valley floor on the north side of small depression, hidden by a bush.

A short passage to a chamber, rather smelly and used by badgers. A second chamber follows with a drop through boulders to a crawl and possible dig. On the left side of the entrance chamber climb down short pitch to mined workings. The cave is named after the last man to be publicly gibbeted at Wardlow Mires, executed for the murder of the toll keeper's wife.

References: Beck, J.S. 1975. Trans. B.C.R.S. Vol.2. No.1. p.8. Beck, J.S. 1978. Bull. P.D.M.H.S. Vol.7. No.2. p.110. Gill, D.W. 1973. British Caver No.60. p.66.

LUMB HOLE NGR 1725 7313 Grade I
(Cressbrookdale Resurgence)
Alt. 630ft (192m) **Length: 80ft (24m)**

On the east side of the gorge section of Cressbrook Dale.

An obvious entrance which can discharge a large stream, above a lava outcrop. It is possible to crawl in for some distance above the stream over breakdown before the way on becomes too tight.

References: Beck, J.S. 1975. Trans. B.C.R.A. Vol.2. No.1. p.8. Beck, J.S. 1978. Bull. P.D.M.H.S. Vol.7. No.2. p.110. Frost, R.V 1956. The Speleologist Vol.1. No.4.

MAGPIE MINE Grade II (Mine)
Shaft: NGR 172 682
Sough Tail: NGR 179 696
Alt. Shaft: 1100ft (330m) Sough Tail: 480ft (144m)
Length: 1 mile (1.5km) approx. **Depth: 600ft (180m) approx.**

No access allowed at present.

Shaft amongst the mine buildings of Magpie Mine, near Sheldon. Sough tail on south bank of River Wye, opposite Black Rock Corner. Gated.

Engine shaft covered. Nearly 600ft (180m) deep.

The sough is over a mile long, mostly waist deep or deeper, with interesting lock-gates and water feeders in cross veins. Blende Vein, 600 yards north of the shaft, has a series of calcite lined pipe-vein cavities which have been pirated by a solution channel in places. Can be followed for about 100 yards and could perhaps be dug further. Extensive workings in vein under shaft no longer accessible owing to partial collapse.

"Chatsworth Cavern" was a large vein cavity now completely submerged.

References: Butcher, N.J.D. 1975. Bull. P.D.M.H.S. Vol.6. No.2. pp.65-70. Survey. Willies, L.M., Roche, VS., Worley, N.E., & Ford, T.D. 1971. P.D.M.H.S. Special Publication No.3. Worley, N.E. 1975. Bull. P.D.M.H.S. Vol.6. No.1. pp.28-32. Survey.

MONKS DALE CAVE   NGR 134 739   Grade I
Alt. 900ft (270m)   **Depth: 30ft (9m)**

Nature Conservancy land. Permission required from N.C.C.

On the west side of the dale, 200ft (61m) above the valley floor, at the base of a small cliff.

First entered and dug by Eldon P.C. 10ft (3m) climb down entrance rift. Two ways on at the bottom. Left leads to 20ft (6m) descent with small wet weather stream sinking in the bottom. Right leads after a few feet to a small wet weather inlet sinking down a 6 inch (15cm) rift. Presumed to resurge directly below the cave in the valley floor at 135 738.

Reference: Gill, D.W. 1973. British Caver No.60. p.67.

MONKS DALE SPRINGS   Digs
Alt. 665 – 690ft (203 – 210m)

On Nature Conservancy land. Permission required from N.C.C.

1: On the east bank at 140 735.

2: Three springs on the west bank and one on the east bank close to 136 740.

3: Spring at 135 738.

4: Large rising at 135 745 on the east bank.

Nos. 1 & 2 are relatively small springs. No. 3. is presumed to be the resurgence of the stream seen in Monks Dale Cave. No. 4. is a large rising on the east bank, and could be a good dig.

Reference: Gill, D.W. 1973. British Caver No.60. p.67.

MONKS HOLE   NGR 134 750   Grade I
Alt. 875ft (262m)   **Length: 25ft (8m)**

On east side of Monksdale 100ft (30m) above the valley floor at the base of a cliff.

A 25ft (8m) crawl dug out by Oldham Hydrological Group in 1955, leading to a short blind pot.

NEPTUNE MINE   NGR 175 745   Grade II (Mine)
(Ney Green Mine)
Alt. 875ft (267m)   **Length: 1142ft (348m)**   **Depth: 92ft (28m)**

On the east side of Cressbrook Dale, 150 yards (46m) south of Wardlow Sough.

An oil drum entrance leads into the adit, which is 650ft (198m) long, with shafts in the floor flooded to varying depths. The first is the main shaft, 60ft (18m) from the surface to the level (shaft capped), with an ancient timber bridge. First level on right is 125ft (38m) long. The second right is 213ft (65m) to a backfilled natural rift which could be a good dig. The only level on the left is 50ft (15m) long.

Reference: Beck, J.S. 1978. Bull. P.D.M.H.S. Vol.7. No.2. pp.113-115.

OLD CRESSBROOK CAVE   NGR 1723 7312   Grade I
Alt. 660ft (201m)   Length: 50ft (15m)

Directly opposite Lumb Hole (Cressbrook Resurgence Cave).

A large cave entrance diminishes in size after 30ft (9m) and a muddy crawl continues to a small chamber.

References: Beck, J.S. 1975. Trans. B.C.R.A. Vol.2. No.1. p.8. Beck, J.S. 1978. Bull. P.D.M.H.S. Vol.7. No. 2. p.110.

OLD WOMAN'S CAVE   NGR 165 708   Grade I (Arch)
Alt. 700ft (210m)   Length: 44ft (13m)   Depth: 20ft (6m)

100ft (30m) above the road, south side of Taddington Dale above crags. Difficult to find in broken ground and undergrowth.

An easy climb down 15ft (5m) into chamber, with small passages leading off. Iron Age pottery in British Museum, London.

References: Brailsford, J.W. 1959. Derbys. Arch. Jour. No.77. p.56. Fox, W. Storrs. 1911. Derbys. Arch. Jour. No.33. pp.115-126.

PERCY'S RESURGENCE CAVE   NGR 138 732   Dig
Alt. 575ft (175m)

Above the road on the south side of the bridge at Millers Dale.

A small resurgence cave which issues a small amount of water. Used to supply the Dale Hotel with water. Has since been dug inconclusively.

PETER'S STONE RISING   NGR 175 753   Dig
Alt. 775ft (236m)

On the hillside opposite Peter's Stone, about 20ft (6m) above the valley floor.

A small choked cave entrance which discharges a considerable stream in very wet weather.

Reference: Beck, J.S. 1978. P.D.M.H.S. Bull. Vol.7. No.2. p.107.

PIPS CAVE   NGR 133 730   Grade I
Alt. 800ft (244m)   Length: 25ft (8m)

On the east side of the dale above the road, near a small crag. Well hidden.

A 25ft (8m) long crawl blocked with calcite. Inhabited by badgers.

Reference: Gill, D.W. 1975. D.C.A. N/L. No.26. p.7.

PITTLE HOLE   NGR 133 783   Grade I (Dig)
(Pittle Mere Pot)
Alt. 1170ft (357m)   Depth: 45ft (14m)

Permission from landowner (first farm on right descending into Peak Forest).

100 yards (91m) north of the main A623 road, immediately west of the minor road from Pittle Mere to Little Hucklow.

At the foot of a dry valley on the edge of a dolerite outcrop. A timbered shaft was excavated for 10ft to enter several open joints. Main joint, heavily fluted, descended for 10ft to tight squeeze into tiny chamber with washed out wayboard penetrable for 20ft. Further drop down parallel rift for 25ft via enlarged squeeze until too tight. Slight outward draught. Site now covered with boulders.

Reference: Beck, J.S. 1978. TSG N/L No.4. p.2.

PORN POT   NGR 133 728   Dig
Alt. 825ft (251m)   **Depth: 12ft (4m)**

Directly above Blackwell Dale Cave.
    A 12ft (4m) deep fissure blocked with earth.
    Reference: Gill, D.W. 1975. D.C.A. N/L No.26. p.7.

PRIESTCLIFFE SPRING 1   NGR 141 721   Dig
Alt. 1000ft (305m)

Near Priestcliffe village.
    Water issues from a bedding plane. Source unknown but old mine workings above.

PRIESTCLIFFE SPRING 2   NGR 151 731   Dig
Alt. 625ft (190m)

On the south bank of the River Wye. A strong spring, possibly a sough. It is thought that it was blocked when the railway was built over its course.

PUTWELL HILL MINE   NGR 179 718   Grade II (Mine)
Alt. 670ft (204m)   **Length: c.300ft (c.90m)**

Walled up entrance by the side of the railway track, but other entrances on the hillside above.
    Immediately inside the former trackside entrance is a 20ft (6m) climb down to the floor of the stope. Stopes in the vein run southwards for roughly 300ft (90m) under the disused quarry.
    References: Bird, R. 1972. Bull. P.D.M.H.S. Vol.5. No.1. pp.54-60. Survey. Shaw, R.P. 1980. Bull. P.D.M.H.S. Vol.7. No.6. pp.342-344. Survey. Thompson,S. 1971. Bull. P.D.M.H.S. Vol.4. No.6. pp.413-416.

RAVENCLIFFE CAVE   NGR 1739 7356   Grade I (Arch)
Alt. 1000ft (305m)   **Length: 25ft (8m)**

In cliffs high on the east side of Cressbrook Dale. West of Hay Tor.
    A single large chamber with a crawl at the back. Archaeologically excavated.
    References: Beck, J.S. 1975. Trans. B.C.R.A. Vol.2. No.1. p.8. Brailsford, J.W. 1957. Derbys. Arch. Jour. No.77. pp.55-56. Bramwell, D. 1974. Archaeology in the Peak District. pp.12 & 62. Fox, W.S. 1910. Derbys. Arch. Jour. No.32. p.141-146. Read, C.H. 1910. Derbys. Arch. Jour. No.32. pp.147-151.

SHELOB'S LAIR   NGR 134 741   Grade I
Alt. 900ft (274m)   **Length: 20ft (6m)**   **Depth: 25ft (8m)**

High on the west side of Monks Dale, north of Monksdale Cave.
    A small entrance opens directly into the top of a rift approximately 25ft (8m) deep, floored with boulders. The rumble of a stream can be heard some way down. Digging is awkward. The cave is a prolific breeding ground for large spiders.

TADDINGTON DALE GROTTO   Lost

The exact location is unknown, but it is most likely to lie in one of the road cuttings on the Taddington by-pass, now grassed over.

Several photographs and vague articles about this cave, apparently very well decorated, appeared in the press in about 1936 during the construction of the Taddington by-pass.

TANSLEY DALE MINE   NGR 171 747   Grade III (Mine)
Alt. 850ft (259m)   Length: 200ft (61m)   Depth: 120ft (37m)

Mine entrance on the south side of the dale floor.

Small crawl entrance enlarges to walking sized level. A shaft in the roof at a kink in the level is slabbed over at surface. The level continues to a shaft in the floor, 120ft (36m) deep to some very unstable workings.

References: Beck, J.S. 1978. Bull. P.D.M.H.S. Vol.7. No.2. pp.113-114.
Gill, D.W. 1973. British Caver No.60. p.67.

TIDESWELL DALE CAVE   NGR 1555 7319   Grade I
Alt. 700ft (213m)   Length: 100ft (30m)

About 200 yards (183m) upstream from the junction of Tideswell Dale and Millers Dale, on the east side of the footpath.

A small bedding cave enlarged by mining. Ends at a small chamber on a mineral vein. Continuation is too tight.

Reference: Gill, D.W. 1974. British Caver Vol.62. p.48.

WARDLOW CRAWL CAVE   NGR 178 756   Grade I
Alt. 810ft (247m)   Length: 10ft (3m)

Situated on the right hand corner of a small terrace just above dale floor level, 410ft (125m) down dale from Wardlow Mires Swallet, on the north west side.

Dug out entrance to 10ft (3m) long flat out crawl blocked by stalagmite. Water can be heard flowing beyond in wet weather when the nearby swallets become resurgences.

Reference: Bridger, R. 1978. D.C.A. N/L No.38.

WARDLOW MIRES SWALLET   NGR 1791 7557   Dig
Alt. 775ft (236m)

A few yards south of the A623 Peak Forest to Stoney Middleton road, in the valley floor at the head of Cressbrook Dale. A stream flowing from the shales is culverted under the road, and sinks in an obvious depression.

In wet weather, the swallet continues to take water until the water table rises above the valley floor, and the swallet and nearby depressions become powerful resurgences. In flood conditions the volume of water rising here and at several places along the north west bank further down the valley may be very large. The water sinking in dry weather is thought to flow to Watergrove Mine. Several depressions have been dug in the past, but have become too tight so far.

Reference: Beck, J.S. 1978. Bull. P.D.M.H.S. Vol.7. No.2. pp.106-115.

WARDLOW SOUGH   NGR 174 748   Grade III (Mine)
Alt. 720ft (219m)   Length 1200ft (366m)

On the east side of Cressbrook Dale at the base of a line of shaft hillocks running diagonally up the hillside.

A timbered passage under a shaft mound (now partly backfilled for safety) led into the sough, which could be followed past two filled shafts to surface, and a large shaft which was climbed for approx. 130ft (40m) to a level through toadstone and some small natural cavities. The sough continued to a complete collapse 950ft (290m) from the tail. A large volume of water issues in wet weather.

Reference: Beck, J.S. 1978. Bull. P.D.M.H.S. Vol.7. No.2. pp.113-114.

WATERGROVE MINE   NGR 189 759   Mine
Alt. 800ft (240m)   Depth: 350ft (107m)

A group of shafts on the east side of the Wardlow Basin around Housley.

The Fairburn Engine Shaft is 350ft (107m) deep, with the sough crosscut at 150ft (46m). The crosscut leads to the Forefield Shaft, from where the Watergrove Pipe was explored for some 300ft (91m) in the 1976 drought. The sough is accessible for some distance in dry weather, passing various other shafts. Other workings have been entered in dry weather, but the whole complex is normally submerged. The workings are used as a water supply to Cavendish fluorspar mill, pumping taking place from the Fairburn Engine Shaft.

The sough tail lies west of the sharp bend in Stoney Middleton Dale, and is described in the Stoney Middleton chapter.

References: Beck, J.S. 1975. Trans. B.C.R.A. Vol.2. No.1. p.8 Beck, J.S. 1978. Bull. P.D.M.H.S. Vol.7. No.2. pp. 106-115.

WATERSAW SWALLETS
NGR 1925 7337 & 1928 7338   Lost
Alt. 1100ft (335m)   Depth: 12ft (4m)

In shallow valley north of the opencast workings on Watersaw Rake.

Two sinkholes which took water from the peat cover were excavated to a depth of 12ft (4m). They were obliterated when the adit to Watersaw Mine was driven.

Reference: Beck, J.S. 1975. Trans B.C.R.A. Vol.2. No.1. p.8.

INDEX

GLOSSARY

ADIT. Level or sloping entrance to a mine, sometimes used for drainage.

ANASTOMOSIS. Random distribution of tubular channels of various sizes in bedding planes; also called spongework.

ARAGONITE. An unusual crystalline form of calcium carbonate.

AVEN. A vertical extension up from a passage, not breaking through to the surface, but sometimes leading to passages at higher levels.

BEDDING PLANE. The parting between two beds of rock, often enlarged to give a wide low cave penetrable by flat-out crawling.

BELAY. Point used for anchoring a ladder or rope, or a lifeline operator. TO BELAY – to attach the rope or ladder. BELAY ROPE – a short length used for anchoring.

BOULDER CHOKE. A mass of boulders blocking progress in a passage.

CALCITE. The commonest crystalline form of calcium carbonate; the chief constituent of limestone and stalactites, etc.

CAVE. A natural underground cavity or passage. The term is often restricted to those cavities not requiring tackle for exploration.

CAVE PEARLS. Small unattached concretions of stalactitic calcite usually formed in pools round nuclei of rock. Clusters of pearls in a pool are often called "nests".

CAVERN. Usually restricted to large chambers in caves or to large cave systems.

CHAMBER. A relatively large part of a cave.

CHERT. A cryptocrystalline form of silica found as nodules, etc., in limestones and often weathered out as projections from walls or forming pebbles on the floors of caves.

CHIMNEY. An ascending or descending shaft which is climbable by back and knee method.

CRAWL. Any passage which has to be traversed on hands and knees or lower, i.e., lying flat out. Often necessary to reverse out – a very tiring procedure.

CURTAIN. Either a rock barrier nearly to the floor of a passage necessitating crawling OR a thin elongated dripstone (stalactite) formation on walls or roof.

DEADS. Stacked boulders, usually mine debris, at the side of a passage. Often "supported" by wood of unknown age and dangerously unstable.

DOG TOOTH SPAR. A pointed form of calcite crystals.

DOLOMITE. A mineral composed of carbonate of calcium and magnesium. Or a rock chiefly composed of that material.

DRIPSTONE. A general term to cover formations deposited by dripping water, i.e. stalactites and stalagmites, etc.

DUCK. A short water-filled passage necessitating complete immersion. Usually restricted to those with a little air-space.

EFFLUENT CAVE. A cave from which water flows out.

ERRATICS. Boulders transported by ice action.

FAULT. A fracture in rocks causing relative displacement of the two sides either vertically or horizontally. Fault-surfaces are often marked by grooving known as Slickensides.

FISSURE. A natural narrow but relatively high passage, often in a joint or fault, but the term does not necessarily signify displacement.

FLOWSTONE. Stalactite or stalagmite formation deposited as a sheet on walls or floors, usually from a film of gently moving water.

FORMATION. Either a group of strata bearing a name, OR any kind of mineral deposit in a cave, such as stalactites, gypsum, clay, etc.

GINGING. The "dry" stone walling supporting the loose ground round the top of a mine shaft. Often unstable and best avoided.

GOUR. A pool rimmed by deposited calcite, usually in association with stalagmites. Also called RIMSTONE POOL.

GROTTO. A cave or chamber well-decorated with stalactites.

HELICTITE. A stalactitic formation of calcite, aragonite, or gypsum, which does not grow vertically, and which may branch. Often wrongly known as Erratics.

JOINT. Natural fractures of rock strata without displacement. Often perpendicular to bedding.

KARABINER. A metal snap-link used for attachment to a rope, ladder or belay.

LEVEL. A horizontal passage in a mine, sometimes the entrance. A "Coffin level" has a cross-section like a coffin and usually dates from before explosives were introduced.

LIFELINE. A strong safety rope attached to anyone negotiating difficult obstacles or climbing ladders, etc., paid out and kept taut by a lifeliner.

LIMESTONE. A rock composed of more than 50 per cent calcium carbonate, the remainder being sand, clay, shale, dolomite, chert, etc., etc.

Dolomised limestone has been altered by the introduction of magnesium after deposition. Reef limestones differ in bedding and jointing characters from most other limestones, and there is some evidence in Derbyshire that they contain more caves.

MASTER-CAVE. A rather hypothetical concept of a "main drain" cave of large proportions which takes all the drainage from an area via many tributaries. Only Peak and Speedwell Caverns approach this concept in Derbyshire.

MOON-MILK. A colloidal form of calcium carbonate, believed to be deposited by bacterial action and usually found near entrances.

OX-BOW. An abandoned stream meander passage, sometimes providing a dry by-pass to a wet section.

PHREATIC. Either a cave or a feature in a cave formed by solution below the water-table.

PIPE-VEIN. A mineral vein elongated along the bedding.

PITCH. A vertical or near vertical-descent usually requiring tackle.

PITON. A metal spike or peg driven into the rock for a belay.

POT. A vertical chamber entered at the top (the same chamber could be an aven entered from below).

POTHOLE. A vertical pitch open to the surface, or a cave system dominated by vertical descents requiring tackle. OR a hollow in a stream bed worn out by stones swirling in the water, also called a ROCK MILL.

RAKE. A large mineral vein whose workings can often be traced across country for a mile or so. Usually near vertical.

RESURGENCE. The re-appearance of an underground stream at the surface whose source is known.

RISING. The appearance of a stream on the surface whose source is unknown.

RIFT. Strictly should apply only to chambers opened by faulting but often applied to any large chamber elongated in the vertical plane.

RIMSTONE. Calcite deposited round the edge of a pool.

RUCKLE. A jumble of large boulders, sometimes large enough to be penetrated by crawling between them.

SCALLOPS. Current-marking or faceting of rock due to turbulent water flow.

SHAFT. A vertical entrance or extension to mine, sometimes used for mine-like pots in caves.

SHACK, SHAKE or SHAKEHOLE. A depression in the ground surface due to the collapse of a cave beneath.

SINK or SINKHOLE. Any place where water disappears underground or has done so in the past.

SIPHON. A term often used incorrectly for a trap or sump, but which should strictly apply only to those with siphon action as evidenced by ebbing-and-flowing.

SLICKENSIDES. Polished, striated or grooved surface of a fault plane.

SOUGH. A mine drainage level; sometimes forms the entrance to a mine or cave.

SPELEOLOGY. The scientific study of caves.

SQUEEZE. A narrow part of a cave passable only with effort. Care about return often necessary.

STALACTITE. A cave formation, usually of calcite, hanging from the roof.

STRAW-STALACTITE. A stalactite of straw-like dimensions and hollow.

STALAGMITE. A cave formation building up from the floor, usually calcite, other forms must be specified.

STEMPLE. A wooden bar set between notches in the rock walls for miners' climbing purposes, often one of a series forming a ladder. Sometimes later used as a support for stacked deads. Usually rotten and not to be trusted.

SUMP or TRAP. A submerged passage, sometimes passable by diving. A sump in a mine can be any short underground shaft.

SWALLET or SWALLOW. Any hole taking a stream underground from the surface, OR in a mine a natural hole draining the workings.

TACKLE. Equipment needed for descending a cave or pothole, i.e., ladders, ropes, etc.

TETHER. A belay or to belay.

TRAP. A short sump which can be passed by diving.

TRAVERSE. A climb along ledges, etc., above the floor of a passage or pothole.

TUBE. A small passage of nearly circular cross-section. A roof-tube is the upper half of a tube left by downward erosion of the floor.

VADOSE. A cave or part of a cave formed by freely running water above or at the water-table.

WATER-TABLE. The surface of the zone of permanent saturation. It may fluctuate with weather and seasons. A perched water-table is held above the usual height by a local barrier to downward percolation.